PEACE LEADERSHIP

Self-Transformation to Peace

"Leadership for what?
What might be obtained by leadership if
peace could not be obtained?"
(Jean Lipman-Blumen)

Endorsements

This book comes at the right time. With so many regions of the world in turmoil through increasing nationalisms, destabilising populism and the clouds of a trade war, the question of peace leadership needs to move centre stage. The views from across disciplines and applications in various fields – the 'spotlight' sections of the book – bring home the message of peace leadership in an innovative manner. A great source- and reference book!

Professor Piet Naude, Director, University of Stellenbosch Business School,
Bellville, South Africa

This pioneering book highlights the importance of 'good leadership and leadership for good' in the peace-building process. To become a personal bridge in such fraught situations calls for outstanding qualities. It is not easy be a catalyst for desirable change!

The authors instance some of these necessary qualities and substantiate them with real-life examples. What they have done is to put on the map the need for selecting and training a new generation of 'peace leaders'. Speaking as one who has toiled long and rather fruitlessly in this field, I am immensely grateful for their contribution. I hope that it will prompt a new conversation among those nations and organisations that have the will and the means to address the broken parts of our precious world.

Dr John Adair, Director, Adair International, Action Centered Leadership Development
Consultants, Cambridge, United Kingdom

The book *Peace Leadership: Self-Transformation to Peace* is going to fill a large gap in the area of sustainable peacebuilding. The combination of peacebuilding and leadership is both innovative and more than needed to establish a field of expertise that is lacking substantial research and a theoretical foundation. The width as well as the scope of the book is impressive. It reflects a broad interdisciplinary expertise of the authors. The book's approach to work with 'spotlights' makes it not only interesting to read, but also very concrete and relevant as it refers to current and historical figures, and developments in politics, social work, academia and sports. The editors of the book are very clear in their approach towards creating 'positive peace' and suggest a 'peace leadership-in-action model' (emotional, social, communal intelligence for a more civilised and flourishing world) which lays the foundation of the book.

Dr Barbara Schellhammer, Faculty Intercultural Education,
Munich School of Philosophy, Munich, Germany

This book has the ability to move readers from the dance floor to the balcony and provides a creative and concrete path in a world that needs to be redefined on the principles of peacebuilding. Never before has a book been written from such diverse perspectives. It resonates truly with what is possible when peacebuilding is cultivated and promoted for a greater global social change. This is a must read for members of non-governmental organizations, the UN and the Diplomatic Corps.

Dr Imbenzi George, Honorary Consul General (Kenya),
Diplomatic Corps Vancouver, Canada

This book highlights a new and innovative perspective on aspects such as emotional, social and communal intelligence associated with peace leadership by applying peace leadership practices instead of the customary focus on how to establish peace.

Professor Hendri Kroukamp: Acting Vice-Rector: Academic as well as Dean:
Faculty of Economic and Management Sciences, University of the Free State

In a progressively changing society, it is crucial to deepen our understanding of peace and leadership as two critically intertwined concepts. This book sheds some much-needed light on contemporary peace leadership though an in-depth exposition of the past, the present and the future of leadership. A must-read for anyone in leadership, but especially those vested in expanding the body of knowledge on peace or leadership.

Professor Francis Petersen, Rector: University of the
Free State, Bloemfontein, South Africa

The title of the book, 'Peace Leadership', is a very appealing and interesting one in the current competitive context. The book proposes a useful framework for studying the efforts made by top leaders in the world and is well grounded in the theory of social learning, emotional intelligence and existing theories of leadership. The idea of self-transformation is very much relevant for top political and business leaders as the journey of leadership begins with a transformation at the level of 'self'. The book has relevance in a wider social and cultural context, indicating the value of its implications for a much wider audience irrespective of cultural and social differences.

Professor Ajay Jain: Director: Institute of Management Studies,
Ghaziabad Business School, Ghaziabad, India

Peace provides a context and environment in which societies engage, grow and thrive. This book explores the often complex and multifaceted approaches to peacebuilding and emphasises the need to nurture and sustain peace. Through detailed analysis and a study of various peace practitioners, it assesses the contribution of selfless men and women who have championed peace processes across the world. This book is a rallying call for leaders in all fields to respond effectively to the urgent imperative to safeguard peace dividends. Leaders are called upon to participate in developing and promoting peace as a global good.

Mmasekgoa Masire-Mwamba, Executive Director, Masire-Mwamba Office,
Former Deputy Secretary-General for the Commonwealth

This book provides informative resources on the topic of peace and security. The text emphasizes the imminent need for peace leaders who can lead the future of humanity towards peace and prosperity. The authors search for successful patterns of qualifications and skills that can define a peace leader.

Dr Rahim Mirshahi, Director for Peace Leadership Curriculum Development
International Peace Leadership College, Philippines

This book provides significant concepts and perspectives in peace leadership, a concept I had not imagined existed despite over 10 years of peace-building work in northern Uganda and South Sudan. It is a must-read for peace-builders who wish to attain progress in their work. It uses practical and simple concepts, and real-life examples of leaders past and present, such as Nelson Mandela, Kofi Annan, Martin Luther King Jr, George W. Bush and Angela Merkel. It provides a simple and holistic three-layered concept of leadership: leading the self, leading with others, and leading with the community. I am certain that many peace-builders elsewhere have not imagined the existence of the concept of peace leadership. Through this book, they can hopefully re-examine their leadership strategies and work towards attaining peace in their regions. I recommend it as a must-read for all peace-building practitioners.

Lino Owor Ogora, Director & Founder,
Foundation for Justice and Development Initiatives (FJDI), Uganda

Dr Campbell compellingly argues that complexity in statecraft calls not just for leaders, but leadership of a particular kind. Using an understanding that such leadership must be an integration of the leader with the led through intelligence expressed as multiple awarenesses, he provides a new framework for leadership toward our shared progress.

Will Salyards PhD Leader Coaching & Mentoring, Sacramento, California

This ambitious book tackles the role of leadership in achieving sustainable peace in the context of recovering and rebuilding failed and fragile states. The book's unique contribution lies in connecting the psychology of individual leaders and their efforts to lead institutional and structural change. The book offers a novel perspective, since it specifically focuses on leaders' 'emotional intelligence', including their capacity for empathy and their ability to practise forgiveness, as essential elements that impact their success in leading states, societies and communities towards sustainable peace. Considering current events on the world stage, the topic could not be more timely.

Dr Mary Hope Schwoebel, Nova Southeastern University, USA

This book is the seminal guide to peace leadership in South Africa and a welcome addition to South African leadership literature. The authors provide a comprehensive conceptualisation of peace leadership as well as suggestions for its implementation. The book covers many topics related to peace leadership, including spirituality, cultural intelligence, health care, technology, entrepreneurship and sport. In addition, the manifestations and implications of peace leadership are illustrated with fascinating case studies representing a range of contexts. I believe that the book fills a gap that existed in leadership literature for too long and is an indispensable book for academics, researchers, and anyone interested in peace.

Professor Roelf van Niekerk, HoD, Department of Industrial and Organisational Psychology, Nelson Mandela University, Port Elizabeth

As a teacher educator, I know teachers would find this book's topic both powerful and engaging. Most teachers I know strive for inner and outer peace, and would love to converse with other teachers about ways to envision peace and to make it happen.

So, when I read the Table of Contents, I immediately desired to create a graduate or undergraduate course on the topic of Peace Leadership that would use this book as the core reading. What a conversation the book's topics might engender! The breadth of the book's vision is commendable. Further, and in the best sense of collaborative community action, what might teachers build together to make peace leadership and action research curriculum both with their students and with themselves? The book holds much hope.

The book also seems an invitation to people of faith to learn how they might engage themselves and others in projects of peace and justice. In my experience, it is the collaborating on projects of peace that invites relationship building. And, relationships edify peace leadership. I look forward to reading more of the book and talking with others about how to move our reading into action. I trust the book may open to those of us who care, a shared space where futures of hope and faith might be built together.

Jim Parsons, Professor Emeritus, Faculty of Education, University of Alberta, Canada

Demilitarization, disarmament and building conditions for durable peace is not only necessary work – it is exceedingly demanding work as we face such massively unjust economic and social structures. Taking the time to reflect, as this useful volume admirably does, on the challenges to build peace while also addressing our human limitations and foibles, is a most welcome gift for those who truly want to lead for peace.

Joe Gunn, Executive Director of Citizens for Public Justice; author of "Journeys to Justice: Reflections on Canadian Christian Activism" (2018)

This is a timely book during an era in which the cost of peace is increasingly threatening the human, economic and environmental sustainability of the world. The authors are commended on a sterling job of integrating lived experiences with sound research and practical tools for implementing peace leadership at all levels. Notwithstanding its significant contribution, this publication is paramount to scholars and readers committed to progressive human development, peace-building, social cohesion and the holistic advancement of communities.

Vusi M. Vilakati (MA, MPhil), Methodist Minister and African Leadership Researcher

First published in 2019.

ISBN: 978-1-86922-761-6 (Printed)
ISBN: 978-1-86922-762-3 (ePDF)
ISBN: 978-1-86922-776-0 (Epub)
ISBN: 978-1-86922-777-7 (Mobi)

Published by KR Publishing
P O Box 3954
Randburg
2125
Republic of South Africa

Tel: (011) 706-6009
Fax: (011) 706-1127
E-mail: orders@knowres.co.za
Website: www.kr.co.za

Printed and bound: Tandym Print, 1 Park Road, Western Province Park, Epping, 7475
Typesetting, layout and design: Cia Joubert, cia@knowres.co.za
Cover design: Marlene de Villiers, marlene@knowres.co.za
Editing and proofreading: Valda Strauss, valda@global.co.za
Project management: Cia Joubert, cia@knowres.co.za

PEACE LEADERSHIP

Self-Transformation to Peace

Edited by Prof Ebben van Zyl
and Dr Andrew Campbell

kr
publishing

2019

Contents

List of figures

About the editors

Professor Ebben van Zyl is currently Professor in the Department of Industrial Psychology (University of the Free State, South Africa). Professor van Zyl has published 48 scientific publications, 39 research projects and has presented 45 papers at national and international conferences with regard to industrial psychology and leadership-related topics. He is inter alia also the editor and co-writer of the book: *Leadership in the African Context* (2009; 2016). He is the co-writer of the chapter: 'Leadership in South Africa' in the book: *LEAD: Leadership effectiveness in Africa and the African Diaspora* (2016). He is the co-writer of the chapter: 'Cultural intelligence as a way for organisational leaders to enhance peace' in the book: *Global Leadership Initiatives for Conflict Resolution and Peacebuilding*. He received the awards: 'Top Performer: Research' in the Faculty of Economic and Management Sciences (1999 and 2015, University of the Free State) as well as: 'Research Excellence' from the University of the Free State (2004). His book, *Leadership in the African Context,* was nominated as one of the best books at the University of the Free State (2017). He also acts as a consultant for various companies in the fields of medico-legal investigations, leadership, conflict and peace management, stress measurement and management, as well as human resource management. Email: vanzyles@ufs.ac.za.

Dr Andrew Campbell is the Director, International Peace and Leadership Institute. He provides emerging leadership research and leadership development and training programs on a leader's role in the international, national and nongovernmental organisation designed for conflict prevention, specifically for conflict resolution practitioners conducting and executing peacemaking, peacekeeping, and peacebuilding activities within post-conflict resolution and peaceful leadership. In addition, Dr Campbell, as a retired senior military officer, works for the Department of Defence specialising in Counter-Terrorism and Global Security Cooperation. Dr Campbell possesses a Doctorate in Global Leadership from the Institute of Indiana Technology, Fort Wayne, IN. and a Master's in Diplomacy in International Conflict Management from Norwich University, Northfield, VT. He is an Adjunct Professor for the Air Force Command and Staff College, Norwich University, and the Federal Executive Institute. Dr Campbell is a recognised national and international speaker on peace leadership and has addressed the World Society of Victimology at The Hague 2012, Peace Leadership Conference 2017, International Leadership Association 2011–2018, and the European Consortium for Political Research 2015–2017. He is widely published in both national and international journals, with a book chapter on such topics as "Leadership Education in Transitional Justice in Promoting Global Peace" and "Civic Engagement through Education and Forgiveness and Reconciliation as an Organizational Leadership Competence in Transitional Justice" in the *International Journal of Servant Leadership*. He recently published a book entitled *Global Leadership Initiatives for Conflict Resolution and Peacebuilding* which explores leadership theories and practice models to conceptualise the intersection of leadership within conflict management and resolution. Email: andrew.h.campbell3@gmail.com

About the contributors

Adrienne Castellon, EdD, is Assistant Professor and Stream Director of Masters of Educational Leadership, Trinity Western University, British Columbia, Canada. She has worked as a secondary school teacher, elementary principal and education consultant. She later worked in North and South America, as the Director of an English Language Institute in Bolivia for two years and presented at conferences in Canada, the USA, England and India. Adrienne works at Trinity Western University in Langley, British Columbia, where, in addition to teaching numerous graduate leadership courses for educators, she enjoys teaching pre-service teachers in the School of Education. Dr Castellon stays current in the K-12 system through government and private consulting and school-related projects. Research interests include Indigenous curriculum and relationships, women in leadership, practices in K-12 education, applied servant leadership, spirituality in leadership and teaching, as well as various social justice related topics. She can be reached at www.adriennecastellon.com or adrienne.castellon@Twu.ca

Dr Carol Dalglish is founder and secretary of Awaken Mozambique, a not-for-profit organisation that supports entrepreneurs in the poorest section of Beira. She was Associate Professor/Senior Lecturer for 15 years in the Faculty of Business at the Queensland University of Technology (QUT), Australia, where she has been acting head of the Brisbane Graduate School of Business, MBA director and faculty director of Internationalisation. She has taught, studied and consulted in Australia, England, South Africa, Mozambique, Denmark, Hong Kong, Taiwan and Canada. She has been a visiting Professor at Stellenbosch University in South Africa, the Copenhagen Business School in Denmark and the Sun Yat Sen University in Taiwan. She has won a number of university teaching awards, an award for best paper and a teaching fellowship. Carol is the author of several books on leadership and intercultural teaching and learning. Her research interests include micro-entrepreneurship in Africa, leadership development and intercultural teaching and learning. Prior to joining QUT, Carol held senior positions in the public service in Australia and the UK and spent five years as a management consultant. Email: carol@awakenmozambique.org.au

Ciara Gallagher is a Graduate in the Peace and Conflict Research Group at the Norwegian Institute of International Affairs. Gallagher holds an International Bachelors in Politics & International Relations and History from University College Dublin with a specialisation in Peace, Conflict and Justice from the University of Toronto. She was previously a Fred J. Hansen Fellow and recipient of the Conor Martin Memorial prize. Gallagher has conducted field research in both Northern Ireland and South Africa as a Fritt Ord Scholar and in Kosovo as part of the Balkans Peace Program, along with shorter scholarly trips to Albania, Montenegro, Macedonia, Croatia, Serbia, Sweden,

Germany, the Mexico-US border and UN Headquarters. Email: ciara.gallagher@ucdconnect.ie

Mrs Martha Harunavamwe is a Lecturer in the Department of Industrial Psychology (University of the Free State, South Africa). She holds a Master's degree in Industrial Psychology. Her area of research interest includes leadership and positive psychology. Martha worked for a few years in the private sector before joining the Management College of Southern Africa where she lectured in Human Resource Management and supervised MBA students. Martha is currently working at the University of the Free State (from 2015 to date) as a Lecturer. She is an emerging researcher who has published four scientific publications and one book chapter, and presented five papers at national and international conferences. Her research work has mainly focused on aspects of industrial psychology such as work engagement, leadership, and cultural intelligence. Email: harunavamweM@ufs.ac.za.

Magda Hewitt (DPhil) is an Associate Professor and currently situated within the Department of Industrial Psychology and People Management (IPPM) at the University of Johannesburg. She leads the Leadership Doctoral and Masters Programs in Personal and Professional Leadership; Leadership in Emerging Economies; and Leadership Coaching. Her research niche areas focus on Entrepreneurial Leadership in an Emerging Economy context. Email: mhewitt@uj.ac.za

Professor Laetus O.K. Lategan is the Senior Director for Research Development and Postgraduate Studies at the Central University of Technology, Free State, in Bloemfontein, South Africa. He completed doctoral studies with the University of the Free State in Philosophy and Theology. He has an extensive background in senior and executive management. His research interest is in the areas of research ethics, healthcare ethics, applied ethics and doctoral education. He is the (co-)author of more than 200 publications in various disciplines. He is the editor of the *Journal for New Generation Sciences* (ISSN 1684–4998) and a South African National Research Foundation rated researcher. His most recent books include *Get ready, Get set, Go! Preparing for your doctoral studies ad doctoral education* (2017, edited by L.O.K. Lategan) and *Healthcare ethics for healthcare practitioners* (2017, edited by L.O.K. Lategan and G.J. van Zyl). Email: llategan@cut.ac.za

Professor Liezel Lues is an Associate Professor in the Department of Public Administration and Management at the University of the Free State. Prior to this appointment she worked in Human Resource Management in the Free State Office of the Premier and the National Department of Water Affairs respectively. She holds a Doctoral degree in Public Management. She serves as chairperson of the Association of Southern African Schools and Departments of Public Administration and Management (ASSADPAM). Her experience and expertise lie within the fields of human resource development, public management and research development. She has published several articles and papers on topics in research development, human resource development and public management. Email: Luesl@ufs.ac.za

Jannie Putter is a well-known South African mental coach of various national and international teams in a variety of sporting disciplines. He has been in practice as a sport psychologist since 1994. He is the author of six books on sport psychology-related topics. Currently, he is the mental coach of the Golden Lions, the best-performing rugby team in South Africa for the past few years. Email: jannie@jannieputter.co.za

Dr Erich Schellhammer recently retired from Royal Roads University, Victoria, Canada after a long career in Justice Studies. He holds a German law degree (Baden-Württemberg) as well as a Canadian M.A. and Ph.D in philosophy (Queen's University). He has taught at universities in Canada and Germany. His research interests have focused on a philosophical justification for the merits of cultural diversity and a phenomenological grounding of human rights in human ontology. He presently uses recent leadership studies to identify a new leadership category, that is, peace leadership. For him, this academic interest is a combination of modern leadership studies with peace and conflict studies to formulate a framework for peace leadership. He has been the inaugural chair of the *Peace Leadership Affinity Group* of the *International Leadership Association* and has published articles on peace leadership. His emphasis is on relating a culture of peace to the internationally agreed upon Sustainable Development Goals and to explore pathways to creating this new actuality for humanity. Email: erich.schellhammer@royalroads.ca

Professor Gert J. van Zyl is a Full Professor and the Dean of the Faculty of Health Sciences, University of the Free State in Bloemfontein, South Africa where he has held this position for more than eight years. He completed a medical degree, postgraduate diplomas in health management and community health, and two master's degrees – one in Business Administration (MBA) and one in Family Medicine. He has a doctoral degree with the University of the Free State in Health Professions Education. He has a background and extensive experience in senior and executive management of more than twenty-five years. His research interest is in the areas of health professions education, family medicine, community health and medical ethics. He is the (co-) author of numerous publications in various disciplines. He was the associate editor of the *African Journal of Health Professions Education* and is also an Inaugural Fellow of the Association of Medical Education Europe. His most recent book is *Healthcare ethics for healthcare practitioners* (2017, edited by L.O.K. Lategan & G.J. van Zyl.). Email: vanzylgj@ufs.ac.za

Introduction

Welcome to the first edition of *Peace Leadership: Self-Transformation to Peace*. Threats to peace are making headlines all over the world, with tension in the Middle East, worldwide economic decline, high unemployment rates and terrorist activities being just a few examples. Peace is a topic of increasing rather than passing or declining interest, as societies begin to see the harsh realities of the cost of non-peace. Besides evidence of these harsh realities in the daily news, we can see the effects in the hearts of people who are beginning to wake up to the importance of peace within and the ripple effect this can have on peaceful relations with others.

Peace per se is not commonly addressed by leaders, and this is a crucial gap that needs to be filled. Only a few leadership studies include concepts such as "leading for peace". While there seem to be many publications on how to establish peace, mainly those in the field of conflict studies, there are not many available on how to establish peace by applying peace leadership practices.

Peace can be established by first leading self, which will enable one to lead with others. By leading self and leading with others, communities can change their focus towards a more civilised and flourishing world. And a more civilised and flourishing world can, ultimately, lead to peace.

Purpose of the book and target readership

The purpose of the book is to give deeper insight into the concept of "peace leadership" and how to implement it. Specific tools and initiatives on how to become a highly effective peace leader will also be provided.

The book is aimed primarily at academics and researchers (first-world consumption and academic settings) because it contributes to the development of the scientific body of knowledge in a systematic way. Practitioners and organisational specialists would also be interested in how peace leadership can be implemented within their contexts. The complexity of the discussions in each chapter and the depth with which peace leadership is addressed would, therefore, appeal to academics and practitioners in peace leadership.

The secondary market could be anyone interested in peace and peace leadership, as well as the average person on the street because living in peaceful communities is a desire shared by most people.

Structure of the book

The book is presented in four sections:

- **Peace leadership in perspective**. This section provides discussions on the nature and meaning of peace leadership, important building blocks for peace leadership, and a peace leadership-in-action model (which forms the basis of the book).
- **Implementation**. Implementation strategies focus on **lead self, lead with others and lead communities. Lead self** includes: leading peace through self, others and the community, the role of wisdom and spirituality in leading self and others, and individual, social and cultural inertia preventing humanity from attaining peace. **Lead others** includes: leadership theories which support peace leadership, the improvement of cultural intelligence amongst peace leaders, and women's role in peacebuilding. **Lead communities** includes: peace leadership in the public and private sectors, healthcare for the vulnerable and its meaning and contribution towards peace leadership, and working from helplessness to serving the community.
- **Tools and initiatives to become a highly effective peace leader.** In this section, the following themes are discussed: information and communication technological innovations for peace leaders and sport as a tool for peacebuilding.
- **Concluding thoughts.** Concluding thoughts are given, with the emphasis on what we have learned and looking ahead.

SECTION 1

PEACE LEADERSHIP IN PERSPECTIVE

CHAPTER 1

THE NATURE AND MEANING OF PEACE LEADERSHIP

Ebben van Zyl

"We need an essentially new way of thinking if mankind is to survive. Men (and women) must radically change their attitudes toward each other and their views of the future. Force must no longer be an instrument of politics … Today, we do not have much time left; it is up to our generation to succeed in thinking differently about peace initiatives. If we fail, the days of civilized humanity are numbered." (Albert Einstein)

Spotlight: Nelson Mandela

Nelson Mandela was born in 1918 in a small village in the Eastern Cape Province, South Africa. His father, a counsellor to the Thembu royal family, died when Mandela was nine. He joined the African National Congress in 1943 as an activist and later became the founder and president of the ANC Youth League. A qualified lawyer, he opened a law practice in Johannesburg with Oliver Tambo. After the massacre of Sharpeville, Mandela launched a campaign of sabotage against the country's economy. Arrested, he was sentenced to life in prison in 1964. In 1990, after the end of the Cold War, President FW de Klerk lifted the ban on the ANC and Mandela was released from prison after 27 years. The ANC and the National Party began talks about forming a new multi-racial democracy for South Africa. In 1993, Mandela and De Klerk were awarded the Nobel Peace Prize. Mandela was elected president in the first democratic elections in 1994. In 1999 he stepped down in favour of Thabo Mbeki. Nelson Mandela died in 2014 at the age of 94 years.[1]

Introduction

The role that peace leaders can play in reconciling people is evident in Nelson Mandela's thinking and actions after being released from prison and during his term as the South African president. As the newly elected South African president in 1994, he took up the challenge of being a peace leader and envisioned a shared, clear and mutually peaceful future for all South Africans. He stated the following when becoming president:

> "A number of obstacles to the creation of a non-racial democratic South Africa remain and needed to be tackled. The fears of whites about their rights and place in a South Africa they do not control exclusively, are an obstacle we must understand and address. I stated in 1964 that I and the ANC are as opposed to black domination as we are to white domination".[2]

As a former political leader, Mr Mandela therefore **transformed himself** from a political leader and freedom fighter to a peace leader, by thinking past his own negative feelings (for instance, hatred toward those people who put him in jail). He also tried to prevent conflict and to reconcile people, even amid negative events. After the murder of the popular leader of the South African Communist Party, Chris Hani, in 1993, several political experts feared that this could trigger civil war. However, Mr Mandela – and not the President, Mr FW de Klerk – addressed the nation that evening in an SABC broadcast, stating:

> "Tonight, I am reaching out to every single South African, black and white, from the very depths of my being. A white man, full of prejudice and hate, came to our country and committed a deed so foul that our whole nation now teeters on the brink of disaster. A white woman, of Afrikaner origin, risked her life so that we may know, and bring to justice, this assassin … Now is the time for all South Africans to stand together against those who wish to destroy what Chris Hani gave his life for – the freedom of all of us".[3]

By working to a common goal which was to work to a non-racial South Africa, helped him to channel his thoughts, attitudes and behaviours in the right direction (self-direction and self-influence) and ultimately to lead the country towards a peaceful democratic transition.

He recognised the fact that **leading self** is a crucial starting point in becoming a peace leader: "I think power comes from within. If you know yourself and have confidence in what you are doing, that in itself constitutes power, and this power is very important when you are trying to achieve something".

Looking beyond oneself (**having self-insight and emotional intelligence**) can help one gain insight into what is important. Mr Mandela said the following:

> "I have always believed that to be a freedom fighter one must suppress many of the personal feelings that make one feel like a separate individual rather than part of a mass movement. One is fighting for the liberation of millions of people, not the glory of one individual. I am not suggesting that man become a robot

and rid himself of all personal feelings and motivations. But in the same way that a freedom fighter subordinates his own family to the family of the people, he must subordinate his own feelings to the movement".

Nelson Mandela was motivated by his belief in the good of ordinary men and women. He was not driven by hatred, as is clear from this statement:

"Those who thrive on hatred destroy their own capacity to make a positive contribution. I never lost hope that this great transformation would occur, because of the courage of ordinary men and women of my country. I always knew that deep down in every human heart, there was mercy and generosity. No one is born hating another person because of the colour of his skin, or his background, or his religion. People must learn to hate, and if they can learn to hate, they can be taught to love, for love comes more naturally to the human heart than its opposite. Even in the grimmest times in prison, when my comrades and I endured emotional, and physical abuse, isolation and degradation, I would see a glimmer of humanity in one of the guards, perhaps just for a second, but it was enough to reassure me and keep me going. Man's goodness is a flame that can be hidden but never extinguished".[4]

For Nelson Mandela, therefore, the process of being a peace leader started within himself before focusing on **leading others** (in order to create **peace**). He also demonstrated **communal intelligence** by demonstrating important values like **inclusiveness, cohesiveness and shared understanding**.

Nelson Mandela's story touches on the peace leadership topics to be covered in this book. His story demonstrates the role that peace leaders can play in bringing peace to the world. Being a peace leader, however, comes with certain challenges (for instance, transforming yourself past negativity in order to lead with others). Practising **emotional intelligence** skills (lead self) will help to lead with others (**social intelligence**). Ultimately, the abovementioned components could lead to **communal intelligence** (for instance, to include everyone in the solution of a common problem: see discussions in chapter 3 on communal intelligence), which may give rise to everyone in the community being involved. All these factors may contribute to the attainment of **peace.**

In order to set a base for the rest of the book, this chapter will start by demarcating the nature and definitions of three important concepts i.e. peace, leadership and peace leadership. Previous research with regard to peace leadership will be discussed next. The role that leaders play in creating peace is vital and therefore this will also be discussed. Finally, the peace leader's characteristics, skills and attributes will be presented.

The nature and definition of peace and peace leadership

In his book *Understanding peace: a comprehensive introduction*, Michael Allen Fox[5] speculated that, if a TV quiz show (with a million dollars in prize money) were to pose the question: "What is peace?", various answers would be offered. Because of these countless perspectives of peace, the monetary value of the correct answer in this instance would be priceless.

Different perspectives on peace and what may influence peace can indeed be identified in the literature. Reychler[6], for instance, focused on forms of violence (e.g., physical, structural, psychological and cultural violence) as threats to peace. Similarly, the Institute for Economics and Peace[7] emphasised terrorist activities as a threat to peace and indicated that these activities have increased by 61 per cent in 2013, with the total number of deaths rising from 11 133 in 2012 to 17 958 in 2013. On the other hand, Tipson[8] argued that natural disasters and environmental events are expected to increase globally in both number and severity and give rise to civil and international conflicts. According to Tipson[9], such disasters might threaten peace due to the resulting non-availability of medicine, food, water, energy, etc. To illustrate, Tipson[10] explained that additional fresh water needs, due to world population growth, will be the equivalent of 20 Nile Rivers by 2030.

Although "peace" is a comprehensive term, Spreitzer[11] indicated that this concept has usually been investigated only by politicians, historians and policy makers. Traditionally, the topic of peace has been viewed as outside the realm of organisational scholarship with its tendency to focus on individual, group and organisational outcomes[12]. In the mid-2000s, however, Jean Lipman-Blumen[13] raised the question as to why leaders do not become involved in peace and reducing conflict. She asked: "Leadership for what? What might be obtained by leadership if peace could not be obtained?"[14]. According to McIntyre Miller[15], these questions gave rise to various panels and discussions among organisational specialists and initiated the Peace Leadership Affinity Group (as part of the International Leadership Association) in 2012 which works to identify and implement peace leadership in research and in practice. The focus of this book will be on peace and the role that leadership can play in enhancing peace in different settings.

Lipman-Blumen[16] defined peace as follows:
> "Peace (whether it be state peace or peace from organisational conflict), as conceptualised here, must be broadly defined to mean far more than the absence of war. Peace must stand on a foundation of justice, equality, sustainability, and all the other societal and human needs required for the world's citizenry to live productively, harmoniously and happily. We must realize Ubuntu in action".[17]

According to Chinn[18], "*peace* is intent, process and outcome". She stated further:
"The intention of peace is the commitment to chosen values and actions that consistently bring about harmony, trust and constructive solutions to differences and disagreements. The process of peace is the interactions that flow from the commitment. The outcome of peace is relationships that give rise to ongoing harmony, trust, and effective solutions to problems. Peace requires that your chosen values guide your actions. Peace is the means and the end, the process and the product".[19]

When defining peace, Kester[20] focused on person-centred awareness of the self (i.e. body, emotions and spirit), interpersonal relations (i.e. trust, openness and interdependence), and global cultural and environmental consciousness.

Galtung[21] (in Barash and Webel) made the important distinction between "positive" and "negative" peace. According to Galtung[22] positive peace denotes the simultaneous presence of many desirable states of mind and society, for example, harmony, justice and equity. Barash and Webel[23] also indicated that positive peace is a mental or spiritual condition marked by freedom from disquieting or oppressive thoughts or emotions. Similarly, Spreitzer[24] mentioned that positive peace is the calmness of heart and mind (positive inner peace), as well as harmony in human or personal relations.

Negative peace has historically denoted the "absence of war" and other forms of large-scale violent human conflict. Attention to negative peace usually results in diplomatic emphasis on peacekeeping (specific defence strategies) or peace restoring (humanitarian interventions). Both peacekeeping and peace restoring are applicable when war has already broken out[25]. Negative peace is a more conservative goal, because it seeks to maintain the status quo, whereas positive peace is more active and bold, laying the foundation for a status quo that does not exist currently[26]. In contrast, positive peace focuses on peacebuilding and the determination to work towards that goal, even when there is no war. Nelson Mandela tried and succeeded in reconciling and creating harmony in South Africa. He was living proof of a peace leader trying to establish positive peace and implement peacebuilding.

Peace in its positive form is more difficult to articulate, and possibly more difficult to achieve, than its negative version; thus, more research/actions regarding positive peace is required[27]. Spreitzer[28] put it as follows: "Future research should conceptualise and examine more positive manifestations of peace, like human and societal flourishing". Dinan[29] (in Van Zyl[30]) argued, central to positive peace is the desire for attitudes, behaviours and thoughts that support a more humanistic world.

Thus, the focus of this book will be on how to create positive peace.

Positive peace however can be created by leaders and effective leadership. Ledbetter[31] referred to the need of social movements such as the Arab Spring and the Occupy Movement to seriously consider the connection between peace and leadership in order to address the challenges of peace we are facing today. Van Zyl's[32] definition of leadership proves useful in this regard: "Leadership focuses on the ability to influence people and resources in a manner that will result in the achievement of identified goals." Peace leadership can, therefore, be defined as leadership that focuses on the ability to influence people and resources in a manner that will result in positive peace, in other words, where there exists a desire for attitudes, behaviours and thoughts that support a more flourishing and humanistic world.

McIntyre Miller[33] conducted a membership survey among the Peace Leadership Affinity Group of the International Leadership Association with the aim to reach a common definition of "peace leadership". According to her, one or more of the following aspects came to the fore: the promotion of a culture of peace in self and in others; challenging conflict; creating a common notion of and space for human and societal flourishing; creating a space for peace; creating a civilised and humanistic world; and, lastly, promoting peace in organisations.

Based on the above, a more comprehensive definition of peace leadership can be formulated: Peace leadership focuses on the ability to influence the self, people and resources so that a state of peace within the self, with others and the community can be promoted, conflict be challenged and a common notion of and space for a more civilised and flourishing world (peace), can be attained.

Research with regard to peace leadership

Although peace leadership seems to be a relatively new field of study, McIntyre Miller[34] mentioned a few studies which have laid the foundations of peace leadership. Boulding[35] (in McIntyre Miller[36]), discussed the American protest action of the 1960s. He compared the social movement action for peace with a peace leader attempting to create positive, peaceful change in people's current circumstances. As mentioned earlier, Lipman-Blumen[37] (in McIntyre Miller[38]) asked (in the mid-2000s) why leaders are not more involved in peace actions, and this eventually led to the establishment of the Peace Leadership Affinity Group in 2012. McIntyre Miller[39] indicated that, during a similar time frame, the Association to Advance Collegiate Schools of Business released a report, *A world of good: business, business schools and peace* which emphasised the fact that big organisations are interested in becoming involved in peace initiatives and connecting leadership and peace.

More recent studies, as indicated by McIntyre Miller[40], have mainly concentrated on conceptual research. Ledbetter[41] (in McIntyre Miller[42]) referred to the moral element in peace leadership research, especially the fact that, if moral progress is neglected in peace operations, peace cannot be created. Spreitzer[43] argued that participative leadership will enhance employee empowerment and, in turn, enhance a peaceful environment where employees can feel they have a voice. Both Ledbetter[44] and Spreitzer[45], therefore, emphasised the importance of inner feelings, attitudes and emotions that are contributing to outer circumstances (e.g., the enhancement of a just and caring environment).

Alomair[46] described the research of McIntyre Miller and Green[47] who presented an integral and holistic perspective to peace leadership. They used the four quadrants of the integral theory[48] to explain and understand the interplay of the practices and experiences of peace leading. The four quadrants are[49]:

- The I-Quadrant, which includes each leader's inner skills such as forgiveness, patience, love, compassion and kind-heartedness. These inner skills facilitate connection and interaction with other people and, in essence, allow connection with the IT-Quadrant.
- The IT-Quadrant, which embodies the leader's external behaviours such as negotiation, dialogue, communication skills, adaptability and openness. These external behaviours are critical in creating change and peace with others.
- The WE-Quadrant, in which leaders create a safe environment and space where peace-keeping ideas can be discussed and practised.
- The ITS-Quadrant, in which leaders focus on global applicability so that peace movements and peaceful systems can be established in order to create peace.

McIntyre Miller[50] pointed to the interconnectedness and interrelatedness of the abovementioned four quadrants in order for peace to be created by leaders.

Fox[51] is of the opinion that peace and peace leadership should be seen from both subjective and objective points of view. Subjectively, peace leadership has its origins from within the self. Fox[52] highlighted the importance of self-awareness and self-knowledge, in other words, of being aware of who you are and how you contribute to your own peacefulness. In order to have peace, one must have the ability to acknowledge, understand and be aware of one's own values, perspectives, strengths, weaknesses and emotional needs[53]. The ability to create positive peace is, therefore, a product that emanates from our state of mind and the signals we are sending out[54].

The objective viewpoint on peace leadership implies the external conditions of peace[55]. These conditions can include national influences (for instance, political and legal factors, health and education as well as economic and financial factors) in a country, which may affect the attainment of peace in a positive or negative way[56] (see chapter 2 where these external influences will be discussed in more depth). Bjerstedt[57] discussed the fact that unjust societal, economic and political structures inflict a form of violence that has no less impact on human suffering than the physical violence of wars and brute repression. These kinds of violence will probably have a negative effect on self-transformation to peace. Fox[58] emphasised a structured system of participation that is shaped by justice, equitable power sharing, trust, responsibility, accountability, recognition of the interdependence, moral status and political enfranchisement of others, mutual respect for their otherness and procedures for resolving conflicts.

Lastly, Dinan's model of Ubuntu leadership focuses on the movement from self-awareness, self-mastery, relational awareness, relational mastery and eventually the creation of a more humanistic world. The movement through these processes is characterised by Ubuntu values like mutuality, compassion, reciprocity, dignity, interconnectedness and humanity in all spheres of life (Dinan, 2012)[59].

The role of leaders in creating peace

Although the term "leader" has a positive connotation for most people, people do have different expectations of leadership. Also, the context can make a difference in the way people define leadership. Business leaders, political leaders or community leaders could all be viewed differently. One of the important things to remember, however, is that leaders have followers, i.e. people whom they **influence**[60] [61].

Ledbetter[62] argued that peace is not commonly associated with the study of leadership. She put is as follows: "In most leadership studies one is not apt to find a chapter dedicated to advancing peace in the world"[63].

According to Lowney[64], leaders (including peace leaders) should be involved in the following:
- Establishing direction: developing a vision of the future – often the distant future – and strategies for producing the changes needed to achieve this vision. The vision could include the creation of positive peace.
- Aligning people: communicating direction in words and deeds to those whose cooperation might be needed to influence the formation of teams and coalitions that understand the vision and strategies. Leaders need to communicate clearly to all stakeholders the details of the vision (i.e. peace) and how the vision should be achieved.

- Motivating and inspiring: energising people to overcome major political, bureaucratic and resource barriers to change by satisfying basic, but often unfulfilled, human needs. Leaders should motivate and inspire subordinates to partake in creating the vision (peace).
- Producing change and creating the vision (peace).

In short, leaders (including peace leaders) should be able to figure out which direction to follow, get other people involved and going in the right direction, get everyone to agree that they need to get there, and rally everyone through the obstacles on the way to achieving their goals (e.g., the creation of peace)[65].

Reychler and Stellamans[66] divided the authority of leaders into two types: formal and informal. Formal leader authority is granted when the holder has promised to meet a set of explicit expectations (based on job descriptions and legislated mandates). Informal leader authority comes from promising to meet expectations that are often implicit (based on ability, trustworthiness, civility, etc.)[67]. It is important to note that formal leader authority brings with it powers of the office, whereas informal leader authority brings with it subtle yet substantial power to extend the leader's reach way beyond the limits of the job description. Again, Nelson Mandela is a good example of a leader implementing informal authority. Before and after his presidency, he used his informal authority to implement several peace initiatives in an attempt to reconcile the country's diverse groups and prevent civil war in South Africa, among other things (see example previously described in this chapter where it was indicated that Mandela – and not President de Klerk – addressed the nation in an SABC broadcast, stating that everyone should stand together, even after Chris Hani was murdered). It is, therefore, not only leaders in formal positions who have an influence on creating peace, but also those in informal positions.

Based on the discussions (and certain examples given) in the previous paragraphs on peace aspects, leadership and peace leadership, a broad schematic description of the concept of peace leadership can be depicted as follows:

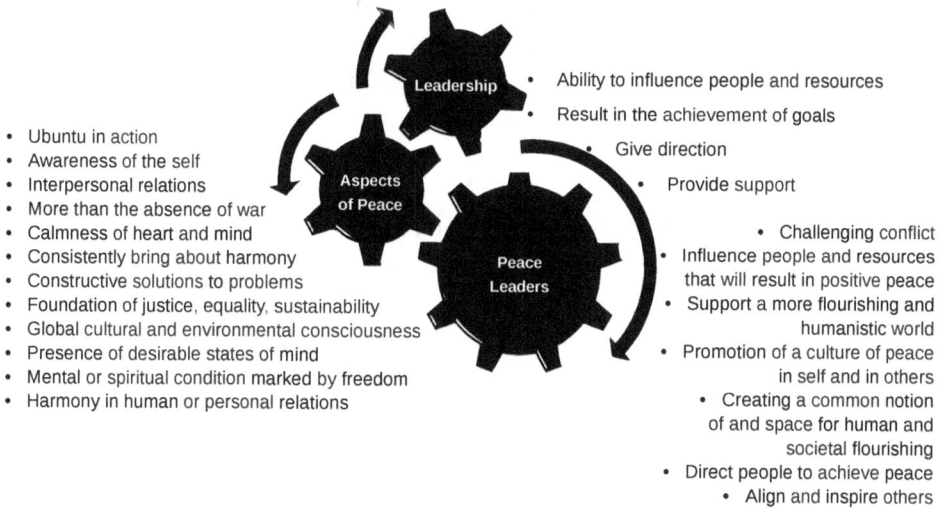

- Ubuntu in action
- Awareness of the self
- Interpersonal relations
- More than the absence of war
- Calmness of heart and mind
- Consistently bring about harmony
- Constructive solutions to problems
- Foundation of justice, equality, sustainability
- Global cultural and environmental consciousness
- Presence of desirable states of mind
- Mental or spiritual condition marked by freedom
- Harmony in human or personal relations

Leadership
Aspects of Peace
Peace Leaders

- Ability to influence people and resources
- Result in the achievement of goals
- Give direction
- Provide support
- Challenging conflict
- Influence people and resources that will result in positive peace
- Support a more flourishing and humanistic world
- Promotion of a culture of peace in self and in others
- Creating a common notion of and space for human and societal flourishing
- Direct people to achieve peace
- Align and inspire others

Figure 1.1: A broad description of the nature of peace leadership

The challenges of being a peace leader

According to Shamir and Eilam[68], any leadership role is highly challenging and requires a high level of energy, resolve and persistence. To lead effectively, especially when leading involves introducing and establishing societal or organisational changes (e.g. in peace initiatives), leaders have to overcome resistance, deal with frustrations and setbacks, sometimes make personal sacrifices, recruit support, and energise others[69]. By staying positive and contributing to peace after 27 years' imprisonment, Nelson Mandela is again a case in point.

Spreitzer[70] discussed the following complexities in the relationship between organisations and peace. Leaders have to deal with and adapt to the following:

- Labour unions are becoming more global in their reach. Employees may engage in strikes to push for political, economic and social reform (and not only for organisational changes). These strikes can turn violent and undermine peace efforts.
- Empowerment of employees is a delicate matter. Empowerment may be a positive manifestation in the modern organisation, but speaking out in countries with totalitarian leadership might not only work against peace, but could also be dangerous and lead to conflict instead of peace. For example, for an Afghan woman, having a significant voice might lead to her arrest, or worse.
- In some countries peace is forced and not sustainable. Totalitarian regimes might create short-term peace through the repression of conflict. However, this is not the kind of peace that is sustainable.

- In peaceful societies leaders might adopt a more participative leadership style, whereas in a hostile, turbulent environment leaders might feel the need to act in a more authoritarian way in order to establish sufficient control to operate effectively. The challenge would be to know which kind of leadership style would be the most appropriate in different contexts.

Van Brabant[71] emphasised a critical challenge to which peace leaders have to adapt, namely understanding and facing cultural differences. For instance, socio-cultural expectations about "leaders" (traits and characteristics of individual leaders) and "leadership" (complex concept requiring multiple capacities) in a given situation differ from one environment to the next. Often people have certain ideas about how leaders should behave, and failure to meet these stereotypes can prevent them from becoming or remaining effective leaders. For instance, if the expectation is for leaders to show themselves as strong, failure to come across as strong could undermine their credibility.

According to Van Zyl[72], general challenges that leaders (including peace leaders) are facing include:
- Working long hours: Leaders are often expected to work for as long as is needed to achieve a goal. This can cause conflict with other commitments, particularly family and community responsibilities. Often leaders undertake these long hours voluntarily without recognising the cost to themselves and others.
- Not enough authority to carry out responsibility: In any kind of organisation, leaders are often held responsible for activities over which they have little or no control. This is also true for peace leadership activities. It is not unusual for leaders to be expected to produce high-quality service with too small a staff and with staffing-level decisions being made elsewhere.
- Loneliness: The higher one rises as a leader, the lonelier one might become (for instance, at times when unpopular decisions have to be made by leaders with which subordinates might differ).

In addition, leadership limits the number of people in whom one can confide. This creates more challenges:
- Too many problems involving people: A major frustration for leaders is the number of human resource problems requiring attention. Leadership is about people. Many of the challenges a leader faces involve getting the best out of many diverse individuals.
- Conflicting goals: Another major challenge for leaders is navigating among the conflicting goals of their followers. The more complex the kind of organisation one leads, the more likely it is that different groups of followers would have different goals that do not necessarily coincide.

Characteristics, skills and traits of peace leaders

Keith[73] distinguished four vital characteristics of peace and leaders:

- Attaining self-awareness: According to Keith[74], if we want to be good peace leaders, we should know ourselves – both our strong and weak points. Developmental areas should be improved so that we can adopt more appropriate ways to interact with people. Self-awareness allows a leader to be more proactive and less reactive because it provides a meta-perspective which is needed for being able to adapt to new situations[75]. Also, self-awareness gives rise to self-mastery, which is to act according to one's core values/life purpose and, in this way, contribute to a just and caring society[76].
- Listening: It is important to attend to the real needs of other people. By applying good listening skills, leaders can attend to the needs of colleagues and customers.
- Changing the traditional hierarchy: According to Keith[77], the traditional hierarchy of boss and subordinates should be changed if real needs are to be met. Two-way communication is more effective than from the top down and provides subordinates with the opportunity to speak their minds.
- Bringing out the best in other people: Peace leaders can bring out the best in other people by focusing on engaging with them, inspiring them and mentoring them.

Reychler and Stellamans[78] emphasised the following skills needed by peace leaders:

- Relational skills which sustain interconnections among people
- Mediation skills which turn conflicts into opportunities
- Wisdom skills which increase understanding, such as innovation, problem solving and judgement
- Elicitive skills which motivate people to act, such as involving others, building coalitions and facilitating

According to Reychler and Stellamans[79], the following personality traits should be practised by peace leaders: courage (they risk their lives and careers), humility (they demonstrate a compelling humility), hardiness (they draw positive energy from painful experiences), sense of humour (humour can be used to relieve strain) and personal integrity (one should always be true to one's values).

McIntyre Miller[80] referred to a study in which the lives of peace leaders such as Abraham Lincoln and Nelson Mandela were analysed. The findings revealed the following essential traits of peace leaders: empathy, optimism about the potential for change, emotional self-control, forgiveness, and propensities toward reconciliation.

McIntyre Miller[81] summarised the traits and characteristics of peace leaders as follows: empathy, optimism, forgiveness, orientation towards reconciliation and service, strong relational skills and interconnectedness, good intellect and imagination, a focus on the future, a holistic viewpoint, flexibility, cultural appreciation, use of narrative, integrity, character, trust building, humility and a sense of humour.

Concluding remarks

From current research on peace leadership (see Fox[82], Ledbetter[83], McIntyre Miller[84], Spreitzer[85]), it is clear that inner works/subjective viewpoints of peace/inner skills should be included in order for peace to be created. At the same time, however, outer works/objective viewpoints of peace/external behaviour and safe environments should also be in place in order for peace to be created by leaders. Researchers agree on the fact that conditions for both inner and outer peace circumstances should be in place in order for peace to be created.

Dinan[86] mentioned that peace leadership starts from the inside out. According to her, for peace conversations to begin successfully, one needs to come from a place of peacefulness, and from that place one can lead others to peace.

References

Alomair, M.O. 2016. International Journal for youth leaders. *Journal of Public Leadership,* 12(3): 227-238.

Barash, D.P. and Webel, C.P. 2014. *Peace and conflict studies*: Third Edition. London: Sage Publications.

Bjerstedt, A. 1993. Peace education: Global perspectives. Stockholm: Wiksell International.

Boulding, K.E. 1967. Towards a theory of protest. *ETC: A Review of General Semantics,* 24(1): 49-58.

Bryant, M. 2012. Harvard System. 'Self-leadership definition', Available from: http://www. selfleadership.com/self- leadership/self-leadership-definition/ (Accessed 22 August 2018).

Chinn, P.L. 2004. *Peace and power: Creative leadership for community building*. Sudberry: Jones and Bartlett Publishers.

Dinan, B.A. 2012. *Ubuntu leadership*. Paper presented at Barrett Values-Based Leadership Conference. Cape Town: South Africa.

Fox, M.A. 2014. *Understanding peace: A comprehensive introduction*. New York: Routledge.

Galtung, J. 1996. *Peace by peaceful means*. London: Sage Publications.

Keith, K. 2010. *The key practices of servant leaders*. Westfield: Greenleaf Centre for Servant Leadership.

Kester, K. 2010. Education for peace: Content, form and structure: mobilising youth for civic engagement. *Peace and Conflict Review,* 4(2): 1-10.

Ledbetter, B. 2012. Dialectics of leadership for peace: Toward a moral model of resistance. *Journal of Leadership, Accountability and Ethics,* 9(5): 11-24.

Lipman-Blumen, J. 2014. 'Peace and prosperity: Make it happen (A connective leadership strategy for global, enduring and sustainable peace and prosperity).' Paper presented at the International Leadership Association 12th annual meeting. London.

Lowney, C. 2003. *Heroic leadership*. Chicago: Loyola Press.

McIntyre Miller, W. 2016. Towards a scholarship of peace. *International Journal of Public Leadership,* 12(3): 216-226.

McIntyre Miller, W. and Green, Z. 2015. An integral perspective of peace leadership. *Integral Leadership Review,* 15(2): 1-8.

Reychler, L. 2006. Challenges of peace research. *International Studies of Peace Research,* 11(1): 1-16.

Reychler, L. and Stellamans, A. 2005. *Researching peace building leadership.* Paper presented at the International Peace Research Association. Hungary.

Schellhammer, E.P. 2016. A culture of peace and leadership education. *International Journal of Public Leadership,* 12(3): 205-215.

Shamir, B. and Eilam, G. 2005. What's your story? A life-stories approach to authentic leadership development. *The Leadership Quarterly,* 16: 395-417.

Spreitzer, G. 2007. Giving peace a chance: Organisational leadership, empowerment and peace. *Journal of Organisational Behaviour,* 28: 1077-1095.

Tipson, F.S. 2013. 'Natural disasters as threats to peace.' United States Institute of Peace (Special Report). Washington.

Van Brabant, K. 2012. *Leadership for peace.* Working paper presented at Inter Peace Conference. Bern: Switzerland.

Van Zyl, E.S. 2009. *Leadership in the African context.* Cape Town: Juta Publishers.

Van Zyl, E.S. 2016. *Leadership in the African context.* Cape Town: Juta Publishers.

Wilber, K. 2000. Peace in the Navajo language and culture: Some Navajo perspectives. *International Journal of Humanities and Peace,* 16(1): 74-75.

Endnotes

1	Reychler & Stellamans, 2005.	20	Kester, 2010.
2	Ibid.	21	Galtung, 1996.
3	Ibid.	22	Ibid.
4	Ibid.	23	Barash & Webel, 2014.
5	Fox, 2014.	24	See endnote 13.
6	Reychler, 2006.	25	See endnote 25.
7	Ibid.	26	Ibid.
8	Tipson, 2013.	27	Ibid.
9	Ibid.	28	See endnote 13.
10	Ibid.	29	Dinan, 2012.
11	Spreitzer, 2005.	30	Van Zyl, 2016.
12	Ibid.	31	Ledbetter, 2012.
13	Lipman-Blumen, 2014.	32	See endnote 32.
14	Ibid.	33	See endnote 17.
15	McIntyre Miller, 2016.	34	Ibid.
16	See endnote 15.	35	Boulding, 1967.
17	Ibid.	36	See endnote 17.
18	Chinn, 2004.	37	See endnote 15.
19	Ibid.	38	See endnote 17.

39   Ibid.
40   Ibid.
41   See endnote 33.
42   See endnote 17.
43   See endnote 13.
44   See endnote 33.
45   See endnote 13.
46   Alomair, 2016.
47   McIntyre Miller & Green, 2015.
48   Wilber, 2000.
49   See endnote 48.
50   See endnote 17.
51   See endnote 7.
52   Ibid.
53   Bryant, 2012.
54   See endnote 7.
55   Ibid.
56   See endnote 5.
57   Bjerstedt, 1993.
58   See endnote 7.
59   See endnote 29.
60   See endnote 32.
61   Van Zyl, 2009.
62   See endnote 33.
63   Ibid, p.11.
64   Lowney, 2003.
65   Ibid.
66   See endnote 1.
67   Ibid, pp 6-7.
68   Shamir & Eilam, 2005.
69   Ibid, p 399.
70   See endnote 13.
71   Van Brabant, 2012.
72   See endnote 32.
73   Keith, 2010.
74   Ibid.
75   Schellhammer, 2016.
76   See endnote 5.
77   See endnote 74.
78   See endnote 1.
79   Ibid.
80   See endnote 17.
81   Ibid.
82   See endnote 7.
83   See endnote 33.
84   See endnote 17.
85   See endnote 13.
86   See endnote 5.

CHAPTER 2

IMPORTANT BUILDING BLOCKS
FOR PEACE LEADERSHIP

Ebben van Zyl

"The sum of my teachings comes down to this: Live in harmony with yourself and be at peace with all humanity." (Confucius: 551-479 BCE)

Spotlight: Kofi Annan

Kgofi Annan is a Ghanaian diplomat who was born in Kamasi, Ghana, in April 1938. He completed his degree in economics at the Macalester College in 1961. He then furthered his graduate studies in economics at the Institut Universitaire de Hautes Études Internationales in Geneva. Annan received a Master of Science Degree in Management as a Sloan Fellow at the Massachusetts Institute of Technology. He joined the UN in 1962 and later served as its Secretary General from 1997 to 2006. He gave priority to reform of the UN by expanding the UN's traditional work in developing countries, maintaining the drive for international peace and security and by promoting human rights, the rule of law and human dignity. He issued a report in April 2000 about the role of the UN in the 21st century and outlined the actions that should be taken in addressing all these aspects. This report was later adopted by many leaders when they signed the Millennium Declaration at the Millennium Summit. As part of the Millennium Declaration, the following values and principles were accepted by heads of state and governments: respect and dignity for others, fairness (including a just society for all), inclusiveness, cohesiveness, equality and mutuality.

During his career at the UN, he occupied senior positions in human resource management, budgeting and finance, and peacekeeping. He took a leadership position in peacekeeping and peacebuilding at a time when the UN had operations around the world and ordered the deployment of almost 70 000 military and civilian personnel. During his career he facilitated and successfully led various challenging special assignments.

In his efforts to create peace, he emphasised the importance of implementing the values and principles of the Millennium Declaration. He also stressed the importance of self-respect, good communication and listening skills, empowerment of others and good interpersonal relations to reach non-violent solutions to conflicts.

Kofi Annan will be remembered for his ability to unite stakeholders from civil society, private business sectors, governments and non-government role players in support of the UN's mission. Through what he called the Global Compact, he took a strong stance to inspire businesses to comply with good practice in environmental conservation, employment laws and human rights in general.

He has received honorary degrees from universities in Africa, Asia, Europe and North America, as well as several prizes and awards for his contributions to the aims and purposes of the UN.[1]

Introduction

Important building blocks for peace leadership are evident in the actions of Kofi Anan during the term he served as the secretary general for the UN. During this period, he demonstrated important emotional and social intelligence in his thoughts and actions. The way he disciplined himself to work very hard in obtaining his goals, as well as the way he approached other people in maintaining good interpersonal relations, are proof of that. Communal intelligence was demonstrated in the way in which different civil societies, businesses in the private sector and government sectors were united and involved in actions towards achieving peace. Important communal values like a just and fair society, as well as inclusiveness and cohesiveness, were implemented by him as a way of uniting communities. Kofi Annan therefore proved himself to be a peace leader.

In this chapter, emotional and social intelligence (as part of emotional intelligence) as important building blocks for peace leadership (focusing on "lead self" and "lead with others") will be discussed. Communal intelligence to create peace in communities will then be discussed. Thereafter the Social Learning Theory is set out as a way of integrating emotional (social) intelligence/communal intelligence with peace leadership. Solutions as well as future research directions and research trends will then be discussed. The chapter will end with concluding remarks.

What are the important building blocks for peace leadership?

Manz and Simms[2] indicated that leaders (including peace leaders), should be able to lead themselves and lead other people in order to be successful. According to Manz and Simms[3], that involves emotional intelligence (which may include social intelligence). Dinan[4] created a model linking emotional intelligence to peace and focused on the fact that leaders should have emotional intelligence skills in order to be good peace leaders.

Veldsman and Johnson[5], are of the opinion that due to new challenges leaders have to face, a leadership style integrating the self (emotional intelligence), others (social intelligence), the organisation and the world, should be implemented.

Campbell[6] in his book *Global Leadership Initiatives for Conflict Resolution and Peacebuilding* referred to lead self, lead people and projects, lead organisations and programs and lead the institution. According to him, leadership skills like forgiveness, interpersonal skills, communication skills, problem-solving skills and the ability to balance work and life, are part of the peacebuilding process. By implementing the mentioned skills, emotional, social and communal intelligence become evident as important building blocks for peace leadership[7].

Jaffe[8] in his book *Changing the world from the inside out*, indicated that emotional and social intelligence skills should be obtained by leaders in order to make a real difference in our world. According to Jaffe[9], leading others (social intelligence), should start with leading self (emotional intelligence). By changing the world from the inside out therefore requires you to know and develop yourself first (emotional intelligence)[10]. Changing the world from the inside out, however, can't be done alone, and therefore other people and communities should be involved.

Fox[11] focused on subjective and objective viewpoints of peace. Subjective viewpoints of peace (according to him), include emotional intelligence. Objective viewpoints of peace include factors outside the individual like political and legal factors (government affairs and laws), economic and financial factors (financial situation of a country) and health and educational factors (how health as well as the development and training of citizens are handled)[12]. Objective viewpoints of peace, according to Fox[13], may enhance or inhibit a climate of peace. For instance, lack of financial support for peace actions may inhibit peace efforts. Also, the hungry and the oppressed whose basic human rights are neglected would probably not take part in discussions around creating peace. Another example may be that of citizens living in a country where they are oppressed. Under these circumstances, peace development and peacebuilding may also be regarded as not being a priority. Furthermore, restrictive laws and legislative measures may also inhibit peace efforts (for instance, in certain countries women leaders may be prevented from taking part in peace actions). Campbell[14] focuses on human security (also as subjective viewpoints of peace), as armed, psychological, structural and cultural violence and the impact of that on the basic essential needs of the population. The physical and territorial security of indigenous populations and institutions are central to the success of stabilisation and reconstruction efforts for sustainable peace[15]. (Objective viewpoints of peace are included in Figure 2.4 as external influences which may support or inhibit peace and peace leadership.)

Fox[16] furthermore emphasised the fact that leaders should encourage inclusiveness and cohesiveness in communities in order to attain peace. Ringer[17] is of the opinion that cohesiveness and inclusiveness in communities indicate a shared way of thinking, and hence communal intelligence. According to Ringer[18], leaders (and peace leaders), should implement communal intelligence in order to have an impact on their world.

Malan[19] indicated that implementing cohesiveness, truthfulness, sharing, inclusiveness, justness and shared understanding are important communal values in Africa. African management focuses on including everyone in a group context, and that the group defines individual performance[20].

Emotional (social) intelligence as an important building block for peace leadership

Mokuoane[21] defined "emotional intelligence" as the ability to comprehend, express, understand and manage emotions in oneself and others. By comprehending, expressing, understanding and managing emotions in oneself and in others, attitudes, behaviours and thoughts that support a more civilised and humanistic world can be cultivated[22]. A more civilised world may lead to peace.

Brackett, Rivers and Salovey[23] described emotional intelligence as a collection of capabilities to accurately perceive, appraise and integrate emotions through information channels to facilitate thoughts, including the ability to understand emotional knowledge and regulate emotions to promote emotional growth. By understanding and regulating the emotions of self and others, a platform is created to address conflict and create a culture of peace.

Ackley[24] focused on the definitions of researchers working in the field of emotional intelligence, namely: Salovey, Mayer and Caruso; Goleman; and Bar-On. These researchers are well-known worldwide for their contributions in the field of emotional intelligence and are associated with widely-used instruments, each of which has proven reliability and validity[25]. According to these researchers, emotional intelligence can be defined as follows:

- Salovey, Mayer and Caruso[26]: "Emotional intelligence is the ability to perceive emotions, to access and generate emotions so as to assist thought, to understand emotions and emotional knowledge, and to reflectively regulate emotions so as to promote emotional and intellectual growth."

- Goleman[27] [28]: "Emotional intelligence is the capacity for recognising our own feelings and those of others, for motivating ourselves and for managing emotions effectively in ourselves and in others. An emotional competence is a learned capacity based on emotional intelligence that contributes to outstanding performance at work."
- Bar-On[29]: "Emotional intelligence is an array of non-cognitive capabilities, competencies and skills that influence one's ability to succeed in coping with environmental demands and pressures."

From the above-mentioned three definitions, it is clear that emotions (in self and in others) are perceived (recognised) and managed (regulated) in different situations/ circumstances. This will influence one's ability to learn from difficult situations (e.g. high-conflict situations) so that one's ability in coping can be influenced. If a person is coping well in difficult situations, this may lead to more positive thoughts, attitudes and behaviours, which could enhance the possibilities of obtaining peace[30].

Summative perspectives

Models of emotional intelligence include the **ability models of emotional intelligence**[31] which view emotional intelligence as a set of mental abilities related to the processing of emotions relevant to the situation[32] [33]. These models also include **mixed models of emotional intelligence**[34] [35] (e.g., the Competency Based Model and the Bar-On Model of Social Emotional Intelligence) and **trait-based models**[36]. In the latter models the focus is not only on mental abilities in the processing of emotions, but also on the personality factors that could have an impact on an individual's emotional intelligence.

According to Ackley[37], Bar-On's refined model has 16 skills grouped into four composites as follows:
- Self-perception, comprising self-regard (respecting oneself, self-confidence), self-actualisation (pursuing meaning, self-improvement) and emotional self-awareness (understanding one's own emotions).
- Self-expression, including emotional expression (constructive expression of emotions), assertiveness (communication of feelings and beliefs, non-offensive) and independence (self-directed, free from emotional dependency).
- Interpersonal, referring to interpersonal relationships (mutually satisfying relationships), empathy (understanding, appreciating how others feel) and social responsibility (social consciousness, helpfulness).
- Stress management, compromising flexibility (being able to adapt emotions, thoughts and behaviour), stress tolerance (coping with stressful situations) and optimism (having a positive attitude and outlook on life).

Goleman identified 25 emotional competencies, sorted into four clusters[38]. These clusters[39] are as follows:

- Self-awareness: Self-awareness concerns knowing one's internal states, preferences, resources and intuitions. The self-awareness cluster contains three competencies: emotional awareness (recognising one's emotions and their effects), accurate self-assessment (knowing one's strengths and limits), and self-confidence (a strong sense of self-worth and own capabilities).
- Self-management: Self-management refers to managing one's internal states, impulses and resources. The self-management cluster contains six competencies: emotional self-control (keeping disruptive emotions and impulses in check), transparency (maintaining integrity, acting congruently with one's values), adaptability (flexibility in handling change), achievement (striving to improve or meet a standard of excellence), initiative (readiness to act on opportunities) and optimism (persistence in pursuing goals despite obstacles and setbacks).
- Social awareness: Social awareness refers to how people deal with relationships and the awareness of others' feelings, needs and concerns. The social awareness cluster contains three competencies: empathy (sensing others' feelings and perspectives and taking an active interest in their concerns), organisational awareness (reading a group's emotional currents and power relationships) and service orientation (anticipating, recognising and meeting customers' needs).
- Relationship management: Relationship management concerns the skill or adeptness at inducing desirable responses in others. The relationship management cluster contains six competencies: development of others (sensing others' developmental needs and bolstering their abilities), inspirational leadership (inspiring and guiding individuals and groups), change catalyst (initiating or managing change), influence (wielding effective tactics for persuasion), conflict management (negotiating and resolving disagreements), and teamwork and collaboration (working with others towards shared goals, creating group synergy in pursuing collective goals).

Riggio and Reichard[40] and Oxoby[41] believe that the social (interpersonal) awareness and relational (interpersonal) management components of emotional intelligence probably refer to social intelligence (as part of emotional intelligence). Social intelligence is about figuring out the best way for people to get along and come out of a situation with a favourable outcome. Even if a person has the qualifications on paper, a lack of social intelligence could lead to strained relationships, as well as lost opportunities. Riggio and Reichard[42] indicated that social skills are key components of social intelligence, and include the following:

- the ability to express oneself in social interactions;
- the ability to "read" and understand different social situations;
- knowledge of social roles, norms and scripts;

- interpersonal problem-solving skills; and
- social role-playing skills.

George[43] pointed out that critical traits for people with high social intelligence (as part of emotional intelligence) are:
- they are excellent listeners;
- they have social expressiveness skills, i.e. they communicate with appropriate and tactful words;
- they know how to approach and handle people by paying attention to what they are saying and how they are behaving; and
- they feel at ease with many different types of personalities.

Social intelligence (as part of emotional intelligence) forms an important building block in peace leadership when people have contact with other people. Both Dinan[44] and Ackley[45] proposed that the following components should at least be included when emotional (social) intelligence is described:
- personal awareness;
- personal management;
- interpersonal awareness; and
- interpersonal management.

Personal awareness and personal management probably have to do with the "self" when peace leadership is implemented. Interpersonal awareness and interpersonal management probably have to do with people and groups when trying to reach peace.

Apart from personal awareness ("knowing one's internal state"), and personal mastery ("managing one's internal state"), emotionally intelligent peace leaders should also be able to handle stressful situations. Stressful situations may be external to the internal state of an individual, and it is important for peace leaders to be able to handle this (as part of their emotional intelligence skills).

Interpersonal awareness ("to deal with others' needs") and interpersonal management ("to induce desirable responses in others") may be regarded as important to emotionally and socially intelligent peace leaders. Additionally to that, peace leaders may also have to deal with difficult environmental factors (as part of social intelligence). For instance: in certain cultures, the rights of women are not acknowledged. As peace leaders, it is important for leaders to take cognisance of the requirements of the situation, but also to take the needs of the individuals into consideration.

Ledbetter[46] argued that the implementation of emotional intelligence skills can lead to the resolving of conflict in societies and in communities. Communal intelligence will be discussed next.

Communal intelligence as an important building block for peace leadership

The nature and definition of communal intelligence

The Oxford Dictionary of English defines "communal" as belonging to and being shared by all groups of a community[47]. Communal intelligence, according to Fayard and DeSanctis[48], is a sense of "us" or "we-ness".

According to Fayard and DeSanctis[49], communal intelligence demonstrates commonality of purpose, values, language and other understandings, such as norms, roles and practices. There is a commitment to the welfare and continuation of the group and its reason for being.

Ringer[50] defined communal intelligence as a shared way of thinking that includes the way the world is perceived and the group's place within it. Members would understand things similarly, for example, what works and what doesn't, what causes a problem and what might resolve it. Korsvold and Ramstad[51] believe that communal intelligence is an active and encompassing awareness of the collective in community context. According to them, this is not only about manifest behaviour (for instance, how the group solves a problem or carries out a task), but also how the group is thinking, how mindful the group is concerning thought processes and member effectiveness as they go about their tasks[52].

The abovementioned definitions of communal intelligence can be summarised as: "A shared way of awareness, thinking, understanding and acting within a community in order to solve problems and carry out tasks for the well-being, welfare and benefit of the community as a whole and for its individual members."

Malan[53] believes that communal intelligence can only be realised when important values are implemented. According to Malan[54] values like forgiveness, compassion, humaneness, good neigbourliness, reluctance to initiate confrontation, the promotion of mutual understanding and the re-establishment of harmony in communities, are essential in attaining communal intelligence. Mbigi[55] discussed the importance of communal values in communities by emphasising the fact that important values focus firstly on the needs of groups and communities, before the needs of individuals are considered.

Communal values as an important way of thinking for peace leaders

Nussbaum[56] explained important communal values by referring to the aftermath of 9/11, when people travelled from across the USA to volunteer any type of support to rescue workers and victims in New York. The desire of both ordinary people and celebrities to raise funds for victims they might not have known and the collective compassion evident during those weeks and months were a natural outpouring of our shared humanity. The billions of dollars raised during the immediate period following the tragedy are the tangible measure of important communal values. The intangible measure of important communal values is simply the movement and feeling of compassion for fellow human beings and the spontaneous desire to act in a caring and compassionate way, in which our selfhood is, in turn, inspired by a sense of collective belonging[57].

Hailey[58] referred to one of the more memorable attempts to explain important communal values, namely during a speech at the British Labour Party's Annual Conference in 2006, when Bill Clinton used this concept to emphasise the need for cooperation and community spirit. He argued that society was important and that any individual, regardless of race or gender, needs others to become fulfilled. He argued that we need to relate to, and engage with, others in the community if we are to thrive and feel positive about ourselves and the way we lead our lives[59].

The abovementioned discussions go to the essence of being human and being part of society. Unfortunately, societies in many parts of the world have moved away from humanity and are more concerned about status, power and money. It is most common in Western industrialised countries to see people working extremely hard and neglecting their families. People become more and more absorbed in collecting possessions and money, and values such as compassion and mutual respect are disappearing. Focusing and acting on communal needs and values seems to propose the exact opposite. People who live according to important communal values are concerned about humanity and other people. Van Niekerk[60] is of the opinion that important values of humanity should be integrated into communities. Values such as forgiveness, compassion, positive group identification, reconciliation, etc. make it easier for people to be sensitive to others' needs and to be an active part of a group or community.

Hailey[61] suggests that important communal values are integral to the notion of peace leadership through the principles of reciprocity, inclusivity and a sense of shared destiny between people and communities. He points out that communal values provide a value system for giving and receiving forgiveness, a rationale for sacrificing or letting go of the desire for revenge for past wrongs or engaging in petty vendettas.

It is a way of culturally re-informing our efforts to promote reconciliation and facilitate the work of peace leaders.

According to Van der Walt[62] and Dinan[63], central to the important communal values are inclusion, cohesiveness, justness and shared understanding. If peace leaders can create circumstances where the abovementioned values exist, peace and peacebuilding could become a reality[64].

The Social Learning Theory as a way of integrating emotional, social and communal intelligence with peace leadership

Emotional, social and communal intelligence have already been defined, and it was emphasised that components of those kinds of intelligences can be connected to peace and peace leadership.

Van Sandt and Neck[65] and Lyons[66] believe that leadership behaviours can be grounded in the Social Learning Theory (see Figure 2.1).

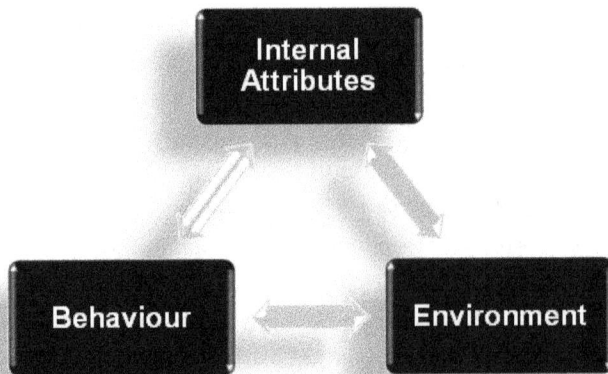

Figure 2.1: Social learning theory[67]

The Social Learning Theory[68] suggests that leadership behaviour can best be explained by a set of continuous, reciprocal interactions among three sets of variables, namely the person's internal attributes (cognition and emotions), the behaviour (actions) and the environment[69]. According to Van Sandt and Neck[70], these three variables interact reciprocally with one another to explain leadership behaviour.

Although peace leadership will be affected mostly by internal attributes of leaders (thoughts and attitudes), environmental factors will also influence peace leader behaviour (such as the way the environment is empowering the leader to implement peace strategies). Environmental factors and the internal attributes of peace leaders might also be affected by behaviour. For instance, when a peace leader recognises and accepts other people, this may give rise to a more conducive environment for peace talks (environmental factors) and the way the leader and other people think and feel about themselves (internal attributes) (see Figure 2.2).

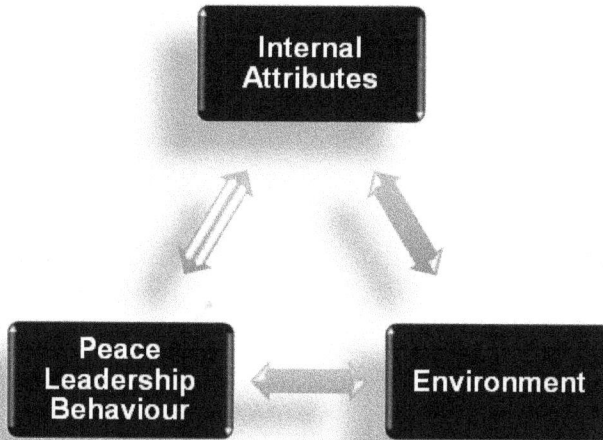

Figure 2.2: Social learning theory application to peace leadership

Emotional, social and communal intelligence behaviour leading to peace can also be integrated into the Social Learning Theory (see Figure 2.3). Emotional, social and communal intelligence behaviour leading to peace will probably be affected mostly by the internal attributes of leaders (for instance, certain emotions and cognitions)[71], but environmental factors (for instance, poor life circumstances) could also affect behavioural actions. On the other hand, emotional, social and communal intelligence behaviour leading to peace (for instance, positive self-management strategies and maintaining sound interpersonal relations) might have a positive effect on the internal attributes of the person (e.g. feeling good about him-/herself) and the environment (e.g. creating a positive climate for peace talks). Another example of effective emotional, social and communal intelligence behaviour and its effect on the environment and internal attributes could be the following: if a peace leader gets different groups to talk to each other and make progress in conflict solutions, the possibilities of a better climate for future talks (environmental factors) and more positive attitudes (internal attributes) could be created.

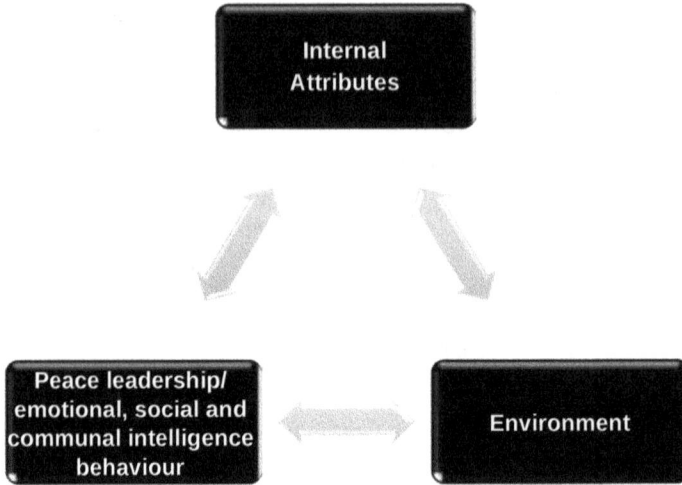

Figure 2.3: Social learning theory application to peace leadership/emotional, social and communal intelligence behaviour

The above-mentioned discussions suggest that effective behaviour (i.e. emotional, social and communal intelligence behaviour leading to peace as well as peace leadership) can be grounded within the Social Learning Theory. It is, therefore, possible to integrate peace leadership, emotional, social as well as communal intelligence into a comprehensive model of peace leadership.

Solutions

Based on what has been discussed in this chapter, important building blocks of peace and peace leadership can be depicted, as in Figure 2.4:

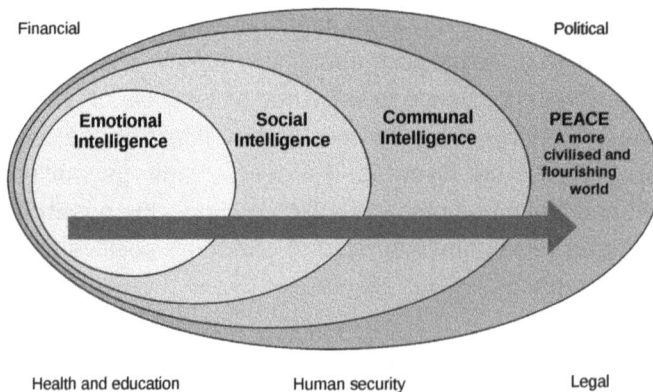

Figure 2.4: Building blocks for peace leadership

The underlying premise of Figure 2.4 is that systematic understanding is an essential component of attaining peace. To create peace, progressing through all the building blocks is essential. By focusing on systems thinking (each part of the model affects the other parts in the system), solutions to a problem which are not obvious, can be created[72].

Future directions/research trends

The key role in striving for peace will most probably be played by individuals and leaders, and not the environment. Future research on how peace could be attained should therefore focus more on what kind of individual behaviours and intelligences may give rise to peace. Collective intelligence (shared or group intelligence that emerges from the collaboration, collective efforts and competition of many individuals and appears in consensus decision-making[73]), is something which may be an additional building block to peace and peace leadership. Where communal intelligence is collective thinking in a communal context, collective intelligence may include collective thinking in a larger context (for instance, between different communities). Problems to be solved in collective intelligence will be more varied than in the case of communal intelligence, and one of the main challenges in implementing collective intelligence would be to achieve unity of purpose, action and thoughts.

Although high-quality individual thinking will always be important in peace efforts, effective collective thinking and communication should be implemented in addition to that. More research/thinking about collective thinking and communication as a way of achieving peace, should be done. Collective thinking as a way of achieving peace follows different rules and requires some additional understandings[74].

Developing standardised measuring devices to measure communal intelligence will help a lot to support groups working within communities on their own processes, relations and abilities.

Concluding remarks

The real-life story of Kofi Annan was discussed as an illustration of a peace leader utilising important building blocks for peace leadership. Important building blocks for peace leadership were then discussed. Emotional, social and communal intelligence were put forth as important requirements for achieving peace. National influences (political and legal influences, health and education, human security as well as financial and economic factors) may influence the building blocks for peace. In addition, it was pointed out that emotional, social and communal intelligence could be integrated with peace leadership via the Social Learning Theory. Lastly, future directions and trends were discussed.

To conclude: "What we need are additional structures, layers of connectivity, objectives, purposes, etc. if we want to achieve peace in our everyday lives. Old truths still hold, but the world is becoming more complicated, which makes it more difficult to achieve peace. Luckily, today we have armies of unused intellectuals, employed for work that uses only a fraction of their potential, ready to deal with it."[75]

References

Ackley, D. 2016. Harvard System. Emotional intelligence: A practical review of models, measures and applications. *Consulting Psychology Journal: Practice and Research*. Available from: http://dx.doi.org/10.1037/cpb0000070 (Accessed 5 October 2017).

Avsec, A. and Kavcic, T. 2011. Importance of the alternative five and trait emotional intelligence for agentic and communal domains of satisfaction. *Psychological Topics*, 3: 461-475.

Bandura, A. 1986. *Social Foundations of Thought and Action: A Social Cognitive Theory*. Englewood Cliffs: Prentice Hall.

Bar-On, R. 1997. *Technical Manual for the Emotional Quotient Inventory*. Toronto, Ontario, Canada: Multi-Health Systems.

Brackett, M.A., Rivers, S.E., and Salovey, P. 2011. Emotional intelligence: Implications for personal, social, academic and workplace success. *Social and Personality Psychology Compass,* 5(10): 88-103.

Campbell, A. 2018. *Global Leadership Initiatives for Conflict Resolution and Peace Building*. Indianapolis: IGI Global.

Creff, K. 2004. Exploring ubuntu and the African renaissance: A conceptual study of servant leadership from an African perspective. *Servant Leadership Roundtable*. Available from: https://www.regent.edu/acad/global/publications/sl (Accessed 5 October 2017).

Dinan, B.A. 2012. *Ubuntu leadership*. Paper presented at Barrett Values-Based Leadership Conference. Cape Town: South Africa.

Fayard, A. and DeSanctis, G. 2009. Enacting language games: the development of a sense of "we-ness" in online forums. *Information Systems Journal*, 2: 1-34.

Fox, M.A. 2014. *Understanding peace: A comprehensive introduction*. New York: Routledge.

George, J.M. 2000. Emotions and leadership: the role of emotional intelligence. *Human Relations*, 53(8): 1027-1055.

Goleman, D. 1995. *Emotional intelligence: Why it can matter more than IQ*. New York: Bantam Books.

Goleman, D. 1998. *Working with emotional intelligence*. New York: Bantam Books.

Hailey, J. 2008. *Ubuntu: A literature review*. Paper presented for the Tutu Foundation. London.

Jaffe, D. 2016. *Changing the world from the inside out*. Colorado: Shambhala Publishers.

Karsten, L. and Illa, H. 2005. Ubuntu as a key management concept: Contextual background and practical insights for knowledge application. *Journal of Managerial Psychology,* 20(7): 611-620.

Korsvold, T. and Ramstad, L. 2004. A generic model for creating organizational change and innovation in the building process. *Facilities*, 11: 303-310.

Larue, C. 2009. Factors influencing decisions on seclusion and restraint. *Journal of Psychiatric and Mental Health Nursing,* 16(5): 440-446.

Ledbetter, B. 2012. Dialectics of leadership for peace: Toward a model of resistance. *Journal of Leadership, Accountability and Ethics*, 9(5): 11-24.

Levy, P. 2010. From social computing to reflexive intelligence: the IEML programme. *Info Science*, 2: 71-94.

Lyons, A. 2011. *Leadership ethics and the corporate function: Leverage HR to mitigate the risk.* Capstone paper, Master of Professional Studies in Human Resource Management. Georgetown: Georgetown University.

Malan, K. 2014. The suitability and unsuitability of ubuntu in constitutional law – intercommunal relations versus public office-bearing. *De Jure*, 2: 12-15.

Mangaliso, M.P. 2001. Building competitive advantage from ubuntu: Management lessons from South Africa. *Academy of Management Executive,* 15(3): 23-33.

Manz, C.C. and Sims, H. 2001. *The new superleadership: Leading others to lead themselves.* San Francisco: Berrett-Koehler Publishers.

Mayer, J.D., Salovey, P. and Caruso, D.R. 2000. Emotional Intelligence: New Ability or Eclectic Traits? *American Psychologist*, 63(6): 503-517.

Mele C., Pels, J. and Polese, F. 2010. A brief review of Systems Theories and their managerial applications. *Service Sciences*, 2: 126-135.

Mbigi, L. 1997. *Ubuntu: The African Dream in Management.* Randburg: Knowledge Resources.

Mogadime, D., Mentz, P., Armstrong, D.E. and Holtam, B. 2010. Constructing self as leader: Case studies of women who are change agents in South Africa. *Urban Education,* 45(6): 797-821.

Mokuoane, M.L. 2014. *The effect of work stress and emotional intelligence on self-leadership amongst nurses in leadership positions in the Ministry of Health and Social Welfare in Lesotho.* Master's dissertation, University of the Free State, Bloemfontein, South Africa.

Nel, L. 2012. *Let's talk about positive psychology.* Essex: Pearson.

Nussbaum, B. 2003. Ubuntu: Reflections of a South African on our common humanity. *Reflections,* 4(4): 21-26.

Oxoby, R.J. 2009. Understanding social inclusion, social cohesion and social capital. *International Journal of Social Economy,* 26(12): 4-12.

Petrides, K.V. and Furnham, A. 2001. Trait emotional intelligence: Behavioural validation in two studies of emotion and recognition and reactivity to mood induction. *European Journal of Personality,* 17: 39-57.

Riggio, R.E. and Reichard, R.J. 2008. The emotional and social intelligences of effective leadership. *Journal of Managerial Psychology*, 23(2): 169-185.

Ringer, T. 2007. Leadership for collective thinking in the workplace. *Team Performance Management*, 3: 130-144.

Runsten, P. 2017. *Team Intelligence: The Foundations of Intelligent Organisations.* Working paper series in Business Administration. University of Stockholm: Stockholm.

Salovey, P., Mayer, J.D. and Caruso, D. 1989. Emotional intelligence. *Imagination, Cognition and Personality,* 9: 185-211.

Shonhiwa, S. 2006. *The effective cross-cultural manager.* Cape Town: Struik Publishers.

Sindane, J. 1995. *Democracy in African societies and ubuntu.* Pretoria: Human Sciences Research Council.

The Oxford English Dictionary. 1989. University of Oxford: London.

Van der Walt, B.J. 2003. *Understanding and rebuilding Africa from desperation today to expectation for tomorrow.* Potchefstroom: The Institute for Contemporary Christianity in Africa.

Van Niekerk, J. 2013. *U'buntu and moral values.* PhD thesis, University of the Witwatersrand, Johannesburg, South Africa.

Van Rensburg, G. 2007. *The leadership challenge in Africa.* Pretoria: Van Schaik.

Van Sandt, C.V. and Neck, C.P. 2003. Bridging ethics and leadership: Overcoming ethical discrepancies between employee and organisational standards. *Journal of Business Ethics,* 43: 363-387.

Van Zyl, E.S. 2013. Self-leadership and happiness within the African working context. *Journal of Psychology,* 4(2): 59-66.

Van Zyl, E.S. 2016. *Leadership in the African Context.* Second Edition. Cape Town: Juta Publishers.

Veldsman, T.H. and Johnson, J. 2016. *Leadership. Perspectives from the Front Line.* Randburg: KR Publishing.

Wanasika, I., Howell, J.P., Littrell, R. and Dorfman, P. 2011. Managerial leadership and culture in Sub-Saharan Africa. *Journal of World Business,* 46(2): 234-241.

Wolff, S. 2005. *Emotional Competence Inventory: Technical Manual.* Boston: The Hay Group.

Endnotes

1	Frangsmyr in Van Zyl, 2016.
2	Manz & Simms, 2001.
3	Ibid.
4	In Campbell, 2018.
5	Veldsman & Johnson, 2016.
6	Campbell, 2018.
7	Ibid.
8	Jaffe, 2016.
9	Ibid.
10	Ibid.
11	Fox, 2014.
12	Ibid.
13	Ibid.
14	See endnote 6.
15	Ibid.
16	See endnote 11.
17	Ringer, 2007.
18	Ibid.
19	Malan, 2014.
20	Mbigi, 1997.
21	Mokuoane, 2014.
22	Dinan, 2012.
23	Brackett, Rivers & Salovey, 2011.
24	Ackley, 2016.
25	Ibid.
26	Salovey, Mayer & Caruso, 1989.
27	Goleman, 1995.
28	Goleman, 1998.
29	Bar-On, 1997.
30	See endnote 22.
31	Mayer, Salovey & Caruso, 2000.
32	See endnote 21.
33	Nel, 2012.
34	See endnote 29.
35	See endnote 28.
36	Petrides & Furnham, 2001.
37	See endnote 24.
38	Ibid.
39	Wolff, 2005.
40	Riggio & Reichard, 2008.
41	Oxoby, 2009.
42	See endnote 40.
43	George, 2000.
44	See endnote 22.
45	See endnote 24.
46	Ledbetter, 2012.
47	*The Oxford English Dictionary,* 1989.
48	Fayard & DeSanctis, 2009.
49	Ibid.
50	See endnote 17.
51	Korsvold & Ramstad, 2004.
52	Ibid.
53	See endnote 19.
54	Ibid.
55	See endnote 20.
56	Nussbaum, 2003.
57	Ibid.
58	Hailey, 2008.
59	Ibid.
60	Van Niekerk, 2013.
61	See endnote 58.
62	Van der Walt, 2003.
63	See endnote 22.
64	See endnote 62.
65	Van Sandt & Neck, 2003.
66	Lyons, 2011.
67	See endnote 65, p. 374.
68	Bandura, 1986; Van Zyl, 2013.
69	See endnote 65.
70	Ibid.
71	See endnote 28.
72	Mele, Pels & Polese, 2010.
73	Levy, 2010, p. 73.
74	Runsten, 2017.
75	Ibid, p. 83.

CHAPTER 3

A PEACE LEADERSHIP-IN-ACTION MODEL: SELF-TRANSFORMATION TO THE CREATION OF PEACE

Ebben van Zyl

"In this postmodern world, cultural conflicts are becoming more dangerous than at any time in history. A new model of coexistence is needed, based on man's transcending himself." (Vaclav Havel: 1995)

Spotlight: Mohandas Karamchand Gandhi

Mohandas Karamchand Ghandhi, known as Mahatma Gandhi and the great leader of the masses in India, has often been described as the spiritual and political leader of India. He led the struggle for India's independence from the British Empire. Gandhi studied law in London. After finishing law school, he returned to India in 1891. In 1893, he went to South Africa where he spent 20 years opposing discriminatory legislation against Indians. In South Africa, he experienced the suffering of Indians due to racial tensions. He personally suffered greatly at the hands of the European colonists who treated Indians as outcasts. He was kicked out of a first-class train compartment even though he had a valid ticket. He was also refused a hotel room and was not allowed to sit inside a stagecoach with white people. This motivated him to fight for the rights of Indians by using non-violence and by "holding on to truth".

When he returned to India, he led Indians to fight the British with the same approach (of non-violence and "holding on to truth"). Inclusion and freedom of all Indians were therefore important values which he lived out in his life. India became an independent nation on 14 August 1947.

He reached his goals in South Africa and India without violence and created a more humanistic world (and peace) for Indians. As a preacher and practitioner of non-violence, best described as passive resistance through soul force instead of active resistance through physical force, Gandhi became world famous and earned the name of Mahatma, which is Sanskrit for "great soul". The world acknowledged his special place when the United Nations flew its flag at half-mast when he was killed. He is the only individual with no connection to a government or an international organisation for whom this has been done.

Gandhi created freedom and peace for India as a nation. He had decided that he would not hold any position in government, but rather remain a humble servant who would sacrifice his life for the cause of India. In doing that, he made an estimation of himself which proved to be the correct decision.

Introduction

A peace leadership-in-action model is evident in the real-life example of Gandhi. By being aware of what he is and what he wanted to achieve (leading self), he used his people skills to collaborate with others (leading with others), giving each person the opportunity to express their individual talents collectively. He changed his community (leading community) to a place of freedom for all where integrity, honesty and truth exist, which has led to a more civilised, humanistic and peaceful world not only for Indian people, but as an example for the whole world[1].

At a leadership conference, someone asked John Maxwell (a well-known writer of leadership books) about the greatest challenge he as a leader has experienced. He responded as follows[2]: "Leading me! That has always been my greatest challenge as a leader." Although some people in the audience were surprised by his response, the more experienced leaders were not. The reason being that they could trace many of their failures to their own personal leadership mismanagement. Maxwell[3] put it as follows: "Isn't that also true for you? If I could kick the person responsible for my problems, I wouldn't be able to sit down for a week"[4].

Maxwell[5] indicated that civilisation will always be in danger if leaders who never learned to obey other leaders are in charge. Only a leader who has followed well has done some self-reflection with regard to self-improvement and how to lead others appropriately. Connecting emotionally with others only becomes possible once you have walked in their shoes. Only then do you know what it means to be under authority and thus have a better sense of how authority should be exercised[6].

Furthermore, good leadership requires an understanding of the community/world you are functioning in. Ledbetter[7] claims that the world needs more leaders in all spheres of life, who focus on the creation of a more civilised and humanistic world. A more civilised world will, inter alia, be characterised by inclusion and engagement of everyone.

In this chapter, we will firstly try to answer the question: Why self-transformation in order to create peace? Secondly, specific solutions are recommended by focusing on a peace leadership-in-action model, as well as global perspectives on the implementation of this model. Future directions are discussed. The chapter ends with concluding remarks.

Why self-transformation in order to create peace?

According to Petrie[8], leadership strategies of the last 50 years were focused on the individual, i.e. what makes a good leader and what should be developed in order for leaders to become successful. The field of leadership therefore has focused a lot on heroic leaders as examples of great leaders who could command and inspire organisations and the community. In the last 15 years, however, this model has become less effective because of new challenges of the environment and the lack of appropriate abilities among these heroic leaders to handle all the demands[9].

New environmental challenges include the following:
- information overload;
- the dissolving of traditional organisational boundaries;
- new technologies that disrupt old work practices;
- the different values and expectations of new generations entering the workplace; and
- increased globalisation leading to the need to lead across cultures[10].

Manz and Sims[11], as well as Ledbetter[12], are of the opinion that our environment is characterised by rapid change, threats to peace, complexity and new high-tech autonomous work roles of the information age.

The constantly changing environment (according to Ledbetter[13]), necessitates the importance of leaders pro-actively adapting to these changes and implementing effective and relevant plans to survive. According to Graig and Snook[14], one way leaders can adapt to difficult changes is to improve the "human-element" in the way leadership is practised. By leading self and with others, the human element in leadership can be improved. By doing that, everyone will be empowered and be willing to help in overcoming difficult challenges.

Manz and Sims[15] however, are of the opinion that leaders (and peace leaders) first have to transform themselves in order to lead themselves. Transforming self means knowing who you are, what your strong points (and not-so-strong points) are, and then developing yourself. To hear and acknowledge your not-so-strong points may at times be difficult. This may be due to the fact that in order to identify aspects of yourself which might improve, you may be required to ask of yourself to work on negative experiences in your past (events in the past may be an indication of present behaviour).

According to Manz and Sims[16], those who are able to lead themselves should demonstrate that to other people. Even if unintentional, this modelling behaviour will help other people to lead themselves as well. Alomair[17] is of the opinion that if innerwork skills of peace leaders can be developed, this will facilitate the leaders' engagement and interaction with others.

The complexity of the new environment and the threats to peace make it impossible for one individual to know the solutions as to how to create peace or even how to define the problem (peace). What is needed is a transformation of the self in order to lead not only oneself, but also to lead with others and to lead the community so that peace can be defined and solutions can be obtained. Manz and Simms[18] as well as Reychler and Stellamans[19] believe that peace leaders cannot achieve peace alone, but only with other people and with communities. McIntyre Miller[20] pointed out that most models of peace leadership (as an emerging area of leadership) are inclusive and interconnected and often focus on peace leadership as a collective capacity as opposed to an individual one.

Ledbetter[21] claims that peace leaders should focus on engagement skills and participative leadership as well as employee empowerment styles to create peace. Spreitzer[22] argues that participative leadership gives employees a sense of empowerment which encourages them to speak up and share their opinions in organisations. If employees have the confidence to speak up in organisational contexts, this may have a spill-over effect to the community outside the organisation, where people feel empowered to change their community for the better. Spreitzer[23] believes that when employees experience democracy and shared responsibility for outcomes at their workplace, they can feel compelled to replicate these conditions in the social context outside of work.

A peace leadership-in-action model: self-transformation to the creation of peace

As indicated in the previous paragraph, a holistic approach in achieving peace includes the following: lead self (as part of emotional intelligence), lead with others (as part of social intelligence) and lead community (as part of communal intelligence) to the attainment of peace (also see chapter 2 where important building blocks of peace leadership were discussed). As also indicated in chapter 2, external influences like health and education, human security, political, financial, legal and financial circumstances all may support or inhibit peace. Moving through different phases (leading self, leading with others and leading your community), will enhance self-transformation (horizontal axis of Figure 3.1) and peace transformation (vertical axis of Figure 3.1) in a positive way. The movement of self-transformation and peace transformation in a positive direction will enhance peace.

Through cycles of action, reflection, learning and adaptation (see Figure 3.1), peace leaders will improve on efforts to obtain peace.

The abovementioned will now be discussed in more detail.

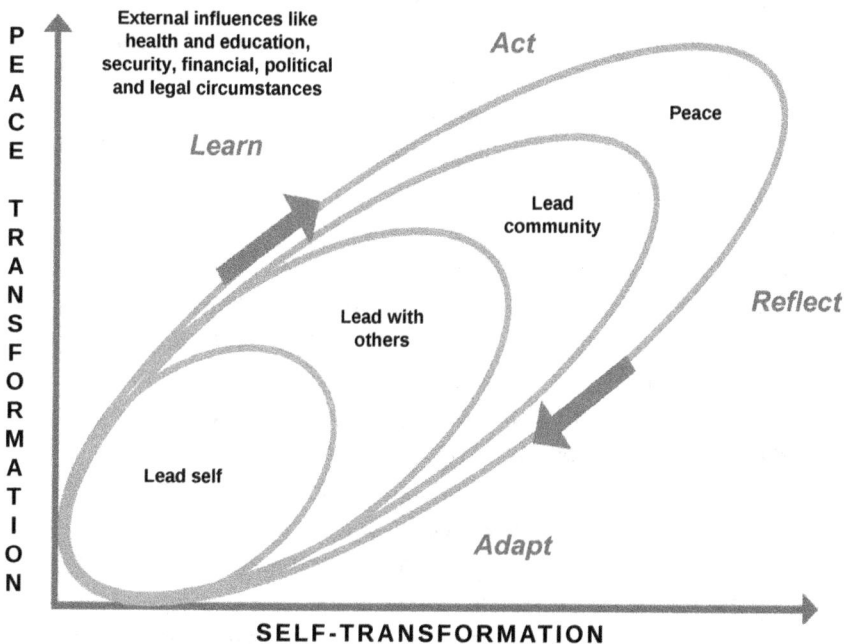

Figure 3.1: A peace leadership-in-action model: Self-transformation to the creation of peace

Leading self

John Maxwell[24] says the following with regard to leading yourself: "Learning to lead yourself is one of the most important things you will ever do as a leader. For almost forty years I have served others as a leader and for more than two and a half decades of that time, I was the senior pastor of a church. My years working with people have taught me an important truth: people seldom see themselves realistically. Human nature seems to endow us with the ability to size up everybody in the world except ourselves. If you don't look at yourself realistically, you will never understand where your personal difficulties are coming from."

Personal awareness and personal management (as indicated in chapter 2) are part of emotional intelligence and should be the starting point (see Figure 3.1) for peace leaders in leading themselves[25].

For peace leaders to have personal awareness means being aware of one's own assumptions, values, principles, strengths and limitations and how you contribute that awareness to being peaceful (in other words, evaluating your own thoughts, actions and emotions and to make sure they are in accordance with your real values and principles)[26]. Think of your own life purpose. Why are you here and what do you want to accomplish (for instance, to live according to your full potential or to help and support those who are in need)? What are your core values and principles (for instance, patience, love, friendship, forgiveness, persistence, compassion, kind-heartedness, sharing feelings, empathy, helping others) that will guide your behaviour/thoughts as you attempt to live your life "on purpose". It is therefore important to note that a correlation should exist between core values/principles and life purpose. Developing a personal vision or mission statement is an effective way for peace leaders to discover their true values/principles/life purpose.

An example of a personal vision or mission statement could be: "To … (what you want to achieve, do, become) … so that … (reason why it is important). I will do this by … (specific behaviours or actions you can use to get there)." After developing a personal vision/mission statement, share that with someone you trust who will regularly check if you are living according to your life purpose/values. According to Mokuoane[27], personal awareness requires one to learn and to listen effectively to internal dialogues through introspection, defeating non-productive emotions and attitudes. It helps one to observe one's own reactions to activities and work relationships, as well as to find out what activities are motivating and to focus on improving one's weaknesses. Dinan[28] indicates that being personally aware is the strongest foundation for peace to be realised because peace efforts start within yourself. Peace leaders should therefore regularly revisit their own awareness when peace is not achieved.

Personal management involves emotional management and personal mastery[29]. Emotional mastery refers to the ability to regulate both the expression and experience of emotions. The competencies associated with emotional management include the following: emotional self-control, transparency, adaptability, achievement, initiative and optimism. Personal mastery is about creating what one wants in life and in work (pursuing meaning in a self-assertive way). It's about taking control of one's life instead of blaming, not allowing external circumstances or mood to define one's choices, continually growing and learning, exercising discipline and taking proactive control of one's own choices, decisions and actions[30].

Peace leaders should therefore deepen their thoughts, attitudes and behaviours to the point of mastery. At this point one may feel a high enough level of self-awareness to know what to focus on for self that will bring about a more peaceful place[31]. For instance, people have identified some thoughts/actions which are not in accordance with their life purpose. Specific action plans can now be formulated to improve their thoughts, behaviours and attitudes. At this stage it might also be possible that they want to add some core values into their lives in order to achieve their life purpose. As an example, let's assume it is part of your life purpose to live according to your full potential. Constant negative thoughts may hamper the realisation of your stated life purpose. Actively focusing on more positive thoughts may help you achieve your life purpose.

Peace leaders have to handle stressful situations external to themselves; therefore stress-handling skills (for instance, time management, problem-solving skills and conflict management), will always be regarded as important.

Leading with others

Leading with others (see Figure 3.1) is important in achieving peace. Peace leaders do not exist in isolation – they exist in context and in relationship with others. Peace cannot be achieved alone, but with and through other people. Social awareness and relational management are therefore important concepts in creating peace.

Dinan[32] indicated that personal awareness and relational management flow logically to interpersonal awareness (being aware of others' emotions and values) and interpersonal mastery (to treat others according to their own chosen emotions and values). The focus is now on self-utilising awareness and learnings and applying those to interactions with others, whether it be within the family, the team, the community, the organisation or globally[33]. Chinn[34] summarised the relation between personal and interpersonal awareness and mastery when she wrote the following: "The kind of peace that we are talking about here requires that you know what you do as an individual when you interact with others. Peace requires that your chosen values guide your actions. Peace is the means and the end, the process and the product."

One takes the learnings from personal awareness and personal management and begins to apply them from self to others. Again, this starts from the place of awareness. Who am I at peace with and who am I not at peace with? Which circumstances am I at peace with and which not? What am I saying "yes" to and what am I saying "no" to in this space? Reasons for not being at peace with others/circumstances should be analysed. Now that peacefulness is understood at a personal level, this awareness is about being able to ascertain whether there is a place to intervene regarding peacefulness with others. Awareness may extend to family members, friends, community members, work teams and colleagues – group members and globally. Once awareness is achieved and aligned with personal awareness and mastery, it is time to achieve interpersonal management.

Building on personal awareness, personal management and relational awareness, this stage of interpersonal management connects self to others in a highly effective and peaceful manner. At this point, one is learning the specific tools and techniques to bring about peacefulness in terms of interacting and thinking about others. As an example, it is possible to feel centred and calm but then get triggered (in a negative way) by someone else. Drawing on awareness skills, one might still engage in a positive and calm way with such a person. Practising self-management should therefore make you aware of typical circumstances and actions of people who may trigger you in a negative way. Plans or tools about how to deal with this should be in place (for instance, putting yourself in the shoes of the other person).

The focus of interpersonal management for peace leaders is to influence, inspire, change and develop other people to attain peace. Working with others towards shared goals (peace), and creating group synergy in pursuing collective goals, is important[35].

Peace leaders may be expected to handle difficult situations (for instance, to have discussions with people from extreme groups), and specialised skills (for instance, negotiation skills), may be needed at times.

Leading your community

Dinan[36] believes that interpersonal awareness and interpersonal management can lead to attributes, behaviour and thoughts that have an impact on the community.

To change a community (see Figure 3.1), all sections of society should be included in actions (inclusiveness). The needs of people should be addressed (for instance, if security is a problem in a specific community, people can be included in making suggestions on how the security problem can be addressed). It is important to be aware of what the needs of diverse cultural groups in the community are. By being aware of everyone's needs, peace leaders can make sure that everyone is included in actions[37].

The quality of forming a united whole in the community (cohesiveness) might be evident in the way people from the community are willing to express themselves about matters of common concern. For instance, let's assume everyone in the community, irrespective of race, age and gender, are concerned about the security situation in the community. If everyone is able to speak in a comfortable and authentic way about it, that means that this community is a cohesive group.

Being just means to be fair and to act impartially[38]. This means that all people from the community are treated fairly and in the same way.

According to Van Niekerk[39], if inclusiveness, cohesiveness and justness exist in a community, it becomes easier to create a collective ownership of new perspectives accepted by the group/community (shared understanding). If, for instance, everyone in a community understands and accepts a common problem and feels included in a fair manner as part of the solution, objectives (for instance peace) can be attained.

Implementing inclusiveness, cohesiveness, justness and shared understanding in communities will make it easier to create a more flourishing and civilised world where people reach out to others and conflicts are resolved in a peaceful manner.

Peace

In chapter 1, the concept "peace leadership" was defined as follows: "Peace leadership focuses on the ability to influence the self, people and resources so that a state of peace within the self, with others and the community can be promoted, conflict be challenged and a common notion of and space for a more civilised and flourishing world (peace), can be attained".

By focusing on leading self (personal awareness and personal management), leading with others (through interpersonal awareness and interpersonal management) and leading your community (by applying the already mentioned communal values of inclusiveness, cohesiveness, justness and shared understanding), the abovementioned definition of peace can be attained.

As already indicated, moving through different phases (leading self, leading with others and leading your community), will enhance self-transformation (horizontal axis of Figure 3.1) and peace transformation (vertical axis of Figure 3.1) in a positive way. The movement of self-transformation and peace transformation in a positive direction will enhance peace.

Through cycles of transformation (action, reflection, learning and adaptation – see Figure 3.1), peace leaders will improve on efforts to obtain peace.

Acting is to implement certain peace strategies to create peace. Learning is about analysing the outcome of the interventions, so that you can identify what works and what not. Adapting means using what works and modifying/changing existing strategies if needed. Reflecting is to constantly think about improving the process of leading self, leading with others and leading the community to peace.

It may be possible (as an example), to create peace and resolve conflict in a community by means of regular discussions on the problem (acting). If the conflict is not resolved, due to not everyone participating in the discussions, it may require different ways to try and involve everyone (learn and adapt). Leading self, leading with others and leading the community in this example therefore becomes crucially important for peace leaders to achieve the needed outcome. Constant reflection on how actions can be improved should take place.

Lastly, although difficult to manage, external influences (health and education, political and legal factors, human security and financial as well as economic factors), may affect lead self, lead with others and lead community, in a positive or negative way (see discussion on this in chapter 2).

Based on the building blocks of peace leadership (see chapter 2) and the self-transformation model of peace discussed above, peace leadership can now be defined as: "focusing on transforming self to the attainment of peace (a more civilised and flourishing world) through lead self (emotional intelligence), lead with others (social intelligence) and lead community (communal intelligence)".

Global perspectives

The way people lead themselves as well as with others may be different within different cultures. This assumes that emotional and social intelligence (like self-awareness, self-management, social awareness and relational management) does not transfer across cultures[40]. Researchers argue that culture influences the ways that emotions and social interactions are experienced depending on which emotions/interactions are valued in the specific culture. Emotional and social intelligence therefore vary across cultures, both in terms of their expression and in their meaning[41].

Molinsky[42], however, believes that emotional intelligence can be linked to cultural dimensions of individualism and collectivism. Individualistic cultures value autonomy and a person's unique attributes. Personal awareness and personal management (as part of leading self), may therefore be applicable within cultures where individualism is regarded as important. The United States is the highest scoring nation on individualism, followed by Central and Western European nations[43].

In contrast, populations in Asia, Africa and the Middle East live in collectivist societies. Collectivist cultures value social harmony, good interpersonal skills and group membership[44]. Interpersonal awareness and interpersonal management (leading with others) as well inclusiveness and cohesiveness (leading the community), may be regarded as important within these cultures.

The challenge therefore is to combine the focus of individualistic cultures (where the focus is on leading self) and collectivist societies (where the focus is on leading with others and leading the community). This ultimately leads to a global civilised and humanistic world.

Molinsky[45] believes that cultural intelligence (see chapter 8) is one strategy for combining different focuses of different societies in implementing peace. Cultural intelligence predicts effectiveness in culturally diverse settings and explains differences in coping and functioning outside one's home culture[46]. Cultural intelligence is a capability that allows individuals to understand and act appropriately across a range of cultures[47]. Livermore[48] indicated that cultural intelligence "picks up where emotional and social intelligence leaves off".

Important communal values (like inclusiveness, cohesiveness and shared understanding) may help in changing communities into being more humanistic. Nussbaum[49] is of the opinion that interdependence is a reality for us all. According to Nussbaum[50], the evidence of Ubuntu values being implemented in all parts of the world is clear. Nussbaum[51] gave the example of the devastating effects of hurricanes and other natural disasters (like flooding), experienced all over the world, where strangers took food and blankets to people who lost their homes. Doctors, nurses and security forces went beyond the limits of their usual job descriptions to help patients. Communal values therefore reflect a humanistic view of leadership and of commitment and loyalty to all people, regardless of the culture they are from[52].

Based on the abovementioned, it therefore seems to be important to implement the self-transformation to peace model in different cultural settings (also in individualistic cultures). As Nussbaum[53] put it: "We should understand that our actions do not truly serve us unless they serve us all. We should look forward to a more just, equitable and inclusive future for everyone. By doing that, whether we are African, European, Muslim or American, we co-create our own safety and peace."

Future directions

Beinhocker and Hanauer[54] as well Reilly and Karounos[55] point out that the global financial crisis we experienced in 2008, the stagnation of the middle class and rising income inequality, the constant attacks by terrorists on civilians, etc., are challenging our deeply held beliefs about how a fair and well-functioning society should be organised. We typically talk about growth in terms of GDP (Gross Domestic Product), but the biggest problem with the GDP is that it doesn't necessarily reflect how growth changes the real lived experience of most people[56]. As an example, one can say that the GDP has improved considerably in the USA (with increased income effects for the top of the income spectrum). The important question to ask is, is life better or worse for all people? How are the gains of growth shared? What about the unintentional effects of the improved GDP (for instance, people working even longer hours to maintain their high standard of living)? According to Beinhocker and Hanauer[57], the GDP cannot answer all these questions.

If the concept of growth is to have significance for all people, it should therefore represent improvements in lived experiences. If the measurement of a society's growth and prosperity is the availability of solutions to human problems, growth cannot simply be measured by changes in GDP. It should instead be measured by the rate at which new solutions to human problems (like conflict) are met.

Growth should therefore be seen as the increase in quality and availability of solutions to human problems. Future leadership developments should therefore focus more on what could improve the quality and availability of humanity and humanness in general. The concept of "humanness" should therefore be emphasised more in future leadership and managerial thinking. Peace and peace leadership are important concepts as part of the improvement and implementation of humanness in communities and in organisations.

More research also needs to be done on how individualistic cultures can be developed/ changed to thinking more collectively. It was proved in the past that individualistic societies can help each other and act collectively, when in crisis. If people in such cultures can act collectively in a more constant way, global peace may be attained more effectively.

Concluding remarks

Peace, as the ultimate goal of peace leadership, should start with leading self. Lead self may lead to leading others and leading the community. Changing communities to be more flourishing and civilised (peace) can be done if the process of leading self and leading with others is implemented effectively.

Nussbaum[58] puts it as follows: "Our own actions (leading self) do not truly serve us unless they serve us all. Serving others, inter alia, means to serve with others in order to reach a common goal. This actually marks a return to the earth-centred values of a long-forgotten time when we all lived closer to nature. It connects us to the forces of the cosmos. The financial markets, in fact, with their short-term focus and narrowly based criteria for performance, militate against such progressive union."

References

Alomair, M.O. 2016. Peace leadership for youth leaders: a literature review. *International Journal of Public Leadership*, 12(3): 227-238.

Barnabas, A. and Clifford, P.S. 2012. Mahatma Gandhi – An Indian model of servant leadership. *International Journal of Leadership Studies*, 7(2): 136-139.

Bagheri, Z., Kosnin, A.M. and Besharat, M.A. 2013. *The influence of culture on the functioning of emotional intelligence*. 2nd International Seminar on Quality and Affordable Education, Istanbul.

Beinhocker, E., and Hanauer, N. 2014. Redefining capitalism. *McKinsey Quarterly*, 31: 1-6.

Canadian Health Leadership Network. 2010. *Lead self: the root of the matter*. Ottawa: Canadian College of Health Leaders.

Chinn, P.L. 2004. *Peace and Power: Creative Leadership for Community Building*. Sudberry: Jones and Bartlett Publishers.

Dinan, B.A. 2012. *Ubuntu Leadership*. Paper presented at Barrett Values-Based Leadership Conference. Cape Town: South Africa.

Graig, N. and Snook, S.A. 2014. From purpose to impact. *Harvard Business Review*, May issue, 21-23.

Karsten, L. and Illa, H. 2005. Ubuntu as a key management concept: Contextual background and practical insights for knowledge application. *Journal of Managerial Psychology*, 20(7): 611-620.

Ledbetter, B. 2012. Dialectics of Leadership for Peace: Towards a Moral Model of Resistance. *Journal of Leadership, Accountability and Ethics*, 9(5): 11-24.

Livermore, D. 2010. *Leading with Cultural Intelligence: The Real Secret to Success*. New York: American Management Association.

Marques, J.F. 2007. On impassioned leadership: A comparison between leaders from divergent walks of life. *International Journal of Leadership Studies*, 3(1): 98-125.

Maxwell, J.C. 2007. *21 Irrefutable Laws of Leadership: Follow them and people will follow you*. New York: Nelson Thomas Publishers.

Manz, C.C. and Sims, H. 2001. *The new superleadership: Leading others to lead themselves*. San Francisco: Berrett-Koehler Publishers.

McIntyre Miller, W. 2016. Toward a scholarship of peace leadership. *International Journal of Public Leadership*, 12(3): 216-226.

Mokuoane, L.M. 2014. *The effect of work stress and emotional intelligence on self-leadership amongst nurses in leadership positions in the Ministry of Health and Social Welfare in Lesotho*. Unpublished Masters Research dissertation, University of the Free State, Bloemfontein.

Molinsky, A. 2015. Emotional intelligence doesn't translate across borders. *Harvard Business Review*: Cross Cultural Management. Available from: https://hbr.org/2015/04/emotional-intelligence-doesnt-translate-across-borders. (Accessed 3 February 2018).

Nussbaum, B. 2003. Ubuntu: Reflections of a South African on our common humanity. *Reflections,* 4(4): 21-26.

Petrie, N. 2014. Future trends in leadership development. White paper: Centre for Creative Leadership. Colorado Springs: Colorado.

Reilly, A.H. and Karounos, T.J. 2015. Exploring the link between emotional intelligence and cross-cultural leadership effectiveness. *Journal of International Business and Cultural Studies*, 1: 1-12.

Reychler, L. and Stellamans, A. 2005. *Researching peace building leadership*. Paper presented at the International Peace Research Association, Hungary.

Spreitzer, G. 2007. Giving peace a chance: organisational leadership, empowerment and peace. *Journal of Organisational Behaviour*, 28: 1077-1095.

Van Niekerk. J. 2013. Ubuntu and moral values. PhD Thesis, University of the Witwatersrand, Johannesburg, South Africa.

Van Zyl, E.S. 2015. The improvement of cultural intelligence: An African focus. *Journal of Psychology*, 3(4): 1-9.

Wolff, S. 2005. *Emotional Competence Inventory: Technical Manual*. Boston: The Hay Group.

Endnotes

1	Barnabas & Clifford, 2012; Marques, 2007.	30	Ibid.
2	Maxwell, 2007.	31	See endnote 26.
3	Ibid.	32	Ibid.
4	Ibid.	33	Ibid.
5	Ibid.	34	Chinn, 2004.
6	Ibid.	35	Wolff, 2005.
7	Ledbetter, 2012.	36	See endnote 26.
8	Petrie, 2014.	37	See endnote 29.
9	Ibid.	38	Ibid.
10	Ibid.	39	Van Niekerk. 2013.
11	Manz & Sims, 2001.	40	Bagheri, Kosnin & Besharat, 2013.
12	See endnote 7.	41	Molinsky, 2015.
13	Ibid.	42	Ibid.
14	Graig & Snook, 2014.	43	Ibid.
15	See endnote 11.	44	See endnote 40.
16	Ibid.	45	See endnote 41.
17	Alomair, 2016.	46	Ibid.
18	See endnote 11.	47	Van Zyl, 2015.
19	Reychler & Stellamans, 2005.	48	Livermore, 2010.
20	McIntyre Miller, 2016.	49	Nussbaum, 2003.
21	See endnote 7.	50	Ibid.
22	Spreitzer, 2007.	51	Ibid.
23	Ibid.	52	Karsten & Illa, 2005.
24	See endnote 2.	53	See endnote 49.
25	See endnote 11.	54	Beinhocker & Hanauer, 2014.
26	Dinan, 2012.	55	Reilly & Karouno, 2015.
27	Mokuoane, 2014.	56	See endnote 54.
28	See endnote 26.	57	Ibid.
29	Canadian Health Leadership Network, 2010.	58	Nussbaum, 2003, p.10.

SECTION 2

IMPLEMENTATION

CHAPTER 4

TRANSFORMATION: LEADING PEACE THROUGH SELF, OTHERS, AND THE COMMUNITY

Dr Andrew Campbell

"We all want peace – don't we?" (Gareth Fitzgerald, Prime Minister of Ireland, 1981–1987)

Spotlight: George W. Bush and Saddam Hussein

A clearer understanding of one's adversaries is a wise strategy in international conflict resolution."[1] Thus, the different personality characteristics of national leaders, their attitudes, and mechanisms toward accomplishing personal and national interests' goals will determine their effectiveness in relating to other countries. To illustrate, a personality leadership comparison of US President George W. Bush and Iraq President Saddam Hussein demonstrates that self-leadership determines the initiation and resolution of conflict. The personality characteristics of Saddam and Bush influenced both the internal and external policies and relations with other countries. Giacomello, Ferrari & Amadori state that international leaders, "by the force of their personalities and the decisions they made, have enduring effects on history."[2] Saddam's personality characteristic of paranoia, narcissistic, aggressive impulses, depressive anxieties, distrust and anti-social behavior prohibited conflict prevention and reconciliation with regional and international power brokers. Coolidge and Segal state that there was "little world leaders could not have done to temper Hussein's sadistic personality disorder tendencies .... [and] .... submitting to negotiations makes antisocial individuals unwilling and hostile".[3] In contrast, Bush's personality characteristics of humor, information-centric, gathering analytical data, listens to various points of view, instinctive, and the need for power-affiliation shaped his decision-making process and the outcome of the conflict.[4] Goldfield[5] suggests that emotionally significant events shape the decision-making process that influences the perception of situations, non-verbal behavior, coping strategies, and leadership behavior. In other words, international leaders who develop a self-awareness of their personality characteristics are better prepared not only to lead others toward confidence-building measures in conflict-affected areas but also influence peace development within the international system.

Introduction

Within the international community, one can expect conflict among nations with certainty. Violent interstate and intrastate conflict is due to a clash of political, religious, ethnic-social ideologies and cultures among nations, communities, individuals. Many of the root causes of violence, such as disintegration in the legitimacy of national instruments of power, socioeconomic inequalities, repression, corruption, intercommunal conflict, racial disparity, competition over natural resources, and religious tension are central concerns for conflict resolution practitioners.[6] Researchers state that conflict prevention means "addressing the sources of conflict in poverty, marginalization, injustice, and building the domestic, regional and international capacity to manage conflict".[7] A violent discourse that spans across transregional boundaries, encompassing multifunctional approaches, and deploying multi-domain capabilities creates an environment where transnational criminal organizations, radicalization, and violent extremist organizations flourish. Additionally, driven by a clash of political wills between state and non-state leaders, it frequently contributes to an ideological crisis that produces hostility among intercommunal actors. In other words, the most important ingredient in understanding interstate and intrastate conflict is that violence operates across many different contexts.

There is an epistemological gap in the literature addressing the complex relationship between the theoretical and application leadership constructs and conflict resolution and peace development frameworks. A comprehensive literature review reflected four articles and two books addressing the role of leadership in the peace development process. As a result, there are no theoretical or application models addressing a leader's role in conflict resolution for practitioners to draw upon. Given that the global environment is characterized by regional instability, failed states, increased weapons proliferation, and global terrorism the need has never been more urgent for greater glocalized leadership – in particular, the transformative mindset of building bridges in resolving intergroup ideological discourse. Current business leadership models do not address the complex requirements of international relations and peace development.[8] Nevertheless, there is a relationship between leadership, conflict resolution, and peace development constructs and frameworks. History shows that changes in leadership may precipitate the change in protracted interstate or intrastate conflict.

Basically, nation-state leaders are responsible for the political, economic, and human security of the nation, institutions, and citizenry.[9] Lieberman[10] argues that domestic governmental leaders, non-state actors, civil society leaders, and communal leaders shape the peacemaking, peacekeeping, and peace-building operational environment toward sustainable peace and stability.

Peace actors must lead key stakeholders toward activities responsible for protecting civilians, humanitarian assistance, promoting human rights, organizing social services, and reconstructing governance institutions. The 2014 *Rethinking Peacebuilding: Transforming the UN Approach*[11] argues that:

> *peace was no longer only about ending wars and withdrawing belligerent armies to ceasefire lines. Now, peace incorporated all aspects of human life from the right to security to democratic rights; access to justice; protection of human rights; the delivery of health, education, and other basic services; and the provision of social and economic opportunities. Peace meant helping overcome old ethnic, religious, and social divisions.*

Fukayama[12] noted that state weakness and failure is the single most critical threat to international security. The peace actor needs to understand the root cause contributing to the vulnerability of societal instability. This understanding is important as peace developers seek an environment that transforms the national and intercommunal political, ethical, religious ideological narrative toward sustainable peace and stability. Noteworthy, stabilization and reconstruction in a post-conflict environment rest with the domestic leader's relationship with the governed elite, belligerents, and the governed to resolve the religious and ethnic ideological tensions among intercommunal parties.

This chapter proceeds in three sections. First, an in-depth discussion linking the failed state framework with peace development activities. This analysis undergirds our understanding of the dynamic nature of moving a country from a failed state to peace and stability. Second, an innovative framework that examines the role of emotional intelligence in leading self and others toward leading intercommunal tension in reconciling ideological worldviews in developing long-term sustainable peace, will be discussed. Peace development actors are global change agents that "empower people to create change themselves and participate in innovation during the transformation process".[13] Third, critical transformative issues for further glocalized leadership research will be addressed as peace development actors lead reconstruction and stabilization of confidence-building measures.

Failed state framework

History shows that internal and external conflict among states also occurs as nation-states rise and fall. Figure 4.1 illustrates the complexity as states transition from a failed state to stabilization and reconstructing the political, socio-economic, and human security institutions toward sustained peace. The failed state framework links national, local, civil society and tribal leadership across a whole range of deterrence as well as stabilization and reconstruction activities needed to end intrastate and interstate conflict. These activities require leadership.

However, "we are currently experiencing a global leadership crisis".[14] Given that leadership is an important element of statecraft, understanding sources and character conflict underpins the complexity that characterizes failed, failing and recovering states.[15]

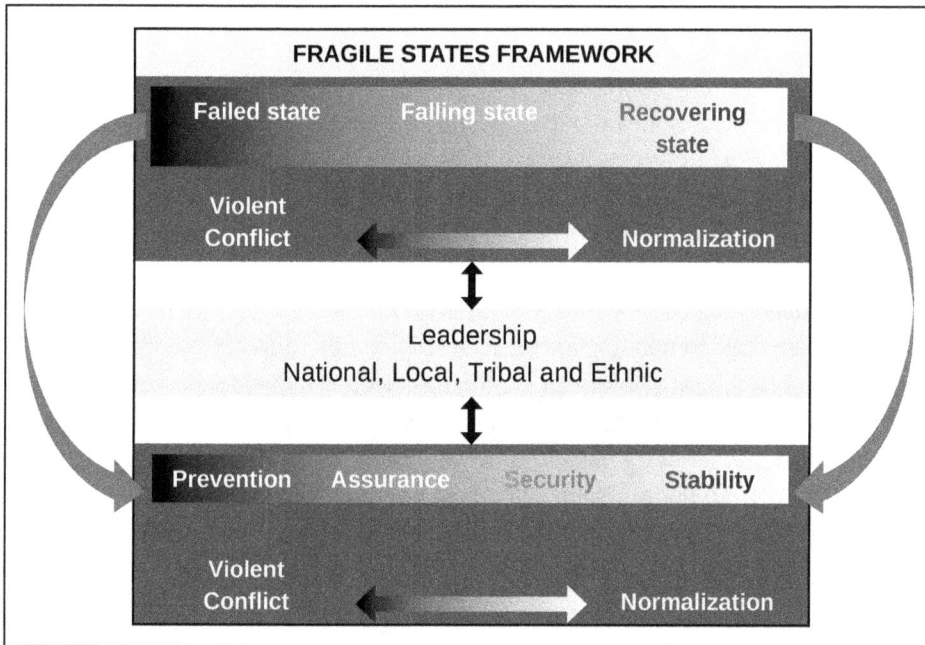

Figure 4.1: Fragile States Framework

Failed State

Scholars suggest the structural characteristics of a failed state cover a broad spectrum across the country's political, economic, human security, rule of law, and territorial integrity domains.[16] A 'failed state' or 'collapsed state' is characterized by conflict at the interstate and intrastate level. The contributing root cause is derived from the socio-disparities, ethnic and religious ideological tensions, conflict over natural resources, and elite corruption.[17] "In most failed states, regimes prey on their own constituents.

Driven by ethnic or other intercommunal hostility, or by governing elite's insecurities, they victimize their own citizens or some subset of the whole that is regarded as hostile."[18] The characteristic of a failed state is that it lacks the capability, capacity, and the authority to employ instruments of national power to protect and govern the population, provide essential services, prevent human rights violations, and foster an environment for ethnic and intercommunity confidence-building activities.

The initiator of peace from structural violence, armed violence, cultural violence, and psychological violence is the peacemaking leader that negotiates and mediates peace agreements, ceasefires, and protective measures for human security.[19] Scholars contend that the aim of "peacemaking is moving toward a settlement of the armed conflict, where conflict parties are induced to reach an agreement voluntarily … aims to change the attitudes of the protagonist".[20] Peacemaking scholar-practitioners postulate that it takes strategic leadership to know when and "whether to address the core issues in the conflict, which tend to be the most difficult or to concentrate on the peripheral issues in the hope of making early agreements and establishing momentum".[21] In fact, it never is an easy thing to move forward the conditions of conflict transformation from unofficial peace agreements to formal peace accords. The reason is the lack of trust, and the fact that relationships among warring parties and peacemakers are strained and frequently polarized within the negative peace and positive peace process. As a result, the vulnerability of violent resurgent and other low-level acts of violence commonly break out when parties break agreements, and when misunderstandings and miscommunication occur. Thus, peacemakers need strategic leadership competencies such as diplomacy, political savvy, intercultural awareness, and external awareness to structurally end violence and restore peace. In doing so, examining and transforming one's own's ideological values and beliefs as a peace development actor shapes the environment of conflict resolution and peace development. In a groundbreaking book Dan Millman[22] states that in forming peace "there are different interpretations of the past and many ways to change the present, there is any number of possible futures".

Failing state

A failing state describes nation-states suffering from weak national instruments of power that are serious enough to threaten the effectiveness and legitimacy of governing institutional structures. On the one hand, transitional authorities are challenged with prioritizing and resourcing instruments of power. For example, the prioritization of human security, providing essential services, and accountability of human rights violations challenge the political stability of transitional authorities. On the other hand, transitional authorities that fail to contain the spread of spoilers and antagonists who seek to exploit ethnic, religious, or other intercommunal tensions, threaten the integrity of peace accords as well as stable governance.[23] The main characteristics of a failed state are:

1. lacks the capability or political will to meet human security and physiological needs
2. fails to protect the territorial integrity of the state
3. comprises of civil wars, genocides, forced evictions and other violent actions
4. corruption of political elite
5. violence and human rights violations by spoilers
6. lack of legitimacy of political, economic, security, rule of law, and governance institutions.

Knodell[24] postulated that peacekeeping processes enable failing states to maintain order and stability by creating the political stability, physical security, rule of law and governance structures as transitional leaders comply with negotiated ceasefires and peace agreements by peacemakers. Peacekeeping initiatives do not address the underlying core issues of societal conflict. However, peacekeeping does address the strategic means to resolve state discourse while in a permissive and non-permissive environment.[25] According to the Brahimi Report, peacekeeping is a multi-dimensional operation that seeks the protection of civilians, monitors ceasefires, conducts security sector reform (SSR) and disarmament, demobilization and reintegration (DDR) activities, protects human rights, and respects the rule of law.[26] As de-escalation of conflict takes hold, peacemakers and peacekeepers build relationships and lead key stakeholders toward not only a shared understanding of resolving socio-political, ethnic, and ideological beliefs but also confident prevention and confidence-building measures. Basically, the multidimensional complexity of peacekeeping operations requires leaders and actors with the strategic foresight to navigate the balance of hard power (armed conflict) and soft power (diplomacy) to create space in which conflict resolution strategies can be built.[27]

Recovering state

As a nation transitions from a failed and fragile state toward stability, it remains vulnerable to spoilers that use violence to reach political objectives. Under extreme circumstances, human security, ceasing conflict, re-establishing the rule of law, and installing a national transitional authority are pre-requisites for establishing a recovering state in a post-conflict environment. Researchers point out that recovery of the state depends on the interaction of political, military, economic, social, infrastructure development, and strategic communication elements.[28] Therefore, to deter war-torn states from the reoccurrence and continuation of armed, structural, cultural, and psychological violence, leaders must look beyond quick solutions toward addressing the root causes of state fragility and shape the stabilization and reconstruction activities within conflict-affected environments.[29] As a result, the characteristics of a recovering state include:

1. a high level of human security from political, ethnic, and criminal violence
2. the civil populace perception of the government as the legitimate authority
3. the ability to offer basic essential services to its citizenry
4. an accountability to the rule of law
5. a stable institutional governance structure
6. economic and infrastructure development
7. a reintegration of ex-combatants into society.

The recovery of conflict-affected states rests with peacebuilding frameworks that integrate not only human security, human rights, and human development processes but also the political dynamics impacting conflict transformation toward sustainable peace. Figure 1 illustrates that linking leadership within the governing dynamics on the local, national, and regional level necessitates peacebuilding frameworks to stabilize post-conflict affected areas toward sustainable peace. Peacebuilding processes are inherently political with an end-state of institutional legitimacy and leadership systems that can peaceably manage conflict and prevent a resurgence of violence.[30] According to United Nations Support Office[31], the UN Secretary-General's Policy Committee conceptually agreed to define peacebuilding as:

> a range of measures targeted to reduce the risk of lapsing or relapsing into conflict by strengthening national capacities at all levels for conflict management and to lay the foundations for sustainable peace and development. Peacebuilding strategies must be coherent and tailored to specific needs of the country concerned, based on national ownership, and should comprise a carefully prioritized, sequenced, and therefore a relatively narrow set of activities aimed at achieving the above objectives.

Effective peacebuilding involves strategic leaders with the ability to navigate the complexity of unilateral or multilateral negotiations, the political savvy to sequence transformational reforms, and the business acumen to mobilize the necessary resources.[32] Basically, sustainable peacebuilding relies on the cohesive human security, governance, and rule of law approach as well as a structural leadership and relational change at the national and intercommunal level.

The next section introduces the concept of peace leadership. The understanding of self-leadership as a peacemaker, peacekeeper, and facilitator of peacebuilding activities provides the underpinning of how peace leaders lead others toward the relational transformation of intercommunal tension as well as reconciliation and sustainable peace.

Peace leadership

Peace development organizations need leaders with the strategic foresight, emotional intelligence, and intercultural awareness capabilities to create key stakeholder networks with a mix of cross-boundary institutional and organizational capabilities in response to a post-conflict environment.[33] Therefore, conceptual definitions of global leadership and global mindset underpin not only the conceptual definition of peace leadership but also the understanding of leading self and its influence in leading others toward establishing sustainable intercommunal peace and stability. Campbell[34] presented global leadership as "a person that builds alliances and coalitions to shape shared values through cross-cultural communication; develops mutual economic, diplomatic, political, and security relationships; and balances corporate, national and international interests". In this context, peace leadership is defined as:

> an individual with the guiding vision and responsibility to lead in multidimensional and multilayered peacemaking, peacekeeping and peacebuilding, a humanitarian operational institution or organization to adapt to the complexity of an uncertain and unambiguous environment by strategically navigating through periods of change, to engage in state conflict prevention and reduction, political and humanitarian crisis management, and stabilization and reconstruction practices, and to have the emotional and social intelligence, global mindset, business acumen, intercultural awareness, and strategic foresight to transform and reassemble the foundations of communal or state political, human security, legal, financial, and socio-economic institutions toward laying the groundwork for sustainable peace and development.

In the remainder of this chapter, the discussion will focus on emotional intelligence as one of the foundational ingredients to peace leadership. In the field of leadership much has already been researched and studied about emotional intelligence (also see chapter 2 where emotional intelligence was discussed as an important building block for peace leadership). However, there is a very limited examination of the theoretical application and implication of emotional intelligence within the peace development domain. Examining the interrelationship reflects a foundational shift for conflict resolution and peace development practitioners from the conventional focus on cross-cutting principles of stabilization and reconstruction to understanding the impact of a leader's emotional intelligence as an additive component of peace development.

Figure 4.2 illustrates an alignment of emotional intelligence components and **expands the discussion of chapters two and three (see chapter 2 where important building blocks for peace leadership were discussed and chapter 3 where a self-transformation model of peace, based on lead self, lead with others and lead community, were discussed)**, as a foundational leadership concept. Peace leader as a central actor shapes conflict prevention, resolution, and peacebuilding processes by leading oneself and others toward leading intercommunal peace. Leadership scholars suggest that emotional intelligence components such as self-awareness, emotional self-regulation, empathy, motivation, and social skills can be developed.[35] Wright and Wright[36] suggest that "no matter what an individual's life circumstances, it's clearly never too late to start" to transform your life and circumstances. Self-leaders influence more through who they are than what they do. Self-change management requires introspection, self-reflection, and meditation. The reason is that the effectiveness of peace leaders cannot rise above the level of their self-leadership. That said, the challenge of leadership frequently overlooked is the ability to lead oneself. Zeilinska[37] writes:

> The hardest person you will ever have to lead is yourself. When you can lead yourself through the challenges and difficulties, you will find that leading others becomes relatively straightforward. By being authentic and true to your beliefs, you can unite people around a common purpose and a set of values and empower them to step up and lead.

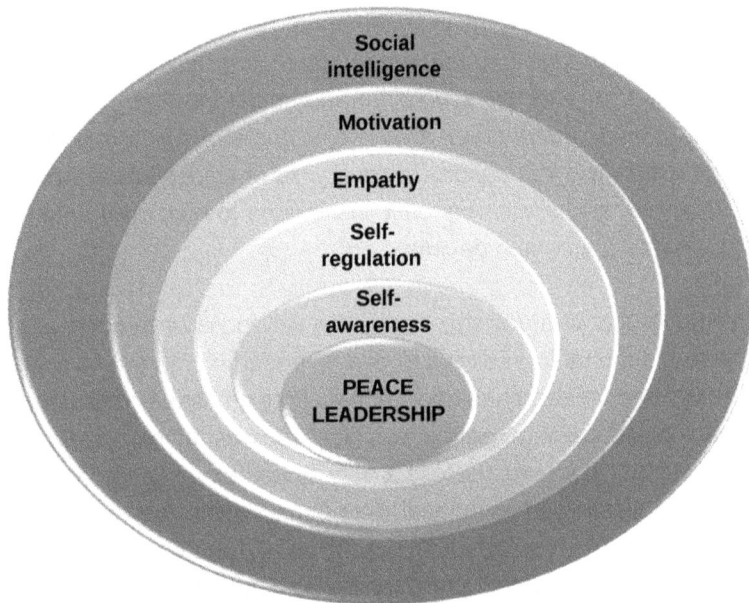

Figure 4.2: Transforming the self to lead others within the community through emotional intelligence

Nevertheless, effective peace leaders in today's complex and uncertain environment, draw on their personal source of ideological knowledge, values, and beliefs to guide leadership decisions and actions. The central question that many peace leaders ask is: 'What kind of peace leader does one want to be'? What is my personal vision and purpose as a peace leader? In other words, what kind of person do I want to be as a peace leader? Scholars suggest that self-leadership in the context of peace development reflects:

1. a positive self-regard for one's strengths and weaknesses with humility
2. the courage to protect the integrity of internalized values and beliefs once challenged by adversaries
3. a defined personal vision and purpose
4. a willingness to accept the personal consequences of difficult decisions
5. the courage to face challenges as opportunities and failures as learning experiences
6. a personal transformation
7. the trust and credibility to adhere to a high set of ethical standards of internalized values and beliefs.[38]

Therefore, emotional intelligence is an important individual leadership skill for peace leaders executing peacemaking, peacekeeping, and peacebuilding activities. Leading self, leading others and leading community will be discussed next. **(The discussion below should be seen as an extension of chapter 3 where lead self, lead with others and lead community, as part of the self-transformation model to peace [see Figure 3.1] were discussed).**

Leading self

Self-awareness

Figure 4.2 shows that the foundational platform of emotional intelligence is self-leadership through self-awareness and self-regulation. Walton suggests that self-awareness is "about understanding ourselves and knowing what pushes our buttons and why. More importantly, it also determines the way we act and the effect we have on others."[39] Developing self-awareness is important for leading self as a peace leader. The reason is that one's inner thoughts, feelings, values and beliefs, and emotional trigger points influence one's behavior and actions.[40] That said, developing a healthy self-awareness requires a sustained personal choice to understand and heal from one's traumatic life events as well as one's emotional trigger points. Leadership research on self-awareness shows that "while much, if not most, typical leadership development takes place in seminars, during a weekend or maybe even over a week of off-site training, that time frame hardly begins the process."[41] Therefore, the peace leader with a healthy self-awareness and attunement to their inner emotional triggers is better equipped to constructively navigate through personal frustration and anger during track-one, track-two, and track-three diplomacy processes as well as mediating and resolving intergroup turf wars. In other words, peace leaders with high self-awareness know their capabilities and emotional trigger points in order to constructively respond to wicked problems without succumbing toward political pressure in resolving key issues.

A peace leader with an unhealthy self-awareness may not have the absorptive capacity for sensemaking or meaningmaking or sense the nature of antagonism and emotional tags between conflictual parties during the diplomacy process. Second, a leader with an unhealthy self-awareness may not be able to recognize hidden agendas or be hypersensitive to others' perception of self and the team. Third, the leader may overtly respond with frustration over the uncooperative nature of conflictual parties in resolving key issues. Finally, when the leader is not self-aware of their inner emotional triggers during intense peace negotiations, frequently response measures may be irrational and demanding, e.g. reacting rashly and blaming others. Effective leaders must not only face but also heal their own demons in order to lead others in resolving intergroup and peace conflict. Bottom line is that with the courage to examine one's self-belief system the emotional self-awareness and self-regulation to authentically lead others with integrity and conviction will develop.

Neuroscience

Emerging research shows that neuroscience is an effective means not only of understanding how an individual leader's values, beliefs, and thought processes are shaped, but also of developing a healthy self-awareness. One could argue that incorporating the development of neuroscience into leadership development programs is a paradigm shift. Leadership development programs are designed for leadership behavioral changes at the cognitive level with often short-term outcomes. However, the nexus of leadership and neuroscience provides a scientific tool for self-examination of innate values, belief system, and emotional structures at the unconscious level, often with permanent outcomes. Wilder[42] postulates that a leader can re-program their value-based belief structure, automatic emotional response architecture, and habits in response to new situations or changes in their environment. In the groundbreaking book *Transformed! The science of spectacular living*, Wright and Wright[43] argue that "we can literally change our brains and our minds, and what we believe, who we are, and how we live. We can transform." They continue arguing that:

> not only are we called to transform, but neuroscience research today definitively demonstrates that we are also uniquely designed to transform, to fulfill our potential. Deep within us, both in our hearts and in our minds, reside the drivers for transformation.[44]

In the context of peace development, the groundbreaking research for "*Neuroscience for the Peacebuilder*", Fitzduff[45] argues that "intuitive/emotional thinking versus cognitive reasoning … is particularly evident and automatic in situations where fear is a factor, which is an emotion that is very present in many of the contexts we deal with as peacebuilder". Hence, integrating neuroscience into the conflict resolution and peace practitioner's toolkit will not only enable the leader to understand and manage the emotional triggering events but also transform how to self-lead with authenticity. In essence, self-leadership is possible when a leader chooses to accept the challenge of investing in the hard work of taking charge of developing their own self-awareness and emotional maturity.

Brain researchers suggest that neuroplasticity "enables transformative brain change via the right insights and training, which translates into new behaviors".[46] For example, the left brain cognitively processes information logically, rationally, analyzes issues sequentially and is solution-focused when solving problems. Within the diplomatic approaches with track one and track two, left-brain leaders tend to not only strategically compartmentalize peace development negotiations on specific individual issues but are also perceptually opinionated when presented with factual details.[47] Leaders who operate from the left brain are relationally disconnected and are fixated on problem-solving at all costs. The result is the tendency to lose trust of others and maintain coalitions built among conflictual parties. The right brain, on the other hand, unconsciously tends to globally examine the interconnectedness of issues and its impact on others within the community, as well as presents problem-solving solutions from a relational and emotional value-based lens. Leaders operating from the right brain are connected to the sensemaking and meaningmaking toward social movements for peaceful change within societal instruments. The problem is that the right brain operates faster than the left brain. Thus, the proverbial saying "we say things and react to situations without thinking and later regret" is alive and well. In essence, peace developers who are self-aware of their own right/left brain dynamics are better able to lead from their core personality and strategically transform their response to emotional triggers during intense track one and track two diplomatic processes.

Self-regulation

Figure 4.2 shows that another foundational element of self-leadership for peace development actors and leaders is self-regulation. Scholars note that self-regulation "refers to the ability to understand and control one's emotions, thoughts, and behaviors to achieve the desired outcomes through self-directed influence."[48] Goleman[49] states that "the signs of emotional self-regulation, therefore, are easy to see: a propensity for reflection and thoughtfulness; comfort with ambiguity and change; and an ability to say no to impulsive urges." Self-regulation is important for effective self-leadership as peace actors in order to control the overt display of inner emotional triggers and inner feelings of frustration in intense situations during track one and track two diplomatic processes. In fact, the leader's lack of emotional control over their impulses frequently prevents or damages the integrative bargaining process in developing joint agreements toward resolving the underlying causes of conflict. The challenge is that leaders' intense desire to act on emotional impulses at the moment is difficult to control not only within the track one and track two processes but also in day-to-day organizational operation. For that reason, peace leaders need the capacity to self-lower the inner emotional intensity of frustration, anger, and manage one's emotional triggers during track one and track two processes. Basically, leading self requires the self-regulation to control one's temperament as well as manage emotional triggers when parties break cooperative peace agreements and peace development outcomes are not achieved.

Mindfulness

Not only does the research note that neuroscience builds the peace leader's self-awareness capability, some literature suggests that mindfulness manages the leader's self-regulation capabilities. "Mindfulness is the skill of being able to be completely present with your actions, your environment or your companions and it makes other skills such as listening and collaboration so much easier."[50] Scientific research reveals that consistent practice of mindfulness strengthens the self-regulation and the sensory awareness of physical messages from emotional triggering events associated with intense situations from challenges associated with an organizational crisis or an intergroup conflict.[51] Furthermore, the practice of mindfulness re-programs the areas of the brain by silencing negative self-talk as well as redirecting one's thoughts from wandering, which transforms the mind into learning how to emotionally control oneself in the heat of the moment. Thus, the consistent practice of mindfulness is a critical tool for self-regulation among peace development actors and organizational leaders. The reason is that without self-regulation the ability for self-control in the heat of intense emotional negotiations or arbitration situations is compromised. Therefore, mindfulness techniques equip the peace leader's capacity, when emotions are running high, to unconsciously self-control their response and calmly and rationally lower the temperature for parties to address the contentious issues associated with stabilization and reconstruction activities. Jha[52] makes a strong case that leaders subscribing to mindfulness encounter fewer performance errors, are more attentive to active listening, and less reactionary to emotionally intense situations. In fact, incorporating mindfulness not only quiets the mind and reduces leadership stressors through self-regulation but also strengthens the peace practitioner's inner resilience to adversity and setbacks. Mindfulness transforms the self-leadership capacity of peace practitioners at the unconscious level by reprogramming the neural pathways that will change not only the long-term leadership behavior but also our lives.

There is a supportive relationship between neuroscience and mindfulness. Incorporating the tools of neuroscience and mindfulness increases not only the peace leader's capacity for self-leadership but also one's sensemaking and meaningmaking skills. Goleman[53] points out that "the key to knowing others' emotional terrain is an intimate familiarity with your own." Personal transformation is at the heart of self-leadership. In fact, an emotionally healthy leader will have the skills to not only listen for hidden meanings and communicate authentically toward a shared understanding but also endure a calm demeanor in the heat of the moment. Note that integrating neuroscience to develop self-awareness and mindfulness that builds self-regulation of one's emotions provides the authenticity, empathy, and motivation to bring discourse parties together in order to understand and address shared concerns and interests. Nevertheless, neuroscience and mindfulness development will strengthen the emotional intelligence rather than transform the personality of peace leaders. In fact, scholars suggest that self-awareness with emotional control lays the groundwork to lead others in understanding the social influence of sensemaking as a function of leadership.[54] That said, if a peace actor or leader cannot lead themselves, how can they lead others?

Leading Others

Figure 4.1 displays leading others as the linchpin in transforming an emerging failed state towards stabilization. Effective peace leaders, driven by their self-awareness and self-management, have the sensemaking and meaningmaking capability to lead others during the conflict resolution and peace development process. Peace development actors recognize that diplomatic leadership is central toward leading others. Figure 4.2 shows that self-leadership is foundational to leading others. The reason is that self-awareness and emotional regulation enable leaders with empathy to effectively lead others through the complex dynamics of conflict resolution. Bass and Bass[55] state that "empathetic leaders can manage conflict with supportive, friendly, obliging, compromising, and integrative efforts to move the parties from a competitive to a cooperative stance." Hence, empathetic leaders transform intergroup dynamics that not only correct misperceptions and develop shared interests but also address the resolution of intra-party conflicts.[56] In essence, the conflict management and resolution necessitate leaders with the empathy to untangle the difficult relationships, conflicting interests, and conflicting ideological worldviews.

Empathy and forgiveness

Research studies show that empathy is an important global leadership competency for peace development actors. Scholars postulate that "sensing what others feel without their saying so captures the essence of empathy."[57] Empathetic peace development actors will sense the potential bottlenecks and seek to circumvent the protracted ideological differences by changing the narrative and reframing issue-specific areas between parties. This includes identifying harm, ideological trauma, and socio-ethnic injustice experienced by victims. That said, peace leaders with empathy sense, read, and attune to another's emotional state during peace negotiations, alternative dispute resolution, and mediation activities. Listening, attuning, and asking questions by civil society leaders and intercommunal leaders will lead others toward understanding the ideological assumptions and beliefs that created instability among identity groups. In fragile states transitioning from conflict to peace, empathetic peace workers sense windows of opportunities to address ethnic, religious, and social divisions with tribal, local, and intercommunal leaders. Thus, leading others with empathy strengthens the evolutionary adaptation to sense points of discourse within the intergroup relationships and diplomatically reduce outer group aggression.[58] In the end, empathy gives peace leaders the diplomacy to reduce the acts of aggression and reintegrate ex-combatants who committed structural acts of violence, human rights violations, and communal genocide back into the community.

Frequently, leaders think they demonstrate empathy in their leadership repertoire. However, empathy is determined by the recipient, not the leader. Therefore, when a leader lacks empathy they are not able to:
1. sense others' emotional cues and perspectives
2. show sensitivity, understand and respond to other people's needs and feelings
3. listen and attune for hidden meaning and messages of others' body language
4. gain the trust of others
5. facilitate forgiveness and reconciliation
6. develop the capacity for building trust[59].

Leaders with a lack of empathy "are inconsistent with sustained political leadership … [and] … when it does occur in the ranks of political figures, it could have catastrophic consequences."[60] Bearing this in mind, it becomes clear that peace leaders without empathy will lack the ability to understand how key stakeholders feel and think during track one and track two negotiations. Also, peace leaders will lack the ability to read the subtle signals between opponents during peace-supporting activities. In other words, peace leaders who lack empathy are unable to build trust, understand diverse worldviews and one's political awareness to influence others toward peace development.

Leadership scholars suggest that a peace practitioner "transforms conflict from a force that can be destructive and divisive into one that is healing and connecting."[61] In fact, Campbell and Johnson[62] agree that empathy creates an interconnective healing environment that restores relationships through forgiveness and reconciliation in a post-conflict environment. Note Campbell, Ferch, Johnson[63] who agree that the most powerful weapon to fight against evil and develop sustainable peace rests with forgiveness. Yergler[64] defines forgiveness as "the act of releasing another from the guilt, shame, or deserved retribution they have merited through their own intentional or unintentional actions directed at another which have resulted in hurt, anger, animosity and relational polarization." Thus, introducing forgiveness as a pathway toward individual and national healing is a paradigm shift within the conflict resolution and peace discipline. In other words, sustainable peace relies on individual healing from the emotional and physical trauma experienced by victims in conflict-affected areas.

Forgiveness is a strategic enabler of statecraft in a post-conflict environment. However, peace development actors and leaders rarely address leading others toward individual forgiveness against perpetrators committing human rights violations. Victims find it difficult to emotionally let go, forgive, and move on from traumatic experiences such as gross human rights violations, ethnic cleansing, and acts of aggression. On the one hand, forgiveness is an internal process of individual courage that cognitively, emotionally, and spiritually transforms the meaning of the traumatic event as well as release of rooted transgression by the perpetrator to wipe the slate clean and restore a cooperative relationship. On the other hand, empathetic peace leaders need to resolve and emotionally heal from traumatic events in their own life in order to lead others toward emotional forgiveness. Emotional forgiveness releases the desire for retributive justice models and builds the restorative justice models toward sustainable peacebuilding frameworks. According to Fehr and Gelfand,[65] "restorative justice values can provide a strong foundation for forgiveness climate post conflict by emphasizing the importance of bringing all parties into the conflict resoution process." "Basically, research shows that empathy leading others toward forgiveness is a critical peace leadership ingredient and opens the way for both sides to live together in peace."[66]

Leading the Community

Social Intelligence

In today's environment, peace development actors and leaders with social intelligence are equipped to lead others through complex intercommunal ideological challenges of forgiveness, reconciliation, and healing.[67] The dual development of self-leadership and leading others builds the peace leader's capability to lead the community through social intelligence. Social intelligence is referred to as a social awareness of personal interactions, empathy in understanding and sensing another's thoughts and feelings, and the ability to listen and attune to another person's concerns.[68] The peace leader's social intelligence provides the relational leadership skills for diplomacy, negotiation, mediation, and conflict resolution. That said, emotionally healthy peace leaders have the social intelligence to mediate conflicting parties from merely coexisting to understanding each other as political elites seek to resolve wicked problems associated with state fragility.

Leadership is more about who you are than the formal reins of intercommunal positions. Sustainable intercommunal peace depends on simultaneous economic development and security. Social intelligence of peace leaders acts as a catalyst of positive change toward resolving wicked problems associated with balancing economic service-delivery programs with security from genocide, ethnic cleansing, or gross violations of human rights. Societies moving away from violence need peace leaders with the relational leadership that builds trust through understanding tribal, local, and intercommunal leaders' experiences and perceptions to facilitate confidence-building measures. Researchers[69] suggest that emotionally significant events shape the decision-making process that influences the perception of situations, non-verbal behavior, coping strategies, and leadership behavior. Therefore, neuroscience and mindfulness develop the peace leaders' ability to influence the social cognition of tribal, local, and intercommunal leadership interactions. One of the prime leadership influences of peace leaders in preventing repeated cycles of violence is opening a dialogue toward intercommunal reconciliation. On the one hand, forgiveness is an individual endeavor. Reconciliation, on the other hand, is an intercommunal process. Reconciliation breaks the cycles of repeated intercommunal violence. Individuals can have forgiveness without reconciliation but cannot have intercommunal reconciliation without individual forgiveness. The problem is that reconciliation has emerged as a specific strategic goal of many peace development programs without peace leaders having the relational foundation to lead intercommunal peace-building activities. Peace leaders need the relational leadership skills to hold dialogues with key stakeholders as well as relationship building with key political tribal, local, and communal leaders to equip peace leaders to facilitate reconciliation through truth telling and memorialization activities. In other words, what distinguishes good peace leaders from great peace leaders rests on the ability to understand one's own emotional dynamics, accurately attune to others' perceptions and beliefs, and move conflict parties toward a shared direction of conflict resolution and peace.[70]

Future trends

The challenge global leadership researchers wrestle with is expanding the theoretical leadership aperture that shapes leader competence-based development, characteristic traits, knowledge, and practical skill sets to meet global challenges outside the business environment. The structural, as well as personal and group transformation to resolve conflict-afflicted areas, is the biggest global challenge for the international community. There is a lack of empirical research on emotional intelligence within the peace development practice. For example, how do peace leaders develop the personal transformation to lead themselves toward a group transformation that leads others in addressing the root cause and preventing a resurgence of conflict?

Second, more work is urgently needed to further develop a standardized peace leadership definition and an empirical application model to prepare peace workers for the volatile, complex, uncertain and ambiguous peace development environment. The reason is that leaders in a peaceful development organization frequently lead organizations and operations by trial and error. Therefore, a standardized definition of peace leadership can be used by researchers to create peace leadership profiles that address the complexities of glocalized ideological political, religious, ethnic, and socio-cultural differences in executing peace operations.

Third, further research is urgently needed to empirically examine the application of theoretical leadership constructs within the international relations and conflict-resolution disciplines. That said, educational institutions and peace organizations need to integrate theoretical leadership models and competencies into training programs. The reason is that they lack leadership application models for peace workers executing the United States Institute of Peace Stabilization and Reconstruction Framework and other peace development models in conflict-afflicted areas.

Fourth, future research is needed to empirically examine the validity of forgiveness as a peace leadership competence. There is a growing body of knowledge recognizing the value of restorative justice and critical elements of forgiveness and reconciliation. Thus the need for conducting research on how forgiveness as an individual and collective competency would assist peace leaders in their understanding of best practices that shape restorative justice and intercommunal reconciliation.

The final issue for further research: How does a peace leader influence the actions of a non-state actor or leader (a terrorist organization) toward peace within the border of another nation state? More importantly, how does a peace development worker lead peace operations when they have no authority and the multiple parties involved do not want to cooperate? An in-depth theoretical exploration and research linking the role leadership plays within conflict resolution, peacemaking, peacekeeping, and peacebuilding are critical as peace practitioners bring peace to conflict-afflicted societies. This is one of the greatest political and economic challenges with national security implications.

Concluding remarks

This chapter presented the role of leadership within peacemaking, peacekeeping, and peacebuilding activities aligned in a failed state framework. This analysis undergirds our understanding of the dynamic nature of moving a country from a failed state to peace and stability. Sustainable peace is a matter of emotional and physical recovery from experiential trauma or human rights violations in the aftermath of conflict. An innovative framework of leading self, leading others, and leading the community toward sustainable peace rests with the emotional intelligence of peace leaders. In other words, emotional intelligence shapes not only the capabilities of peace leaders' organizational and operational peacemaking, peacekeeping, and peacebuilding activities but also the facilitation of conflict-resolution processes and confidence-building measures. Basically, the emotional intelligence transformation of a peace leader builds the internal leadership capability toward leading others and shapes the intercommunal long-term sustainable peace.

References

Ashton, L. (2016). Wise leadership. In T. H. Veldsman and A. J. Johnson (Eds.), *Leadership: Perspectives from the front line* (pp. 431-442). Randburg, South Africa: KR Publishing.

Bass, B.M., & Bass, R. (2008). *The handbook of leadership: Theory, research, and managerial applications* (4th ed.). New York, NY: Free Press.

Baylis, J., Smith, S. and Owens, P. (2008). *The globalization of world politics: An introduction to international relations* (4th ed.). Oxford, NY: Oxford Press.

Beck, A. T., Davis, D. D., & Freeman, A. (2015). *Cognitive therapy of personality disorders* (3rd ed.). New York, NY: Guilford Press.

Bellamy, A., Williams, P. and Griffin, S. (2010). *Understanding peacekeeping* (2nd ed.). Cambridge UK: Polity.

Brooks, D. (2015). *The road to character*. New York, NY: Random House.

Buisson-Narsai, I. and Radecki, D. (2016). Neuroscience in leadership. In T. H. Veldsman and A. J. Johnson (Eds.), *Leadership: Perspectives from the front line* (pp. 41-58). Randburg, South Africa: KR Publishing.

Campbell, A. (2013). In-depth analysis of global leadership challenges. *Journal of Business Ethics, 5*, 69-76.

Campbell, A. (2017). Forgiveness and reconciliation as an organizational leadership competence within the transitional justice. *International Journal of Servant Leadership, 11*, 114-128.

Campbell, A. (2018). Leadership influence in conflict resolution and peacebuilding. In A. Campbell, *Global leadership initiatives for conflict resolution and peacebuilding* (pp. 1-26). Hershey, PA: IGI Publishing.

Cashman, G. (2014). *What causes war? An introduction to theories of international conflict* (2nd ed.). Lanham, MD: Rowman & Littlefield.

Cohen, T. and Insko, C. (2008). War and peace: Possible approaches to reducing intergroup conflict. *Perspectives on Psychological Science, 3*(87), doi: 10.1111/j.1745-6916.2008.00066.x.

Coolidge, F. L. and Segal, D. L. (2007). Was Saddam Hussein like Adolf Hitler? A personality disorder investigation. *Military Psychology*, 19(4), 289-299.

Crocker, C. A., Hampson, F. O. and Aall, P. (2007). *Leashing the dogs of war: Conflict management in a divided world*. Washington DC: United States Institute Peace Press.

Dechesne, M., Van De Berg, C. and Soeters, J. (2007). International collaboration under threat: A field study of Kabul. *Conflict Management and Peace Science*, 24, 225-36. doi: 10.1080/07388940601102811

Doyle, M. W. and Ikenberry, J. G. (1997). *New thinking in international relations theory*. Boulder, CO: Westview Press.

Du Toit, D., Veldsman, T. and Van Zyl, D. (2016). Leadership Maturity. In T. H. Veldsman & A. J. Johnson (Eds.), *Leadership: Perspectives from the front line* (pp. 41-58). Randburg, South Africa: KR Publishing.

Dursun-Ozkanca, O. (2016, Fall). The peace assembly-line model: Towards a theory of international collaboration in multidimensional peacebuilding operations. *International Journal of Peace Studies*, 21(2), 41-57. Retrieved from https://www.gmu.edu/programs/icar/ijps/vol21_2/Durson-Ozkanca%20FINAL.pdf

Fehr, R. and Gelfand, M. J. (2012). The forgiving organization: A multilevel model of forgiveness at work. *Academy of Management Review,* 37(4), pp. 664-668. Retrieved from http://dx.doi.org/10.5465/amr.2010.0497

Ferch, S. R. (2012). *Forgiveness and power in the age of atrocity*. Plymouth, United Kingdom: Lexington Books.

Fitzduff, M. (2015). An introduction to Neuroscience for the peacebuilder. Retrieved from http://www.academia.edu/10234805/An_Introduction_to_Neuroscience_for_the_Peacebuilder

Fukuyama, F. (2004). *State building-governance and world order in the 21st century*. New York, NY: Sage.

Furlong, G. T. (2005). *The conflict resolution toolbox: Models and maps for analyzing, diagnosing and resolving conflict*. Mississauga, Ontario: John Wiley and Sons.

Gerzon, M. (2006). *Leading through conflict: How successful leaders transform differences into opportunities*. Boston, MA: Harvard Business School.

Goldfield, B. A. (2007, Summer). Saddam Hussein: "The unconscious mind of the butcher of Baghdad–New tools reveal what the world does not know. *The Forensic Examiner*, 39-43.

Goleman, D. (1998). *Working with emotional intelligence*. New York, NY: Bantam Dell.

Goleman, D. (2004). What makes a leader. *Harvard Business Review*, R0401H, 1-10. doi: www.hbr.org

Goleman, D. (2011). What makes a leader. In P. Drucker, D. Goleman, & B. George (Eds.), *On leadership* (pp. 1-22).

Goleman, D., Boyatzis, R., & McKee, A. (2002). *Primal leadership: Learning to lead with emotional intelligence*. Boston, MA: Harvard Business School.

Gurr, T. R. (2002, June). Attaining peace in divided societies: Five principles of emerging doctrine. *International Journal on World Peace*, 14(2), pp. 27-51. https://doi.org/DOI: 10.2307/20753354

Hames, R. D. (2007). *The five literacies of global leadership: What authentic leaders need to know and you need to find out*. San Francisco, CA: Jossey-Bass Publishing.

Ikenberry, J. G. (2001). The future of international leadership. *Political Science Quarterly*, 111(3), pp. 385-402.

Jha, A. R. (2018, Spring). The pursuit of happiness: Being in the now. *Scientific American Mind*, pp. 54-61.

Johnson, C. E. (2009). *Meeting the ethical challenges of leadership: Casting light or shadow.* (3rd ed), Thousand Oaks, CA: SAGE Publications.

Junk, J., Mancini, F., Seibel, W. and Blume, T. (2017). *The management of UN peacekeeping: Coordination, learning, and leadership in peace operations.* Boulder, CO: Lynne Rienner Publishers.

Kanter, R. M. (2010). Leadership in a globalizing world. In N. Nohria and R. Khurana (Eds.), *Handbook of Leadership Theory and Practice: A Harvard Business School Centennial Colloquium* (pp. 1-41). Boston, MA: Harvard Business Press.

Knodell, K. (2015). Failed states and refugee crisis prompt peacekeeping surge. World Politics. http://www.humanosphere.org/world-politics/2015/10/failed-states-and-refugees-prompt-peacekeeping-surge/

Lake, D. A. (2003). International relations theory and internal conflict: Insights from the interstices. *International Studies Review*, 5(4), pp. 81-89.

Lieberfeld, D. (2009). Lincoln, Mandela, and qualities of reconciliation-oriented leadership. *Peace and Conflict: Journal of Peace Psychology*, 15(1), 27-47. doi: 10.1080/10781910802589857

Lijn, J., Verkoren, W. and Millar, G. (2013). Peacebuilding plans and local reconfigurations: Frictions between imported processes and indigenous practices. *International Peacekeeping*, 20(2), 137-143. https://doi.org/DOI: 10.1080/13533312.2013.791556

Mendenhall, M. E., Osland, J. S., Bird, A., Oddou, G. R., Maznevski, M. L., Stevens, M. J. and Stahl, G. K. (2013). *Global leadership: Research, practice, and development* (2nd ed.). New York, NY: Routledge.

Millman, D. (1991). *The peaceful warrior collection.* New York, NY: MJF Books.

Oola, S. (2015). Forgiveness: Uncovering as asset in peacebuilding. *Refuge Law Center.* Retrieved from http://refugelawproject.org/files/others/forgiveness_research_report.pdf

Paruk, S. (2016). Change leadership. In T. H. Veldsman and A. J. Johnson, *Leadership: Perspectives from the front line* (pp. 41-58). Randburg, South Africa: KR Publishing.

Ramsbotham, O., Woodhouse, T. and Miall, H. (2008). *Contemporary conflict resolution: The prevention, management, and transformation of deadly conflicts* (2nd ed.). Malden, MA: Polity Press.

Raymont, J., & Smith, J. (2011). *MisLeadership: Prevalence, causes, and consequences.* Burlington, VT: Ashgate Publishing.

Rotberg, R. (2003). *When states fail: Causes and consequences.* Princeton, NJ: Princeton University Press.

Ruben, B. D., & Gigliotti, R. A. (2016). Leadership as social influence: An expanded view of leadership communication theory and practice. *Journal of Leadership and Organizational Studies*, 1-13, doi: 10.1177/1548051816641876.

Salicru, S. (2016). *Leadership results: How to create adaptive leaders and high-performing organizations for an uncertain world.* Melbourne, Australia: John Wiley and Sons.

Schulenburg, M. (2014). Rethinking peacebuilding: Transforming the UN approach. Retrieved from https://www.wiltonpark.org.uk/wp-content/uploads/WP1355-Rethinking-Peacekeeping-Transforming-the-UN-Approach-IPI.pdf

Story, J. S. (2011). A developmental approach to global leadership. *International Journal of Leadership Studies*, 6(3), pp. 375-389. Retrieved from http://www.midwestacademy.org/Proceedings/2008/papers/Story_46.pdf.

Van Dijk, T. A. (2000). *Ideology: Multidisciplinary approach.* Thousand Oaks, CA: SAGE Publications.

Verwey, A., Minnaar, R. and Mooney, P. (2016). In *Leadership excellence dimensions* (pp. 341-360). Randburg, South Africa: KR Publishing.

Wright, J. & Wright, B. (2013). *Transformed! The science of spectacular living.* Nashville, TN: Turner Publishing.

Walton, D. (2012). *Emotional intelligence: A practical guide.* New York, NY: MJR Books.

Warner, M. and Wilder, J. (2016). *Rare Leadership: 4 Uncommon habits for increasing trust, joy, and engagement in the people you lead.* Chicago, IL: Moody Publishers.

Wilder, J. (2015). *Passing the peace: After a crisis.* East Peoria, IL.

Zartman, W. and Rasmussen, L. (1997). *Peacemaking in International Conflict: Methods and Techniques* (7th ed.). Washington DC: United States Institute of Peace.

Zielinska, M. (2012). Developing authentic leadership. *Traniningzone*, 1-3. Retrieved from http://www.kenexa.com/Portals/0/Downloads/Devel

Endnotes

1   Coolidge & Segal, 2007.
2   Giacomello, Ferrari & Amadori, 2009, p. 248.
3   Crocker, Hampson, & Aall, 2007, p. 296.
4   Brookhiser, 2003.
5   Goldfield, 2007.
6   Campbell, 2013; Rotberg, 2011.
7   Du Toit, Veldsman & Van Zyl 2016, p.109.
8   See endnote 25; Fukyama, 2004; Lieberfeld, 2016.
9   Baylis, Smith, & Owens, 2008; See endnote 23.
10 Lieberman, 2016.
11 Schulenburg, 2014, p. 5.
12 Fukayama, 2004.
13 Paruk, 2017, p. 537.
14 Salicru, 2016, p. 4.
15 Crocker et al., 2007.
16 Schulenburg, 2014; Rotberg, 2011.
17 Crocker et al., 2007.
18 Rotberg, 2011, p. 6.
19 See endnote 14.
20 Ramsbotham et al., 2008, p. 30.
21 Ibid, p. 172.
22 Millman, 2006, p. 56.
23 Fukayama, 2004.
24 Knodell, 2015.
25 Junk, Mancini, Seibel, & Blume, 2017.
26 Bellamy, Williams & Griffin, 2010; Dursun-Ozkanca, 2016.
27 Baylis et al., 2008; Bellamy et al., 2010; Dursun-Ozkanca, 2016; Junk et al., 2017.
28 Dursun-Ozkanca, 2016; Junk et al., 2017; Ramsbotham et al., 2008.

29 Baylis et al., 2008; Crocker et al., 2007; Dechesne, Van De Berg & Soeters, 2007.
30 US Department of State, 2018.
31 United Nations Support Office, 2010, the UN Secretary-General's Policy Committee, p. 5.
32 See endnote 30.
33 Mendenhall et al., 2013.
34 Campbell, 2013, p. 54.
35 Goleman, Boyatzis & McKee, 2002.
36 Wright & Wright, 2013, p. xxii.
37 Zeilinska, 2012, p. 2.
38 Mendenhall et al., 2013.
39 Ibid, p. 25.
40 Walton, 2012.
41 Goleman et al., 2002, p. 258.
42 Wilder, 2016; Wright & Wright, 2013.
43 Wright & Wright, 2013, p. 4.
44 Ibid.
45 Fitzduff, 2015, p. 8
46 Buisson-Narsal & Radecki, 2016.
47 Warner & Wilder, 2016.
48 Anton, Minnaar & Mooney, 2016, p. 347.
49 Goleman, 2011, p. 13.
50 Ashton, 2016, p. 438-439.
51 Jha, 2018.
52 Jha, 2018.
53 Goleman, 1998, p. 136.
54 Ruben & Gigliotti, 2016.
55 Bass & Bass, 2008, p. 335.
56 Cohen & Insko, 2008.
57 Goleman, 1998, p. 135.
58 Ibid.
59 Campbell, 2018; Brooks, 2015; Walton, 2012.

60   Coolidge & Segal, 2007, p. 290.
61   Gerzon, 2006, p. 50.
62   Campbell, 2017; Johnson, 2009.
63   Campbell, 2016; Ferch, 2012; Johnson, 2009, p. 119.
64   Yergler, 2005, para. 10.
65   Fehr & Gelfand, 2012, p. 670.
66   Johnson, 2009, p. 119.
67   Goleman, 2006.
68   Ibid.
69   Campbell, 2008; Du Toit, Veldsman & Van Zyl 2016; Goldfield, 2007: Junk et al., 2017.
70   See endnote 69; Goleman, 2001

CHAPTER 5

THE ROLE OF WISDOM AND SPIRITUALITY IN LEADING SELF AND OTHERS

Adrienne Castellon

"When we love and respect people, revealing to them their value, they can begin to come out from behind the walls that protect them." (Jean Vanier)

Servant Leadership requires a strong orientation to values that allow leaders to serve their people well while engaging in efforts that transform the organisation.[1] The undergirding value is human dignity as philosopher Immanuel Kant admonishes:

"Act so that you treat humanity, whether in your own person or in that of another, always as an end and never as a means only".[2]

Servant leadership is an appropriate model for peace leaders as shown by the lived examples of Catholic social justice-oriented leaders Dorothy Day and Jean Vanier illustrated in this paper. As servant leaders, Day and Vanier:

"serve[d] others by investing in their development and well-being for the benefit of the common good. ... aspire[d] to be great only in their service to others... with integrity, humility, sincere concern, a generous, forgiving and giving heart, and self-discipline... by investing, empowering, caring for, and consulting others".[3]

All peace leaders, whether deriving strength from a theistic worldview or not, or from spiritual traditions other than Catholicism, can identify and formulate the principles Day and Vanier used in their lives to create a role model for their leadership.

In considering the role of wisdom and spirituality in leading self and others, it is helpful to distinguish between religious and spiritual beliefs. While Day and Vanier espouse religious beliefs, I would argue they also have a spiritual worldview as defined by Hood and Chen[4]:

> "Religious beliefs typically refer to the more institutionalized aspects of belief in supernatural beings, such as within traditional religious communities. In contrast, spiritual beliefs refer to the individual and personalized beliefs regarding the transcendent or sacred, which are often based on personal experience rather than tradition".

Therefore, religious and spiritual beliefs can be integrated in a person's worldview, particularly when spirituality is understood as a personal experience of religion. To put it another way, to be religious does not preclude being spiritual. This integration is evident in the unique insights of neuroscience into the topic of neurocognitive mechanisms underlying religion and spirituality and predictive processing of people who self-identify as either religious or spiritual. Predictive processing, that is, using prior cognitive models to predict and perceive the world, is important to consider in relation to leadership since prior beliefs, influenced by context and culture, are hierarchically structured and influence decision-making, expectations, beliefs and emotions.[5] The extant literature on neuroscience as it relates to religion and spirituality and implications for leadership, though fascinating, is beyond the scope of this paper.[6]

Spotlight: Jean Vanier and Dorothy Day

Canadian philosopher and humanitarian Jean Vanier (1928-) is the founder of 149 L'Arche homes in 38 countries around the world.[7] In these homes people with intellectual disabilities (the residents) live and work side by side with the nondisabled (their assistants) as peers in "mutually transformative relationships". Jean Vanier emphasizes the great discovery of his life: "Above all, I have discovered how people with a disability can be a source of peace and unity in our terribly divided world, provided we are willing to listen to them, to follow them and to share our lives with them."[8] Among his over thirty inspiring books, *Becoming Human (1998)*[9] is one I keep coming back to at various stages and roles in my life. The inclusivity Vanier proposes is a powerful reminder of the value of the heart, of wisdom and of spirituality in leadership. Jean Vanier is one of Canada's most inspiring and influential leaders. His quiet nature, insightful wisdom, deep faith, and humble yet radical hospitality have made an impact for peace in our world.

Similar in her selfless dedication to the vulnerable, Dorothy Day's life demonstrates a disciplined and purpose-filled way to promoting peace. Born in 1897 in Brooklyn, New York, Day was a social activist involved in women's suffrage, free love, and labor unions. For 50 years, Dorothy lived with the poor, conducted conferences, and published a newspaper while being a single mother, devoted grandmother and loyal friend. She lived a gritty and hard life dedicated to advocating for justice for the homeless in New York City and establishing the Catholic Worker Movement. Seventy-five houses of hospitality were established during her lifetime. She was an avid peacemaker and a prolific author who was accepted by communists, bohemians, non-religious and religious people. She was also shunned by many, but this did not deter her, though the tension and fear did lead her into depressions at times. She felt the burden of leadership saying: "Few there are who will accept authority and exercise it. And plenty to taunt and criticize, to tear down and discourage."[10] She carried on despite the challenges and lived radical inclusivity right up to her death on November 29, 1980 in New York City, where she spent her final months among the poor. Today there are 245 Catholic Worker Communities committed to fostering peace through nonviolence, voluntary poverty, prayer and hospitality for the homeless, exiled, hungry and forsaken[11].

Vanier and Day are peace leaders whose lives illustrate how leadership benefits when grounded in wisdom and spirituality. Their thinking and actions demonstrate how leaders can foster peace in the world through acceptance and inclusion of the marginalized. Their personal dispositions, focused on the dignity of the human person, the value of community and the need for justice, can be emulated by other leaders wanting to privilege relationships and striving to foster peace in their organisation.

Introduction

As founders of internationally recognized communities (L'Arche and The Catholic Worker), Vanier and Day model for leaders how to build community by valuing the human person no matter their background or beliefs, abilities or disabilities, wealth, prestige, poverty or insignificance. Both leaders see unity and the possibility of integration in a pluralistic world. We might readily agree with these principles and aspirations but what is remarkable is that for these leaders, "their inner and outer lives are in accord."[12]

Leaders everywhere can learn from their practicality, humanness, ability to inspire hope and empower generativity. Vanier and Day are grounded in the real concerns and needs of people and through this, affirm the struggle and beauty of ordinary life. Just as much as they write and speak about the importance of the work for and with marginalised people, they actually do the work, involving themselves in the complexity and messiness of change with determined conviction and a strength rooted in faith. They had to be very practical to truly help people – both of them lived in community with the people they were helping. They both had their high ideals "but at the same time, never let them interfere with the reality of the present moment."[13] They lived life in all its nuances and were with people, getting to know them in their joys and sufferings. Vanier recognized the 'mysterious potential' of being able to be with people in their difficulties and why, rather than focusing on the hopelessness of a given situation, leaders are called to greater hope and humanity[14]. Their leadership shows service *with, not to,* people. With a sense of humor and the strength of their convictions, both leaders demonstrate how to be human – to work through difficult relationships, build understandings with people who have different views, not to be separate from but with others, and take the time to celebrate. Both Vanier and Day celebrate humanity and togetherness regardless of challenging circumstances. They foster a sense of belonging and purpose such that each individual is included and brings something to the collective purpose.

The lives and words of Vanier and Day can inspire passion and hope among leaders who care for people and want to use the privilege of their positions to make a social impact for a more peaceful and humanistic world. Vanier and Day are leaders who demonstrate an ability to empower generativity. They equip others to do the work with them and their legacy is evident in the houses of hospitality they established and the many others that were founded subsequently. Their ability to resource through encouragement, mentorship and advocacy allows the impact of their work to multiply. Vanier's words are a call to action for leaders no matter the context:

> "It is always good for individuals, communities and indeed nations, to remember that their present situation is a result of the thousands of gestures of love or hate that came before. This obliges us to remember that the community of tomorrow is being born of our fidelity to the present. We discover that we are at the same time very insignificant and very important because each of our actions is preparing the humanity of tomorrow; it is a tiny contribution to the huge and glorious final humanity".[15]

Leaders focused on peacebuilding can learn from Vanier and Day to value and involve people, be inclusive, do the work with people, inspire hope, mentor and equip others and build community. Peace leaders need to acquire emotional self-control, a spirit of forgiveness, empathy, optimism about change and potential, and propensities towards reconciliation. Such traits are facilitated through servant leadership practices and assist in preparing an individual to confront the challenges of peace. Thus servant leadership provides a good foundation for peace leadership. The founder of servant leadership, Robert Greenleaf[16] said:

> "The servant-leader is servant first...It begins with the natural feeling that one wants to serve, to serve first. Then conscious choice brings one to aspire to lead. That person is sharply different from one who is leader first, perhaps because of the need to assuage an unusual power drive or to acquire material possessions...The leader-first and the servant-first are two extreme types.

Between them there are shadings and blends that are part of the infinite variety of human nature".[17]

The chapter will provide an integrated leadership model applicable to peace leaders. Background information will be given on why we need wise and spiritual leaders in a secular age. Towards the end of the chapter, the focus will be on general strategic approaches that peace leaders may use to ensure peacebuilding. The chapter closes with implications for peace leaders, which include encouraging individuals to be servants before they serve.

Background: why we need wise, spiritual leaders in a secular age

Canadian contemporary philosopher Charles Taylor's views on the secular age and individualism help to contextualize why we need wise, spiritual leaders in a secular age. By 'spiritual' I am referring to a belief in a reality beyond the senses – whether theistic or not – that provides a framework or horizon of significance giving direction to life. Taylor defines a secular age as a time largely devoid of hierarchical order and a general 'flattening' of society[18] when all goals beyond human flourishing are eclipsed and individualism overwhelms the common good[19]. People used to see themselves as part of a larger order that gave meaning and purpose to their lives. However, this is not the reality of most people in a secular age.

Generally, the emphasis for the majority of people in a secular age is self, self-fulfillment, recognition and accomplishments. People in a secular age, Taylor argues, are consequently less concerned with others and society and there is less civic engagement. This does not negate the large public responses to tragedies that are indeed wonderful examples of people coming together through suffering. Taylor's point is to say that daily life in a secular world is more individualistic than communal. His explanation reveals that most people lack a guiding philosophy that informs decisions and social networks, and that there is, rather, a focus on neutrality and an ethic of libertarian thinking where "people should be permitted to run their own lives as they wish [and] nobody would [have] a right to force his way of life upon his neighbor".[20] Forcing a way of life does not sound desirable in any case, but Taylor contends that excessive individualism goes as far as to say that people in a secular age generally let other people lead their own lives and do not necessarily see a common responsibility to intervene or help them – that's the more impersonal role of government. For Taylor, individualism is the primary 'malaise of modernity'[21], since it is inherently inegalitarian; not everyone has equal access to the 'good life'. Self-determination, a focus on efficiency and instrumental reasoning overwhelm a sense of true authenticity, purpose beyond the self and concern for the common good.

Perhaps a result of excessive individualism has led to what Karin Jironet, Sufi theologian and psychoanalyst, calls a "widespread reaching out for spirituality".[22] Can spirituality inform leadership in a secular age? Indeed, wise spiritual leaders can play a significant peace-keeping role as they strive to maintain neutrality while advocating for inclusion and the common good – what the Dalai Lama refers to as 'universal responsibility' or in Swahili *harambee* meaning 'all pull together'. Such leaders have a sense of purpose beyond themselves and are motivated by service to the growth and betterment of others. This servant leadership approach seeks to transform the challenges of competing needs into a community. The way of the peace leader is to continuously define and courageously protect the general good while trying to educate the various stakeholders of each other's needs. Taylor suggests cultural retrieval is necessary whereby leaders "instead of dismissing the culture altogether, or just endorsing it as it is, ought to attempt to raise its practice by making more palpable to its participants what the ethic they subscribe to really involves", that is, viewing the work of leadership with a deep understanding of the pluralistic, globalised world and commitment to true authenticity, tolerance, universal benevolence and solidarity.[23]

Vanier and Day are examples of servant leaders who consistently broadcast, through word and action, a compelling message about the dignity of the human person, the value of inclusion and primacy of social justice. As their lives testify, peace leaders in a secular world are educators, philosophers, poets, artists, inventors, workers, realists, idealists and advocates.

Taylor's philosophical and anthropological writings suggest that there are universal 'goods' including a conception of human dignity and the value of human life that can provide guidance for our decisions and behaviors. This assertion should be welcome among leaders seeking clarity about the direction to pursue within their organisation and with their people. An understanding of common good or universal responsibility is essential to a peaceful society. Common good is in contrast to corrupt governance and self-interest; it is about higher purposes and public interest as opposed to private interests. Leaders seeking the common good are concerned about fairness to protect equal chances for everyone and in their practice they include processes as a way to determine what the community as a whole desires. For leaders then, policies and procedures are important in the pursuit of fair public deliberation to determine the common good and everyday conversations and interactions reflect this fairmindedness. Respecting and working toward the common good involves combining in our lives and in our work "the full development of individual potentials with commitment to a greater whole".[24]

An essential common good according to Taylor, is self-interpretation[25]. A vital component of identity, self-interpretation is what a person thinks of herself. The universal good related to self-interpretation relies on relationship since a person learns more about themselves in relationship. A leader needs to take the time to understand how people self-interpret and what is important to them, including purposes that have special significance for them. This goes beyond knowing empirical information about a person such as race, class, occupation age, background etc. Understanding what a person thinks about themselves, even if erroneous, inflated or deluded, can greatly assist a leader in working with a person to accomplish both personal and organisational goals, and beyond that, establish a workplace conducive to growth.

The secular world needs peace leaders rooted in wisdom and spirituality to advance a more humane and peaceful society. Challenges related to individualism and other practical realities of work face even the most well-intentioned leaders. Some of these challenges include the preoccupation with maintenance of the status quo rather than an openness to change, finding time and discipline for reflection, our need for recognition and, if we're honest, the attractions of power, wealth and self-image. The realities of work life in the twenty-first century such as mobility, the transitory nature of work, fragmentation of personal and work life also add to the leader's list of challenges to overcome in the quest for community and peace. There are however certain dispositions and skills that leaders can hone to meet these challenges.

Solutions: dispositions and skills to develop as peace leaders

In the following section four dispositions and skills will be explored. These are seen as the basis for every person to develop as a peace leader.

Be faithful to people

"Pressed to identify his own strengths, Jean Vanier referred to his faithfulness to people, the fact that once he had entered into real personal contact with someone it was rarely something he broke".[26] When we walk alongside people, get to know them in their strengths and weaknesses, joys and sufferings, they are reassured, feel needed and confidence increases, leading to more innovation and overall efficacy. In a large organisation the leader may need to strategically invest in division heads and encourage these individuals to do the same with their reports. Taking the time to do this builds a culture of dialogue and working together in the same direction, towards a shared vision. Even when there is disagreement, listening to difference can lead to greater understanding, people feeling that they have been heard and overall fewer misunderstandings. Sometimes disagreement manifests in behaviors such as resistance or stonewalling and the leader is challenged to figure out what is underneath it. Upon further investigation they may discover a feeling of inadequacy and fear of failure when faced with change. Therefore, it is best for a leader to interpret the thoughts and actions of others with a charitable disposition and suspend judgment until more dialogue can occur. True community depends on dialogue.

Inviting vulnerability and seeing the potential for growth through the appropriate supports and equipping, reduces the fear that inhibits innovation and causes mistrust. Dorothy Day certainly believed in this, saying: "Failures are inseparable to a work of this kind, and necessary for our growth".[27] Modeling vulnerability is an important part of leadership since it gives permission for people not to be perfect. A leader can model vulnerability by admitting to mistakes and also taking opportunities during meetings to facilitate deepening connections by asking people to share their challenges and how they overcame them.

Take time for self-reflection

A leader needs to take time to be reflective and notice their reactions so as to grow in self-awareness and autonomy – in the sense of not being dependent on the opinions of others. Margaret Wheatley suggests inner work exploring these types of questions: How do I process what's going on? What are my ways of gaining the big picture? What are my practices for restoring a sense of peace and possibility?[28] Some people find journaling to be an efficient tool, others a coaching relationship.

The research of Deana Raffo[29], Assistant Professor of Management, as well as that of former Medtronic CEO Bill George[30] identifies self-reflection as the missing point between self-awareness and authenticity. The rationale for engaging in reflection is clear in the research of David Sable[31] with undergraduate students. His evidence points to contemplative practices as enabling people to feel more connected and empathetic with others. Admittedly, this may be challenging given the fragmentation of the role of a leader, time constraints, proclivity towards action as well as expectation to be transparent and interactive both on and off line. These challenges serve to amplify the need for a leader to take time to think about and include the needs of others rather than being driven solely by their own.

A reflective leader is one who is better able to create a sense of belonging to community and is better equipped to face the challenges of leadership. Taking the time to be reflective leads to mindfulness, greater understanding of oneself and more unified functioning. While there are many reflective practices, the important thing is to take time to think, discern, learn and improve. As Margaret Wheatley asserts, it's important not just for the leader to do individually but: "A leader can do the most good in creating an organisation that is healthy by creating the conditions for people to come together and be thoughtful again."[32]

Work for a purpose beyond yourself

An essential question for leaders to reflect on is: What matters to me and how can my work advance this in some way? Discovering and acting upon a purpose beyond oneself brings meaning to work and can motivate followers to find meaning in work also. This leads to a deeper commitment and sense of fulfillment. Having a greater purpose creates unity and fights fragmentation in the activities of work.

A personal emphasis on human dignity in interactions can also be scaled up to an ethic of care in a wide range of settings including mental health, homelessness, elder care, child protection, asylum seekers, indigenous peoples, marginalized communities of all description and humanitarian aid. Pease & Vreugdenhil argue for political ethics of care models so that a more progressive approach to leadership in international social world and social development practice in humanitarian aid may result. Their interdisciplinary approach moves the emphasis on human dignity to the scale of leadership in wider contexts while staying within similar values and purpose.

Being spiritual may also help one be more focused on human dignity. The experience of self-transcendence may help one to cope with difficulties and to experience higher feelings of purpose and meaning.[33] Piff et al found that experiencing awe can result in a diminishment of the individual self and its concerns, increase pro-social behavior and ethical decision-making and predict greater generosity: "Awe shifts people away from being the center of their own individual worlds, toward a focus on the broader social context and their place within it."[34] Several other studies have shown that spiritual and religious experiences can foster environmental awareness and pro-social behavior, possibly through a process of enhanced identification with the surrounding world and a strong feeling of interconnectedness.[35]

Commit to beauty

Committing to beauty is perhaps an unusual call to action for leaders but it can be an effective tool for a peace leader. "Beauty appeals to what is good in us"[36] – not manufactured or superficial beauty focused on the self, but a natural or created beauty that inspires to innovation, creativity, love, generosity, sacrifice and selflessness. In the life of Dorothy Day we see the power of natural beauty as a healer:

> "There were tiny flower gardens and vegetable patches in the yards. Often there were rows of corn, stunted but still recognizable, a few tomato plants, and always the vegetables were bordered by flowers, often grateful marigolds, all sizes and shades with their pungent odor. I collected odors in my memory, the one beauty in those drab streets. The odors of geranium leaves, tomato plants, marigolds; the smell of lumber, of tar, of roasting coffee; the smell of good bread

and rolls and coffee cake coming from the small German bakeries. Here was enough beauty to satisfy me."[37]

A leader can empower and inspire motivation for a common good or shared vision through beauty in language (speech, poetry, literature), the visual and performing arts, music, prayer and ritual. There is power in art, music, literature and nature that leads to wonder and gives us a clearer vision into the depths of reality. Those who experience them can become moved towards unity, fullness and community.

The mission of Dorothy Day and the aesthetically unattractive Catholic Worker House serve as an example of paradoxical beauty. With its poverty, random alcoholic tenants, basic furnishings, endless pots of watered-down soup and pots of mashed potatoes, the willingness of those within to spend time with criminals and vagrants, to write for their newspaper – this is a beauty that has the potential to overcome loneliness, create unity and commitment. To see the good amid the challenges, find hope amid despair and be able to "conquer the bitterness, the sense of futility and despair"[38] is leadership that people long for. Dorothy Day took inspiration from Dostoyevsky's statement: "The world will be saved by beauty, and what is more beautiful than love?"[39] Peace leaders can indeed use beauty as a tool for peace.

Leaders who commit to people, are reflective, pursue a purpose bigger than themselves and who appreciate and nurture beauty are often able to promote peace more effectively. Our conceptual understanding of leadership and associated behaviors will not however change overnight. It involves persistent focus and commitment to incremental change of attitudes and habits. Knowing what should be done and having the means to do it are useless without personal commitment. Subhanu Saxena, managing director and global CEO of Cipla, a large Indian pharmaceutical company, emphasizes this, saying: "The practice of leadership means that you practice like an Olympian athlete. Every day in the office is your gym to become a better leader."[40] Even seemingly small shifts in our awareness and behaviors can have positive effects. The process of change involving spirituality seeking wisdom may be less of a complex process than about disciplined personal commitment.

Implications for peace leaders

As Vanier and Day illustrate, leaders are called to be bold, vigorous and visionary in their commitment to people, particularly the vulnerable. Peace comes through justice and human flourishing at the level of one-on-one interactions, organisational policies and procedures, and societal laws. The lives of Vanier and Day illustrate the importance of working on each of these levels. Their spirituality and emphasis on justice and human flourishing on an individual basis translate to peace leadership on a macro level for organisational, institutional and social change.

As peace leaders we are meant to confront the reality of ordinary life by inquiring and seeking to understand what lies beyond ourselves in a spiritual quest for wisdom. This better equips us to engage daily challenges and inform wider-reaching practices. At the same time, it presupposes critical discernment and continual personal transformation focused on honing the dispositions and skills of a peace leader. Committing to this endeavour requires a tenacity of spirit and comfort with ambiguity amidst the complexity of life and ever-increasing amount of information we are asked to incorporate.

It is important to note, lest we become disillusioned in our efforts, that in spite of our spiritual quest, critical discernment, commitment to personal transformation and tenacity of spirit, conflict will inevitably arise. However, drawing strength and wisdom from all of these efforts, we can engage respectful dialogue and a restorative approach to conflict. Such an approach has the potential of revealing previously unforeseen considerations to inform the peace process and enrich decisions. Reflection and discernment will also help to live the wise words of Thomas More: "Happy is the person who can distinguish between a rock and a mountain; it avoids so many inconveniences."[41]

In her edited volume *Leading with Spirit, Presence, and Authenticity*, Kathryn Goldman Schuyler presents a model of embodied leadership[42] that includes many of the dispositions and practices a peace leader grounded in wisdom and spirituality should keep in mind. She particularly mentions "ongoing awareness practice, ongoing commitment to sustainability and people and ongoing engagement with the possible/potential". American systems scientist Peter Senge affirms this leadership approach saying:

> "Until you can stop the habitual flow of your mind, you cannot see what's around you. If you're going to be in a position of authority, you'd better have a high level of awareness of what's going on. Otherwise, all you can do is project your inner dynamics on the other world".[43]

Ongoing attention to honing these dispositions and practices is recommended for effective peace leadership. Since leaders are often very busy individuals with an imperative to prioritise their responsibilities, the implication is that fostering these dispositions and practices is worthy of scheduled time. It is important to recognise that consistently fostering this way of being leads to purposeful action and the potential of peace. The cumulative effect of leaders intentionally practising these disciplines and approaches has the potential to effect macro-level social change.

Perhaps discussion of leadership disciplines and macro-level social change seems esoteric and hard to implement faced with the myriad of questions and problems leaders try to solve:

- What works in conflict resolution?
- How do I manage team dynamics?
- What do I need to know about ethical and political issues in the public sphere?
- What are the current hot topics in my field and how do these fit my framework of good education? Good business? Good healthcare....
- How do I effectively supervise and evaluate others?
- How to I lead adults in continual learning?
- How do I collect, present and analyse data?
- How do I allocate the budget?
- What is ethically acceptable in regards to relationships in community?
- What resources (human and other) shall I utilise?
- How can I best work with various stakeholders and manage varied expectations?
- What method of performance review shall I use?

These essential questions face every leader and if we consider them in light of power dynamics, restorative principles, inform them with foundational concepts such as people, process and results, we might better be able to see the role of an individual's dispositions in this context and relevance to peace leadership.

The Pugwash Group is a good illustration of the significance of an individual's decisions and dispositions. The Pugwash group, founded in Pugwash, Nova Scotia, Canada is a Nobel Peace Prize winning group of scientists involved in global security, related scholarly research about the prevention and resolution of armed conflict and environmental threats. The work of these scientists informs government policy nationally and internationally.[44] It is remarkable to note the individual oath that each scientist involved pledges:

> "I promise to work for a better world, where science and technology are used in socially-responsible ways. I will not use my education for any purpose intended to harm human beings or the environment. Throughout my career, I will consider the ethical implications of my work before I take action. While the demands placed upon me may be great, I sign this declaration because I recognise that individual responsibility is the first step on the path to peace".[45]

These peace leadership dispositions are important foundational principles for which to strive in various contexts. As a Canadian educator one key challenge is the mandate to indigenise the curriculum. This is part of a broader call to educational leaders to work toward healing and reconciliation. It is peace leadership in action. In Canadian history, education was used as a tool of assimilation to extricate children from their culture and language. A statement of the   Indigenous Healing Foundation succinctly summarizes the gravity of this call to action:

"No other population group in Canada's history has endured such a deliberate, comprehensive, and prolonged assault on their human rights as that of Indigenous people. Yet, despite growing recognition of past wrongs, many Canadians remain unaware of the full scope of these injustices or their impacts".[46]

We need to realize our moral responsibilities to relate accurately and acknowledge fully our regrettable past. The effort educators in Canada are undergoing parallels that of peace leaders in other contexts. This has been, and continues to be, a process of developing knowledge of our own ignorance, discovering our prejudices and myths, and having the courage to change views and practices. It has required the disposition to work through intellectual and emotional complexities that have caused confusion and frustration. We must be willing to be disturbed and unsettled though! An approach of intellectual humility, curiosity and respect for all people has taken much of the fear of 'doing it wrong' away. This work is offered in a spirit of solidarity with all peace leaders.[47]

What follows is a prayer from an indigenous group in British Columbia, Canada. This Stolo prayer expresses well the importance of prioritizing peace leadership for the present and the future:

A prayer for a better future:
> "Help us use the wisdom of our ancestors, the knowledge of our   elders, the strength of our leaders, the vigor of the youth and the purity of the unborn to make a better tomorrow for our children. Together it will be done".[48]

Concluding remarks

What we value, we prioritize and this directs our work and lives, shaping not just what we do but who we become. We need to start practising now who we want to be in the future.[49] Since who we are impacts the culture of our organisations and further impacts society, if we want peace we need to be peace leaders.

This chapter, with the spotlight figures of Jean Vanier and Dorothy Day, has painted a vivid picture of how it is possible to dedicate oneself to a higher purpose in life, help others find and work towards their purpose and the common good while living this action-filled life with relative inner calm. It has caused the reader to ask new questions while considering their own life stories and listening for new possibilities in their practice of leadership. The aim of this chapter is to argue that there are universal principles for positive peace that can be derived from the work of spiritual leaders and can be equally applied by followers of other spiritual traditions as well as by secular leaders.

Our world is in need of leaders with a wideness of spirit dedicated toward the welfare of others.[50] This is magnanimity – what Aristotle called the crowning virtue in his hierarchy of virtues. A peaceful world is possible if leaders and followers work together in serving people and purpose.

References

Abbey, R. 2000. *Charles Taylor*. NJ: Princeton University Press.

Aristotle, Nicomachean Ethics H. Rackham, Ed. (n.d.). Retrieved from http://www.perseus. tufts.edu/hopper/text?doc=Perseus:text:1999.01.0054:book=4

Bregman, P. 2016. You need to practice being your future self. *Harvard Business Review*. Boston: Harvard University Press. Available from: https://hbr.org/2016/03/you-need-to-practice-being-your-future-self

Canadian Pugwash Group. 23 December 2017. *About Canadian Pugwash Group*. Available from: https://pugwashgroup.ca/#.

Castellon, A. 2017. *Indigenous Integration: 100+ Lesson Ideas for Secondary and College Teachers*. Victoria: Tellwell.

Day, D. 1952. *The Long Loneliness*. New York: Harper and Row Publishers Inc.

Gardner, H., Csikszentmihalyi, M. and Damon, W. 2001. *Good Work: When Excellence and Ethics Meet*. New York: Basic Books.

Garrido, A. 2013. *Redeeming Administration*. Notre Dame, Indiana: Ave Maria Press.

George, B. 2015. *Discover your True North*. San Francisco: Jossey-Bass.

Goldman Schuyler, K. 2012. *Inner peace – global impact: Tibetan Buddhism, leadership, and work*. Charlotte, NC: Information Age.

Goldman Schulyer, K., Baugher, J. E., Jironet, K. and Lid-Falkman, L. 2014. *Leading with Spirit, Presence, and Authenticity*. San Francisco: Jossey-Bass.

Goldman Schulyer, K., Baugher, J. E., Jironet, K. 2016. *Creative Social Change: Leadership for a Healthy World*. Bingley, UK: Emerald Group Publishing Ltd.

Greenleaf, R.K. 1970. *The servant as leader*. Robert K. Indianapolis, IN: Greenleaf Publishing Center.

Hennessy, K. 2017. Dorothy Day: *The World will be Saved by Beauty*. New York, NY: Simon and Schuster Inc.

L'Arche Canada. 2014. *Meeting Ground Newsletter*. Montreal, Quebec. Available from: http://www.larchecommons.ca/en/national/news/open_to_mutual_relationship_april_ may_2014_2013-10-25

L'Arche. (nd). *A brief history of L'Arche*. Available from: http://www.larche.ca/about-larche/our-history.

Langley School District, British Columbia. Aboriginal Enhancement Agreement, p. 5. Available from: https://www.sd35.bc.ca/news-events/community-engagement/aboriginal-enhancement-agreement/

Rogers, S. and Degagne, M. 2012. *Speaking my truth: Reflection on reconciliation and residential school*. Ottawa: Aboriginal Healing Foundation.

Spink, K. 2006. *The Miracle, The Message, The Story: Jean Vanier and L'Arche*. London: Hiddenspring.

Taylor, C. 1985. *Philosophical Papers I: Human Agency and Language*. Cambridge: Cambridge University Press.

Taylor, C. 2003. *The Malaise of Modernity*. Toronto: House of Anansi Press.

Taylor, C. 2007. *A Secular Age*. Cambridge, Massachusetts and London, England: Belknap Press of Harvard University Press.

The Catholic Worker Movement. (nd). Love in Action. Available from: https://www.catholicworker.org/communities/

Vanier, J. 1989. *Community and Growth*. New York: Paulist Press.

Vanier, J. 1998. *Becoming Human*. Toronto: ON: House of Anansi Press.

Endnotes

1   Atha, Castellon, Strong, Wu, 2017, p. 29.
2   Rachels, J., 1986, p. 1.
3   Atha, Castellon, Strong, Wu, 2017, p. 1
4   Hood and Chen, 2013.
5   Van Elk, 2017.
6   Apps & Tsakiris, 2014, Clark 2013, Kamitsis & Francis, 2013, Piff et al 2015, Risen, 2016, Seth, 2013, Zhang et al, 2014
7   L'Arche, (nd).
8   L'Arche, 2014, p. 1.
9   Vanier, 1998.
10   Hennessey, 2017, p. 169.
11   The Catholic Worker Movement. (nd).
12   Hennessey, 2017, p. XIV.
13   Hennessey, 2017, p. 285.
14   Spink, 2006, p. 238.
15   Vanier, 1989, p. 152.
16   Greenleaf, 1970.
17   The Centre for Servant Leadership www.greanleaf.org/what-is-servant-leadership
18   Taylor, 2003.
19   Taylor, 2007, p. 20.
20   Friedman, 1973: 1.
21   Taylor, 1991.
22   Jironet in Goldman Schuyler et al, 2014, p. 4.
23   Taylor, 1991, p. 72.
24   Gardner et al, 2001, p. 244.
25   Abbey, 2000, p. 58.
26   Spink, 2006, p. 157.
27   Hennessey, 2017, p. 185.
28   Wheatley in Shuyler et al, 2016, p. 36.
29   Raffo in Schuyler et al, 2014, p. 179.
30   George, 2015.
31   Sable, 2014.
32   Schuyler et al, 2016, p. 31.
33   Nygren et al, 2005.
34   Piff et al, 2015.
35   Kamitsis & Francis, 2013; Piff et al, 2015; Schnall et al, 2010; Zhang et al, 2014.
36   Clayton, 2015, p. 18.
37   Day, 1952, p. 52.
38   Hennessey, 2017, p. 258.

39   Hennessey, 2017, p. 213.
40   Saxena in Schuyler et al, 2014, p. 22.
41   Garrido, 2013, p. 124.
42   Schuyler et al, 2014, p. xxiii.
43   Schuyler et al, 2012, p. 326.
44   Canadian Pugwash Group, 2017.
45   Gardner, et al, 2001, p. 235.
46   Rogers & Degagne, 2012, p. 8.
47   Castellon, 2017.
48   Langley School District Aboriginal Enhancement Agreement, p. 5.
49   Bregman, 2016.
50   Aristotle, Nicomachean Ethics H. Rackham, Ed. (n.d.).

CHAPTER 6

INDIVIDUAL, SOCIAL AND CULTURAL INERTIA PREVENTING HUMANITY ATTAINING PEACE

Erich Schellhammer

"There is no way to peace, peace is the way." (A.J. Muste)

Spotlight: European Union and Willy Brandt

Two Nobel Peace Prize laureates are analyzed in the third part of this chapter. They illustrate that the power of habit and inertia can be broken for a new actuality. These are the European Union, recipient in 2012, and Willy Brandt, who received the award in 1971.

The European Union was credited for maintaining peace among European nations for over six decades, advancing democracy and human rights. It developed out of efforts mainly between France and Germany after World War II. Previously, both nations perceived each other as arch enemies engaged in conflicts over interests that were often attempted to be resolved by war and the humiliation of the losing party.

In the historical process of European integration more and more European nations got involved to establish a political formation most commentators call a political construct *sui generis*. The European Union maintains the diversity of its cultures and generates commonly agreed guidelines creating *supra-national* law that has priority over national legislation. Its main objective is to work towards free movement of member state citizens as well as the free movement of goods, services and capital within the European internal market.

As of 2012, the European Union, despite many challenges, was able to ally 28 member states in a complex economic and political union comprising approximately 510 million people. Nineteen member states use a common currency, the Euro, in the so-called Eurozone. Twenty six European countries are signatory to the Schengen Agreement of 1985 and the Schengen Convention of 1990. Both agreements resulted in abolishing internal border controls. The European Union also developed the EU Charter of Fundamental Rights protecting citizens' rights. Since 2009 these are binding for all European states and cases can be brought for enforceable adjudication to the European Court of Justice. Moreover, the European Union is committed to protecting human rights, democracy and the rule of law worldwide.

Willy Brandt was credited for easing the tensions between the two major political blocs of his times. This reduced the threat of war between the Western Bloc and the Eastern Bloc. It was also an important step towards greater European integration.

Brandt fled Germany in 1933 for his belief in democracy and freedom. He returned to Germany after the war to build "a democratic Germany together with other freedom-loving people."[1] It is fair to say that he embodied the new German and the new Germany, a Germany that has as its highest legal and constitutional norm the principle that human dignity is inalienable. As was noted in the Award Ceremony Speech, this new perspective led to the Rome Treaty and the European Community[2] and its consequent developments towards the European Union as we know it today.

Introduction

Since 1945, a remarkable change in human self-understanding emerged.[3] It is primarily the discourse on human rights and peace that has gained universal validity.[4] It has been held back (among other factors) by the *Realpolitik* of colonialism, the Cold War, Machiavellian power politics and the transition from the *Industrial Age* to the *Information Age*. However, a culture of peace and human rights is now intrinsically connected to sustainable development in the General Assembly resolution 70/01[5] (2015) entitled *Transforming our World: the 2030 Agenda for Sustainable Development*:

> "We are determined to foster peaceful, just and inclusive societies which are free from fear and violence. There can be no sustainable development without peace and no peace without sustainable development."

It seems to be such a long time since World War II. However, in terms of generations, it is not. It is difficult for individuals, societies and cultures to adjust so quickly to the newly envisioned actuality of a worldwide culture of peace, as outlined by the United Nations, because of the force of habit – established ways of action and thought that provide comfort and direction. Most cultures up to the end of World War II, and many even afterwards, embraced war as a quasi-natural occurrence. War was perceived to serve legitimate purposes, which justified the sacrifices in the wake of unleashing violence. Habits are maintained through inertia and the development towards a culture of peace needs to address both impediments. This chapter explains habit and inertia to suggest a methodology, namely mindfulness in combination with peace leadership and systems theory, to change established ways of thought and practice.

Consequently, the chapter demonstrates that individuals and cultures are not necessarily captive to habit and inertia. Still, this also requires a sensitivity to habit and inertia that favour the status quo. The first part thus explains how habit and inertia works. This is followed in the second part by an analysis of the two cases in the spotlight where a successful transition from a culture of war to a culture of peace happened. The third part explores ways to change mindsets. The self can direct itself to a new actuality through being mindful and implementing neuroplasticity. Also, peace leadership in combination with systems theory provides additional tools for individual and cultural changes.

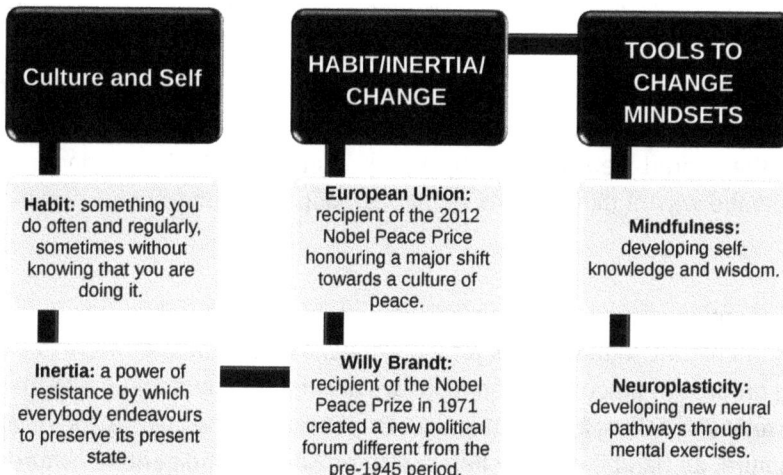

Culture and Self	HABIT/INERTIA/CHANGE	TOOLS TO CHANGE MINDSETS
Habit: something you do often and regularly, sometimes without knowing that you are doing it.	**European Union:** recipient of the 2012 Nobel Peace Price honouring a major shift towards a culture of peace.	**Mindfulness:** developing self-knowledge and wisdom.
Inertia: a power of resistance by which everybody endeavours to preserve its present state.	**Willy Brandt:** recipient of the Nobel Peace Prize in 1971 created a new political forum different from the pre-1945 period.	**Neuroplasticity:** developing new neural pathways through mental exercises.

Figure 6.1: A broad overview of chapter

Habit and inertia: Essential parts of identity and culture

Habit is defined as "something you do often and regularly, sometimes without knowing that you are doing it."[6] Though occasionally despised by us, such as those who try to quit smoking, it gives the comfort of a routine. Often this is accompanied by being good at something, such as the athlete practising the same sequence until it becomes her *second nature*. The repetitions implied in habitual behaviour translates into *body memory*, seemingly suggesting that the body knows what to do without much reflection.[7]

Habit also characterizes attitudes, feelings and thoughts as has been well formulated by B.R. Andrews in 1903: "habit, from the standpoint of psychology, (as) a more or less fixed way of thinking, willing, or feeling acquired through previous repetition of a mental experience."[8] Cultures develop habits as is the case with individual habits. Such cultural habits can be life enhancing. However, they can also sustain unjust circumstances that are not even noticed. This has been already formulated by Marquis de Condorcet in 1790: "habit can familiarize men with the violation of their natural rights to the point that among those who have lost them no one dreams of reclaiming them or believes that he has suffered an injustice."[9]

The self and culture – mutually enforced through habit

There is a mutually enforcing dynamic between the Self and culture. Both are not static. Rather, they change over time. Culture is also more than ethnographic features which only play a role if they influence the world views of its members. Much folklorist tradition and rituals are reminders of historical influences upon one's cultural ancestors that might still resonate in one's identity but has lost its grip upon one's Self. Practising traditional rituals adds colour and excitement though a sole focus on them to understand a culture is too narrow to understand the complexity of habit. Rather, culture is the shared web of meaning of individuals. A culture thus depends on the Self, that is the way of thinking, the emotional responses and behaviours individuals exhibit.[10]

The web of meaning and its accompanying habits are formed by being exposed to an environment that, in turn, is set for individuals by their culture. There is a mutually enforcing process in place between a culture and its members that make their web of meaning relatively robust and sustainable. Depending on the culture, the environment can be nature, as has been and often is still the case for indigenous cultures. It also can be other *natural* environments such as urban centers which has become the actuality for most people. Those are just two examples of the wide range of possible identifiable influences. Others would be early childhood experiences, intellectual and spiritual traditions, educational experiences, etc. Often, the Self is not even aware of what impacts its habitual way of thinking and feeling, a fact that, as will be explored, can be remedied through mindfulness.

An excellent study of *habitus* has been done by the sociologist Pierre Bourdieu. Bourdieu considers habitus to be a "structured structure" as well as a "structuring structure", both being conditioned by the conditions of existence.[11] Habitus then produces "classifiable practices and works" as well as "schemes of perception and appreciation" resulting in life-styles with "classified and classifying practices."[12]

It tends to become a self-edifying system often without a chance of critical self-reflection. A good example to illustrate the working of habitus is *post-truth politics* where perceptions based on emotions and false information override facts and a rational point of view. This has occurred, for example, prior to the Brexit vote and the last US presidential election. The "regime of post-truth" has been analysed by Jayson Harsin.[13] Harsin blames communication that targets populations with misinformation, repetitions, lack of easily accessible different points of view, information overload and with user adjusted information.[14] This, combined with the diminished authority, trust or accessibility of respectable sources as well as the inability to critically assess available information creates perceptions that, from an *objective* point of view are deemed to be incredulous.

The examples of post-truth politics also demonstrate that the workings of habitus, despite the numerous analyses of propaganda, the knowledge generated by sociologists such as Bourdieu, and communication experts, is still operational. It probably is a feature inherent to the Self and culture. It also challenges the fading Enlightenment position that people are rational agents, who, with the right amount of education can and will always revert to an objective point of view. Rather, the Self must be understood to be *situated* and the world is constituted accordingly.

The standing power of habit: inertia

Situated world views are connected to habit making them robust against change. This resistance against change is further cemented through individual and cultural inertia. As with habitus, inertia works through individuals who form the base for a culture. Using the term 'inertia' implies an analogy to classical physics for which Isaac Newton defined inertia as "a power of resistance by which everybody, as much as in it lies, endeavours to preserve its present state, whether it be of rest or of moving uniformly forward in a straight line."[15]

Naturally, separating inertia from habitus is an analytical tool to get a better understanding of both. Both habitus and inertia are intrinsically connected and hard to separate. Inertia is an intrinsic part of habitus and inertia is characterised by habits.

Bourdieu argues that habitus tends to support inertia by emphasising the merits of the status quo. Societal structures are self-enforcing by encouraging individuals to "accept the social world as it is, to take it for granted, rather than to rebel against it, to counterpose to it different, even antagonistic possibles."[16] It works through power where individuals engage in relationship exercising influence that is accepted by others. In turn, it requires members who recognise and accept the authority of those enforcing existing symbolic structures. These complex interactions serve to maintain a societal common sense, or the "legitimate vision of the social world."[17]

However, this is not a *closed* system. Rather, habitus and inertia generate a strong tendency within individuals to adapt, replicate and enforce the prevailing mindset.[18] Thus, developing a new way of *seeing* the world and organizing actuality accordingly most likely occurs within an existing web of meaning and its values, customs and symbolic interactions. This also entails the imminent danger that invention or new ways of perceiving the world might be abandoned in times of crises in exchange for the comfort of the old habitus. All this is now also confirmed by findings in neuroscience.

Neuroscience as a tool to understand habit, inertia and change

Neuroscience, that is the study of the nervous system, reveals that individual and cultural features can be traced to neural networks. Neural networks are neurons that have established connections with other neurons through synapses. Neurons also have axons which are threadlike and can transmit information to other cells. According to Antonio Damasio, this creates *neural patterns* or *maps*[19] which are necessary for the "the management of life".[20]

Maps are also the base for *images* which constitute the mind. Maps are created through interactions with the outside world as well as with the *brain's memory banks.*[21] The mapping represents a *mimicking* of both the external as well as the internal experiences of the individual, which is not a passive copying.[22] Impressions thus might go unnoticed, get altered in translation or are emphasized due to their relationships with existing maps. Over time the mind can use its memory to exert *value-stamped* selection being applied to experiences – this can occur consciously as well as unconsciously.[23] Still, these maps can change based on our experiences, resulting in a permanent redrawing of our images.[24]

Inertia is related to the mind's tendency to minimize effort and cost.[25] The resulting *laziness* of the brain means that existing maps are used whenever possible to react to stimuli. This has the result that existing neural pathways get stronger. Using the illustration by Don Mihaloew in his lectures, the brain develops pathways that are then preferred in processing information. They become analogous to highways that prevent explorations of other paths, or ways of *seeing* things.

To sum up: the workings of habit and inertia are relevant for peace leadership because they explain the reluctance to embrace a culture of peace if individuals are accustomed to a culture of structural violence. In such cases, a re-modelling of mindsets according to the principles of a culture of peace is a formidable task for peace leadership. Still, the goal, a culture of peace, is sufficiently clear and internationally agreed upon due to The Sustainable Development Goals among other international efforts. Powerful examples of the possibility of a major shift from a culture of war to a culture of peace shall be explored in the following part.

European integration and the desire for peace

This part will showcase the European Union, recipient of the 2012 Nobel Peace Price, honouring a major shift within individuals and cultures towards a culture of peace. It will also showcase Willy Brandt, whose détente policy during his chancellorship greatly contributed to the development of the European Union as we know it today. Brandt received the Nobel Peace Prize for this in 1971. Both examples illustrate that a fundamental shift from an established habitus is possible at the individual, civil society as well as state level.

The European Union: recipient of the Nobel Peace Price 2012

In accepting the Nobel Peace Price for the European Union the President of the European Commission, José Manuel Durão Barroso, quoted Spinoza: "Peace is not mere absence of war, it is a virtue … a state of mind, a disposition for benevolence, confidence, justice".[26] He uses this quote to illustrate the prevalent disposition of most Europeans that "places the person and respect of human dignity at its heart. Because it gives a voice to differences while creating unity."[27]

There has been a miraculous shift in attitude in most European countries since the end of World War II. The two world wars have instilled in most citizens, civil society and among politicians an abhorrence of war across ideological, cultural and national boundaries. The total war proclaimed by Joseph Goebbels on 18 February 1943 became a total nightmare for most Europeans. Consequently, war was equated with unimaginable destruction, suffering, loss of home and identity as well as unbelievable human deprivation such as the industrial murder of millions of innocent human beings. The shared stories enforced the notion that peace is necessary to maintain the veneer of civilization constraining the human capacity to horrendous and too often *banal* evil.[28]

In his Nobel Lecture, Herman Van Rompuy, President of the European Council, pointed out important stepping stones[29] towards greater integration of European countries, driven by passion for a new actuality for its citizens, such as the Coal and Steel Treaty of 1951; the Élysée Treaty, a treaty of friendship, signed by Charles de Gaulle and Konrad Adenauer on January 22, 1963; the Treaty of Rome of 1957 establishing the European Economic Community, and the 1992 Treaty of Maastricht founding the European Union.

The European Union is an ongoing project with many challenges. However, it creates a forum for dialogue, economic integration and mobility, all factors that promote peaceful conflict resolution. Still, peace requires more than political agreement as seems to be evident by the failure of the Kellogg-Briand Pact, the 1928 international agreement signed by most other states of the day. The Pact states that war is not to be used to resolve "disputes or conflicts of whatever nature or whatever origin they may be, which may arise among them."[30] The Pact could not prevent World War II and it is little consolation that it was used to prosecute perpetrators at the Nuremberg trials in 1945 and 1946.

The idea of European integration has been driven by the strong desire among its citizens to break the cycle of violence and to create a new actuality for European citizens. There have been many peace manifestations by the general populace, even during the tenacious Cold War period, drawing, for example, 500 000 people to the capital of West Germany, Bonn, on June 10, 1982 during a visit by President Reagan. They protested the deployment of Cruise Missiles and Pershing II missiles on a very hot day, unintimidated by heavy military helicopters flying over the crowd. Another example is the winding chain of people, totalling 1.3 million participants on October 22, 1983 between Stuttgart and Ulm or the 400 000 demonstrating for peace in Brussels on October 23, 1983. This sentiment for peace was also prevalent on the other side of the Iron Curtain as, for example, manifested through the *Schwerter zu Pflugscharen* movement in East Germany.

Willy Brandt: recipient of the Nobel Peace Prize in 1971

The desire for peace and reconciliation permeated also the actions of high-profile politicians in Germany and other European countries. They symbolized that politicians also had turned away from the violent habit of the past, intent on creating a new political forum that was markedly different from the cycles of war politics pursued in the pre-1945 period.

For example, on December 7, 1979 the chancellor of Germany, Willy Brandt, fell to his knees to commemorate the victims of the Warsaw Ghetto Uprising. He demonstrated an attitude of humility, penance and deep regret for World War II German violence. During the same visit, Germany and Poland signed the Treaty of Warsaw, agreeing on not using violence for conflict resolution and acknowledging the existing borders.

Brandt thus had broken with a century-old tradition of prioritizing so-called national interest. As noted in the Award Ceremony Speech, "Brandt's Eastern European policy is an attempt to bury and seek reconciliation across the mass graves of war."[31] He symbolizes the new trajectory of German politics marked by reconciliation and peaceful relations with other nations and particularly with Poland.[32] After the Cold War, these principles were re-confirmed in the German-Polish Treaty of 1990 that came into force on January 16, 1992.[33] The Treaty affirmed the borders between Germany and Poland, the sovereignty and territorial integrity of both states, and relinquished territorial claims.

In order to understand the significance of this departure from the German traditional approach to foreign policy, it is important to know the historical context. The Polish–German relations were tenacious for centuries and war was considered a legitimate means to pursue national interests. Germany inflicted unspeakable suffering on the Polish people through Hitler's maniacal goal to secure *Lebensraum* for Germans. When the tide of war luck turned, it was decided that ethnic Germans should be expelled from the territory of Czechoslovakia and the newly constituted territory of Poland as well as from the part of Poland that became part of the Soviet Union after World War II. Between 12 to 14 million Germans either fled from the advance of the Red Army or, after the war, were forcefully expelled from their homelands and resettled in West and East Germany.[34]

Though losing one's ancestral home is a hardship, it is notable that the organization representing those who were resettled from Czechoslovakia early on made clear that any resolution to this obvious conflict must be done through peaceful means. On August 4, 1950 the Arbeitsgemeinschaft zur Wahrung sudentendeutscher Interessen signed a resolution, *Das Wiesbadener Abokommen*,[35] with the Czech National Committee in London. It declares the desire of Germans to return as legitimate though it is agreed that force is not condoned when nations pursue their self-determination.

To sum up: The European Union, despite its challenges, symbolizes a major shift from often century-old traditions of narrowly understood nationalism and foreign policy that is marked by exclusion and war. It is a miracle that within the span of a generation from World War II it is possible to cross state borders along past war zones still pitted with abandoned bunkers and graveyards of fallen soldiers without even showing a passport. It is a development that arose from the ruins of World War II carried by the majority of Europeans represented by their politicians who, without being branded by their electorate, often compromised so-called national and individual interests for greater European integration. In the end, this course of action led to peace, greater prosperity and the protection of human rights for Europeans that also extends to the rest of the world through the commitment to human security by the European Union:

> "In a more contested world, the EU will be guided by a strong sense of responsibility. We will engage responsibly across Europe and the surrounding regions to the east and south. We will act globally to address the root causes of conflict and poverty, and to promote human rights."[36]

The role of peace leadership in sustaining a culture of peace

This part explores the role of peace leadership in developing a habit sustaining a culture of peace. Most likely, peace leadership needs to be change leadership, that is, transforming individual mindsets and cultures from a habit that accepts violence and the denial of human security to a life that considers a culture of peace as essential for one's wellbeing and as part of our human responsibility towards others. An important tool for individual change is mindfulness.

Mindfulness as a tool to become self-aware, to change and to create peace

Identity is rooted in the Self, who, in community with like-minded others, constitutes a culture. Individuals like to be comfortable, and the customary and habitual gives a sense of belonging and wellbeing. Even in dire conditions, humans need the *meaning of life*, a hold on one's spiritual Self that gives hope and reason for survival.[37] Viktor Frankl has observed this among fellow concentration camp inmates.[38] In more life-conducive conditions the meaning of life goes beyond survival. It is a conglomerate of halos or adumbrations of past experiences resulting in an initial confusing mix of beliefs, values and customs. This conglomerate constitutes the stuff of our identity that often takes care of us though we don't necessarily care about it. Still, there are ways of establishing clarity about one's Self, its meaning within one's life, and to alter our identity according to our visions.

An effective tool to facilitate becoming aware of one's Self is the practice of meditation and gaining wisdom through mindfulness, that allows the mind to focus on the present moment and "gradually develop self-knowledge and wisdom."[39] It is best known through Buddhism though it is part of many other spiritual traditions. In the Western World it came to prominence through the work of Jon Kabat-Zinn. Kabat-Zinn presents mindfulness meditation as a method to escape our habits and to take advantage of our potential.

Mindfulness can be used to find a deeper understanding of the Self, its meaning within one's life and its cultural embeddedness. Mindfulness is also a powerful tool to develop a peaceful actuality by aligning one's Self with the established features of a culture of peace. There is also evidence that lifestyle and habit can influence the genome.[40] Thus, the transition from a culture of war to a culture of peace might also change the genetic make-up: a culture of peace will then be the habit of future generations. This transformation can be helped through peace leadership building on modern leadership theory and systems theory.

Neuroplasticity as a way to develop new thinking

For Northouse, 21st century models of leadership, though manifold, share the basic premise that they assist individuals in achieving a common goal.[41] For peace leadership this common goal is a culture of peace whereas the Sustainable Development Goals can be used as the latest internationally agreed upon guideline for what a culture of peace entails. The prominent modern leadership models, such as authentic leadership, spiritual leadership, servant leadership, adaptive leadership and transformative leadership as well as a combination of these models can be employed based on the situational context of individuals, societies and cultures.

As demonstrated, neuroscience can explain habit and inertia. This knowledge can be employed by peace leadership to work towards a culture of peace. Habit and inertia are based on the synaptic connections that are responsible for the mindset: "mental activity stimulates brain firing as much as brain firing creates mental activity."[42] Daniel Siegel further illustrates this with the phrase "as neurons fire together, they wire together."[43] Thus, a mindset and habit can be changed if the mind is directed towards a different experience which then "stimulates new patterns of neural firing to create new synaptic linkages."[44] Siegel calls this ability of the mind to transform itself *neuroplasticity.*[45] Developing new ways of thinking and experiencing thus becomes analogous to exercising specific muscles for an athletic activity. The more it is used, the stronger it gets. Peace leaders can use this insight for transformative processes to actualize a culture of peace. An additional important impetus for peace leadership can be found in change models based on systems theory.

For example, for transformative peace leadership intervention leaders can use Robert B. Dilts' *logical levels* for learning and change, a model that has been successfully employed by coaches for transforming habits in clients. Building on the work in anthropology of Gregory Bateson and in logic of Bertrand Russell, Dilts argues that there is a natural hierarchy of processes or systems in the brain that need to be integrated.[46]

Dilts consequently identifies six different levels, "that influence and shape our relationships and interactions in the world."[47] Working from the bottom up these are my:

> "*environment*, the external context, the constraints and opportunities or the where and when;
> *behaviour*, what I do or have done, the actions and reactions or the what;
> *capabilities*, strategies and states, maps and plans, or the how;
> *belief system*, the values and meaning or one's mission that is the why;
> *identity*, that is who I am or wish to be, one's motivation or the who;"[48]

A peace leader can use these insights to work with followers to accept peace as the foundation for human wellbeing. The peace leader can then demonstrate or develop concepts of what kind of identity is required to honour peace, what beliefs and values accompany this identity, what capabilities are required to honour the vision of a peaceful world, what behaviour is needed and what kind of environment is conducive to peace.

Most likely, there is not a template for humanity a peace leader can draw from, that is beyond the vision underlying the culture of peace as it has been developed by the international community. Rather, cultural diversity as well as individual identities and their history require sensitivity towards the cultural and individual contexts. Peace leadership thereby becomes necessarily situational.

To illustrate this, the transformation of German culture to adopt a European identity is and needs to be different, for example, from the Dutch development, being a member of the European Union. The evolution of German culture after 1945 has been and is still driven by the deep-seated conviction that Germany should never again impose unbelievable atrocities and hardship on people, basically denying their humanity, as had been propagated and done from 1933 to 1945. This is not a driving force in Holland whose people suffered immensely under German occupation during World War II.

Concluding remarks

The Sustainable Development Goals and other international agreements on a culture of peace are founded on a mindset of solidarity and care asking for a global partnership involving "governments, the private sector, civil society, the United Nations system and other actors and mobilizing all available resources."[49] It is a small miracle that all countries in the world accept them.[50]

Humanity has a goal that is a world without structural violence, where there is no poverty; no hunger; good health and wellbeing; good education; gender equality; clean water and sanitation; affordable and clean energy; decent work and economic growth; industry, innovation and infrastructure; reduced inequalities; where there are sustainable cities and communities; where there is responsible consumption and production; climate action; protection of life below water and of life on land; where there are peace, justice and strong institutions, and where we experience partnerships for these goals.[51]

With the Sustainable Development Goals, peace leadership has a vision to rally its followers. The challenge, though, is to lead individuals, civil society and states to adopt a mindset that underlies a culture of peace – a mindset of solidarity, care and conviction of the value of human dignity. This is a formidable task considering that it is barely a generation ago that the world was engulfed in a global violent conflict.

However, there is justified hope that the transition towards a culture of peace will be successful. There are many tools available that can be employed to help us to understand ourselves and propel the Self and cultures towards a culture of peace. In addition, leadership theory can easily be aligned with peace leadership.

References

Andrews, B.R. 1903. Habit. *The American Journal of Psychology,* 14(2): 121-49.

Arbeitsgemeinschaft zur Wahrung sudentendeutscher Interessen and Tschechischer Nationalausschuß 1950. *Das Wiesbadener Abkommen.* Available from: http://www. mitteleuropa.de/wiesbabk01.htm [Accessed 21 June, 2018].

Arendt, H. 1963. *Eichmann in Jerusalem. A report on the banality of evil.* London: Penguin Books Ltd.

Barroso, J.M.D. 2012. From War to Peace: A European Tale. *European Union (EU)-Nobel Lecture.* Available from https://www.nobelprize.org/nobel_prizes/peace/laureates/2012/ eu-lecture_en.html [Accessed 21 June, 2018]

Bourdieu, P. 1984. *Distinction. A social critique of the judgement of taste.* Transl. by Richard Nice. Cambridge: Harvard University Press.

Bourdieu, P. 1985. The social space and the genesis of groups. *Theory and Society* 14(6): 723-744.

Cambridge Advanced Learner's Dictionary and Thesaurus 2018. Cambridge: Cambridge University Press. Available from https://dictionary.cambridge.org/dictionary/english/habit [Accessed 21 June, 2018]

Condorcet, N. 1789. Sur l'admission des femmes au droit de cité. *Journal de la Société de 1789,* 5.

Corr, P. and Matthews, G. 2009. *The Cambridge handbook of personality psychology.* Cambridge, UK: Cambridge University Press.

Damasio, A. 2010. *Self comes to mind. Constructing the conscious brain.* New York: Vintage Books.

Dilts, R. 2014. *A brief history of logical levels.* Available from: http://www.nlpu.com/Articles/ LevelsSummary.htm. [Accessed 21 June, 2018].

European Union 2016. *Shared vision, common action: A stronger Europe. A global strategy for the European Union's Foreign and Security Policy.* Available from: https://eeas. europa.eu/archives/docs/top_stories/pdf/eugs_review_web.pdf [Accessed 21 June, 2018].

The Federal Republic of Germany and the Republic of Poland 1990. *Treaty between the Federal Republic of Germany and the Republic of Poland on the confirmation of the frontier between them, 14 November 1990.* Available from: https://www.un.org/Depts/los/ LEGISLATIONANDTREATIES/PDFFILES/TREATIES/DEU-POL1990CF.PDF [Accessed 21 June, 2018].

Frankl, V. 2006. *Man's search for meaning.* Boston: Beacon Press.

General Assembly Resolution 70/01 2015. *Transforming our world: the 2030 agenda for sustainable development.* Available from: https://sustainabledevelopment.un.org/post2015/transformingourworld [Accessed 21 June, 2018].

Hagura, N., Haggard, P. and Diedrichsen, J. February 2017. Perceptual decisions are biased by the cost to act. In *e-Life Sciences* 6.

Harsin, J. 2015. Regimes of post-truth. Postpolitics, and attention economies. *Communication, Culture and Critique* 8(2): 327-333.

Hassad, C. 2014. *Playing the genetic hand. Epigenetics and how to keep ourselves healthy.* Melbourne: Michelle Anderson Publishing.

Kabat-Zinn, J. 1994. *Wherever you go there you are. Mindfulness meditation in everyday life.* New York: Hyperion.

Karunamuni and Weerasekera 2017. Theoretical foundations to guide mindfulness meditation. A path to wisdom. *Current Psychology,* 1-20.

Kellogg-Briand Pact 1928. Available from: http://avalon.law.yale.edu/20th_century/kbpact.asp [Accessed June 21, 2018].

Lionæs, A. 1971. Award ceremony speech. *The Nobel Peace Prize 1971. Willy Brandt.* Available from: https://www.nobelprize.org/nobel_prizes/peace/laureates/1971/press.html [Accessed June 21, 2018].

Newton, I. 1846. *Newton's Principia: the mathematical principles of natural philosophy* (A. Motte, Trans.). New York: Daniel Adee.

Norton, P. 2016. *Leadership. Theory and practice* (7th ed.). Thousand Oaks, CA: Sage Publications.

Siegel, D. 2010. *Mindsight. The new science of personal transformation.* New York: Bantam Books.

Slotte, P. and Halme-Tuomisaari M. (Eds.) 2015. *Re-visiting the origins of human rights.* Cambridge: Cambridge University Press.

Statistisches Bundesamt 1958. *Die deutschen Vertreibungsverluste.* Wiesbaden.

Van Rompuy, H. 2012. From War to Peace: A European Tale. *European Union (EU)-Nobel Lecture.* Available from: https://www.nobelprize.org/nobel_prizes/peace/laureates/2012/eu-lecture_en.html [Accessed June 21, 2018].

Welton, D. (Ed.) 1999. *The body.* Oxford: Blackwell Publishers Ltd

Endnotes

1 Lionæs, 1971.
2 Lionæs, 1971
3 Slotte & Halme-Tuomisaari, 2015.
4 Slotte & Halme-Tuomisaari, 2015.
5 General Assembly Resolution 70/01, 2015.
6 Cambridge Advanced Learner's Dictionary & Thesaurus, 2018.
7 Welton, 1999.
8 Andrews, 1903: 121.
9 Condorcet, 1790: 1.
10 Corr & Matthews, 2009.
11 Bourdieu, 1984: 171.
12 Bourdieu, 1984: 171.
13 Harsin, 2015.
14 Harsin, 2015.
15 Newton, 1846: 72
16 Bourdieu, 1985: 728.
17 Bourdieu, 1985: 731.
18 Bourdieu, 1985: 734.
19 Damasio, 2010: 67-69.
20 Damasio, 2010: 67.
21 Damasio, 2010: 67, 68.
22 Damasio, 2010: 68.
23 Damasio, 2010: 76, 77.
24 Damasio, 2010: 69, 70.
25 Hagura, Haggard & Diedrichsen, 2017.
26 Barroso, 2012.

27   Barrosa, 2012.
28   Arendt, 1963.
29   Van Rompuy, 2012.
30   Kellog-Briand Pact, 1928.
31   Lionæs, 1971
32   Lionæs, 1971
33   The Federal Republic of Germany and the Republic of Poland, 1990.
34   Statistisches Bundesamt, 1958.
35   Arbeitsgemeinschaft zur Wahrung sudentendeutscher Interessen & Tschechischer Nationalausschuß 1950.
36   European Union, 2016.
37   Frankl, 2006.
38   Frankl, 2006.
39   Karunamuni & Weerasekera, 2017.
40   Hassed, 2014.
41   Northouse, 2016, p. 4.
42   Siegel, 2010, p. 39.
43   Siegel, 2010, p. 40.
44   Siegel, 2010, p. 41.
45   Siegel, 2010.
46   Dilts, 2014.
47   Dilts, 2014.
48   Dilts, 2014
49   General Assembly, 2015, section 39.
50   General Assembly 2015, section 5.
51   General Assembly, 2015

.

CHAPTER 7

LEADERSHIP THEORIES SUPPORTING PEACE LEADERSHIP

Martha Harunavamwe

To be an effective and relevant leader who finds personal meaning and inner peace in using his or her God-given gifts, one must be a servant leader, dedicated to making better for others[1].

Spotlight: Jane Addams

Jane Addams is a perfect example of a leader who thrived for peace.[2] She was available when economic, social and industrial forces exposed individuals to substandard conditions. Such conditions she considered as obstacles of inner peace for the vulnerable. Jane was born 1860 in Cedarville, Illinois, and graduated from Rockford in 1881.[3] She took a Grand Tour of Europe, where her interest in the lives of others started to show. Her visit to Toynbee Hall, a settlement in the slums of London, affected her and influenced the work she undertook when she returned to the United States.

Jane's desire to assist those in need tormented her, thus leading to the establishment of the Hull House in Chicago where she assisted those living in poverty and focused her attention on child welfare[4]. She developed services and programs based on the needs identified by people[5]. Following a severe economic depression in 1893, Addams realised the connection between poverty and public policy, and directed her attention towards policies and laws, the roots of poverty.[6] That triggered her desire to become a political activist and she worked for the vulnerable, tirelessly lobbying for legislation designed to protect labourers, immigrants, women and children[7]. Less widely known, is the depth of her concern about peace, but her idea of serving the needs of others indicates her desire for equality and freedom[8]. She was passionately committed to the abolition of war and the restoration of peace. World War I appeared to mark the beginning of Jane's public commitment to the peace movement. However, she had already begun earlier to articulate her position concerning peacebuilding. A series of lectures at the Chautauga Institute provided her with an opportunity to advance her view for peace. She became involved in the Women's Peace Party and served as head of the commission to find an end to the war[9].

Addams outlined her thoughts concerning peace in the book *Newer Ideal of Peace,* arguing for the necessity of international peace. In *Women at the Hague* (1915), she detailed the work of the 1915 International Congress and its efforts to advocate for peace. In her third book, *Peace and Bread in Time of War*, Addams recounts her experiences during and after World War 1[10]. The three books expose the destructive impact of war on human relationships and the intimate connection between peace and meeting the basic needs of all humans[11]. Jane's commitment to peace was clearly revealed when peace-making efforts failed and war broke out. She vehemently protested and openly criticised the failure of national leaders to find peaceful solutions. Analysing Jane Addams through the lens of servant leadership can be enlightening. Some of the major teachings peace leaders can draw from her is that the best way to improve oneself is to improve others. Peace leaders with the qualities of a servant leader are not dictatorial and are willing to serve others. Jane was authentic, accepting, present and useful; she displayed qualities which, if adopted by peace leaders, would contribute a lot to the mission of sustaining peace.

Introduction

We exist in a world characterised by many functioning systems of war, violence and discrimination. This makes the role of peace leaders in building and maintaining peaceful systems critical. Central to the concept of peace leadership is the desire for inclusion and cohesion, the experience of inner peace that should be spread around the world. There is a dire need to provide strategies that peace leaders can utilise to build and sustain peaceful conditions, and guarantee long-term peace across the world. When appropriate leadership theories are properly applied to peace leadership, pressing matters become less pressing, and previously hidden connections between groups of people and ideas are clearly revealed. The desire to spread peace becomes uncontrollable as in the case of Jane Addams[12].

Although peace leadership becomes noticeable when there are culminating events that confront some area of injustice, the level of preparation necessary for such action is seldom fully known. Peace leaders are called to strengthen the social contract and guarantee justice, equality, dignity and basic security, but they rarely receive proper knowledge on how to achieve this. Thus, the implementation of strategies that can be utilised by peace leaders involves taking into consideration important theoretical teachings of transformational and servant leadership. This chapter focuses on the strategies that can be used to implement peace leadership by providing an explanation of the processes through which societies can utilise the existing two leadership theories to implement and sustain peace. The chapter begins with a review of two leadership theories that possess elements that can be utilised to foster peace leadership. These include transformational leadership and servant leadership.

The chosen leadership theories adhere to elements such as believing in people, strong interpersonal relationships, facilitating a shared vision and valuing others' contributions, which are the pillars of peace leaders and thus these two theories adhere to the significant requirements of peace leadership[13]. Peace leaders need to acquire emotional self-control, a spirit of forgiveness, empathy, optimism about change potential and propensities towards reconciliation[14]. Such traits are facilitated through servant leadership practices and assist in preparing an individual to confront the challenges of peace. Thus, servant leadership will be discussed in detail since it provides a good foundation for peace leadership. The chapter focuses on describing two leadership theories and how they can be applied to achieve peace. The discussion will then be concluded with an integrated leadership model that informs how transformational and servant leadership theories can be applied in practice during peacebuilding. The chapter closes with future directions, which include encouraging individuals to be servants before they serve.

Utilising existing leadership theories as strategies for peacebuilding

Generally, there are four major classifications of leadership theory: trait theories, behavioural theories, contingency theories and the integrative theories. Trait theories focus on explaining distinctive characteristics accounting for leadership effectiveness and traits related to leadership success are identified. However, most research on leadership has shifted from trait theory to behavioural theory. Thus, behavioural leadership theories explain the different styles applied by effective leaders. Scholars identified two generic dimensions of leader behaviour – task- and people-oriented leadership – which are more significant in describing leadership effectiveness.

Researchers then discovered that there is no one best leadership style in all situations. In fact, the situation determines the required style and thus the contingency leadership theories emerged. The contingency theories explain the appropriate leadership style based on situational factors including the nature of the work, external environment, follower characteristics and the leader as an individual. In recent years, leadership has shifted to the integrative paradigm that ties the theories together. The two theories in question, as highlighted earlier, include transformational leadership, viewed as part of the new leadership paradigm that ties theories together[15], and servant leadership which fit well within the behavioural theories. Both theories fall into the category of behavioural theories and both are people-oriented leadership theories, so that an integration of the two produces elements from which peace leaders can derive great benefit[16]. A close analysis of these two leadership theories indicates the existence of some similarities between servant leadership and transformational leadership[17]. These two theories correlate very well regarding elements such as believing in people, strong interpersonal relationships, facilitating a shared vision and valuing others' contributions. These are some of the strong pillars of peace leadership. A detailed discussion of each leadership theory will be presented.

Conceptualisation of transformational leadership

Transformational leadership is a leadership approach that facilitates change in individuals and social systems enhancing the motivation, morale and performance of followers through a variety of mechanisms[18]. Its elements include motivation, encouragement, honesty, team-orientation, respect, effective communication, reliability, trustworthiness, empathy, empowerment, optimism and inspiration[19]. Referring back to chapter one, these elements are key factors that contribute to the success of peace leaders. This leadership approach is guided by the transformational leadership theory which focuses on directing the followers towards positive change whereby they can care for each others' interests and act in the group's interest as a whole[20]. The main purpose of transformational leadership is to transform individuals and organisations inside a literal logic and to modify them in the mind and heart. It is aimed at enlarging vision, insight and understanding. It simplifies reasoning, makes behaviour congruent with values and concepts, and brings about lasting changes that are self-perpetuating and momentum building[21].

Perspectives of transformational leadership applied in peace leadership

Transformational leadership theory manifests itself in four perspectives, which include idealised influence, individual consideration, intellectual stimulation and inspirational motivation[22]. Idealised influence is concerned with behaviour that instils pride in the followers for being associated with the leader. This indicates that the leader will go beyond their individual self-interest for the greater good of the other group and make personal sacrifices for others' benefit. A very good example is what Jane Addams did with immigrants at Hull House. The idealised behaviour encompasses the aspect of a leader leading by example such that the team may emulate him, treat him with high esteem and adopt his beliefs and principles[23].

Inspirational motivation is another transformational leadership perspective that clearly communicates the organisational goals and vision for the future. The inspirational leaders identify needs and talk about what should be accomplished; they express confidence that those goals will definitely be achieved. Through building confidence and trust in the followers, the transformational leadership style positively affects the followers' performance. This type of motivational behaviour in the peace leadership context encourages a sense of team spirit, creating general enthusiasm, especially towards difficult challenges. The enthusiasm and motivation are needed in order to maintain optimism throughout the peace negotiating processes[24].

Another very important aspect of the behaviour and attributes of transformational leaders that greatly contributes to peace leadership is intellectual stimulation. This aspect implies that transformational leaders seek differing perspectives when solving problems; they always have alternative paths to address challenges and get others to look at existing problems from a different angle[25]. In general, what makes transformational leadership more relevant in peace leadership is that it triggers radical ideas that dramatically stimulate project team initiatives and inspire unusual motivation, both of which enhance overall productivity. Transformational leaders provide mentorship, spend time coaching and counselling their followers, and in so doing, promote self- development. They treat others as individuals rather than simply group members, and identify the differing needs, abilities and aspirations of those individuals; they listen to others' concerns and help others to develop their strengths[26].

A recent study showed the existence of a strong positively significant relationship between transformational leadership and peacebuilding[27]. Transformational leadership and peace leadership are deeply engrained in mission-focused work, and this leadership approach is an ideal lens through which to facilitate change and lead socially minded institutions[28]. One successful example of global peacebuilding and conflict transformation where transformational leadership style played a significant role was the ending of the armed conflict in Northern Ireland and the transition to a more peaceful society. The conflict, which began in August 1969, formally ended with the signing of the Belfast/Good Friday Agreement in April 1998 by the British and Irish governments, with the support of Northern Irish political parties[29]. In addition to that, there have been concerted efforts to enhance peacebuilding in Somalia through transformational leadership, mainly through the use of traditional leaders who are highly esteemed among their respective clans[30].

Transformational leaders largely use soft power, such as the art of persuasion, empowerment and enrichment, which is a major requirement in peace leadership. When implementing this type of leadership approach in peace contexts, transforming should not be understood to be the drastic and mechanistic transposition of external rules-based policies and models, regardless of the realities of local governance.

Instead, transformation should come from within: external support then becomes more an element of facilitation and fuelling of such mechanisms rather than one of authoritative guidance. Empowering the local people and the followers is key to the process of transformation. Thus, existing capacities should be strengthened, new ones introduced, and old rules must be accommodated and made to fit into renovated frameworks.

Servant Leadership

Servant leaders distinguish themselves from ordinary leaders by a desire to serve first, then lead, rather than to lead first, then serve[31]. Jane Addams was living testimony of such a leadership style in her desire to assist those in need. She worked tirelessly and stood for the poor and the oppressed, and in so doing, she sacrificed her own joy, happiness and relationships for the sake of the deprived. Servant leaders ensure that followers' needs are being served such that they grow as individuals.

Conceptualising servant leadership

Greenleaf[32] defined servant leadership as a way of life, which begins with "the natural feeling that one wants to serve, to serve first an inward lifelong journey". It describes an individual who is by nature a servant, whose servant nature is the real man, not bestowed, not assumed, and cannot to be taken away. Servant leaders are distinguished by both their primary motivation to serve (what they do) and their self-construction (who they are), and from this conscious choice of 'doing' and 'being' they aspire to lead[33]. The nine functional attributes of servant leadership that make it crucial to peace leadership include: vision, honesty, integrity, trust, service, modelling, pioneering, appreciation of others, and empowerment[34]. These operative qualities and distinctive characteristics of servant leaders have a lot in common with the qualities of peace leaders as well as the elements of transformational leadership.

Consistent with the functional attributes, Linden[35] identified nine behaviours that define servant leadership: emotional healing, (being sensitive to others), creating value for the community, empowering, helping subordinates grow and succeed, putting subordinates first, behaving ethically, servanthood, knowing and understanding others. Russell[36] also articulated the importance of honesty and integrity, concern for others, fairness and justice as important values of servant leaders. Thus, the utmost rule of servant leadership is to have personal concern for the least privileged in society in terms of whether they will benefit, or at least, not be further deprived. This facilitates freedom and peace for the oppressed. This was actively practised by Jane Addams at Hull House, as well as by Mother Teresa, Moses, Harriet Tubman, Lao-tzu, Mohandas Gandhi and Martin Luther King[37]. In addition, the ultimate example of servant leadership can be traced back to Jesus Christ's life of servanthood and his teachings to his disciples[38] [39].

Scholars have developed models outlining attributes and characteristics of servant leadership. Barbuto and Wheeler[40] developed an integrated model of servant leadership that synthesised the attributes of servant leadership into five categories: altruistic calling, emotional healing, persuasive mapping, wisdom, and organisational stewardship. In addition to that, Dierendonck[41] provided a conceptual model that identified six key characteristics of servant leadership: empowering and developing people, humility, authenticity, interpersonal acceptance, providing direction, and stewardship. From the mentioned models, it is clear that servant leadership is not about power, but it is about service. Thus, rather than embarking on a quest for personal power, servant leaders embark on a quest to identify and meet the needs of others. The servant leader surveys the needs of a group and looks for what is missing. Servant leadership is not a new idea but an inspired practice. Matthew 20:28 indicates that Christ came to serve, not to be served. He healed the sick, fed the hungry and comforted the outcast, and that is what servant leaders should learn from – concern for others and putting others first. This makes servant leadership a unique leadership style from which peace leaders can benefit a lot.

Servant leadership as a unique attribute for peace leaders

What makes servant leadership unique is that it provides the leader with something that power and its trappings cannot provide: personal meaning and inner peace. This gives servant leaders a reservoir of spiritual strength to draw upon. This makes it possible for the servant leader to go on, to continue striving and serving others, no matter how difficult it may be. This inner strength is like a flowing river that never dries up until peace is achieved. Servant leadership is completely against the use of power and force. In fact, servant leaders believe that, rather than healing and building, factional warfare results in more hurt and more fragmentation, and should always be avoided[42]. Jane Addams, a servant leader, maintained that war is not a natural activity for mankind and that it was abnormal for men to fight against each other. She believed that the more natural tendency was for "men to come together into friendly relationships, human beings are more similar than they are different and what unites is stronger than what divides"[43].

It is time that societal leaders move away from focusing on power when leading towards focusing on service so that the society will reap the benefits: peace and freedom. Applying the principles of servant leadership in peace contexts obliges peace leaders to be concerned about the needs and wellbeing of those who are often excluded from the decision-making table. It makes them realise that they have a social responsibility to be concerned with the have-nots and to recognise them as equal stakeholders. Jane Addams believed that the essence of peace is the "nurture of human life" and that the "abolition of degrading poverty, disease, and ignorance" were at the heart of peacebuilding[44]. The contribution of servant leadership to peace leadership can be explained through Jane Addams' understanding of peace that was deeply rooted in her sense of optimism about humanity, and which was fed by her experience of serving the immigrant population in the settlements. Observing immigrants from diverse backgrounds working together to address common needs affirmed Addams' belief that friendly and cooperative relationships among people were possible and that the experience of working together inevitably increased mutual understanding and a sense of fellowship. As people came together and worked on issues such as health and sanitation in their neighbourhood, they realised they shared a common concern and that it was possible to work together to address these concerns. These friendly and cooperative relationships can pave the way to new "internationalism"[45]. Ultimately, Addams believed that the new form of internationalism would lead to "a moment when virile good-will, will substitute the spirit of warfare" and peace will be achieved[46]. In short, servant leadership can be utilised to address ethical dilemmas and social imbalances that are leading to war.

Solutions and recommendations:
an integrated model to facilitate peace leadership

At various stages of peace implementation, effective flow of the process can be maximised through the integration of different leadership theories. At the centre of the notion of peacebuilding is the idea of meeting the needs of people, which is the pillar of servant leadership for security and order, for a reasonable standard of living, and for recognition of identity and worth, and this can be achieved through servant leadership[47]. From the discussion it is clear that both transformational and servant leadership focus on understanding the needs of followers and empowering them. Thus, a combination of the elements of transformational leadership and the attributes of servant leadership can possibly provide peace leaders with a list of key success factors of sustaining peace. These factors should however be appropriately utilised at different stages in the process of implementing peace. As indicated in Figure 7.1, transformational leadership and its components may be more relevant during the initial stages of peacebuilding when leaders are trying to win the hearts of the masses. A very good example is when leaders are seeking to understand the causes of conflict as well as trying to address the needs of people. Servant leadership then assists in the implementation phase and some of the dimensions from servant leadership facilitate the development of peace leadership. These qualities, in turn, enable both servant and peace leaders to maintain and sustain peace.

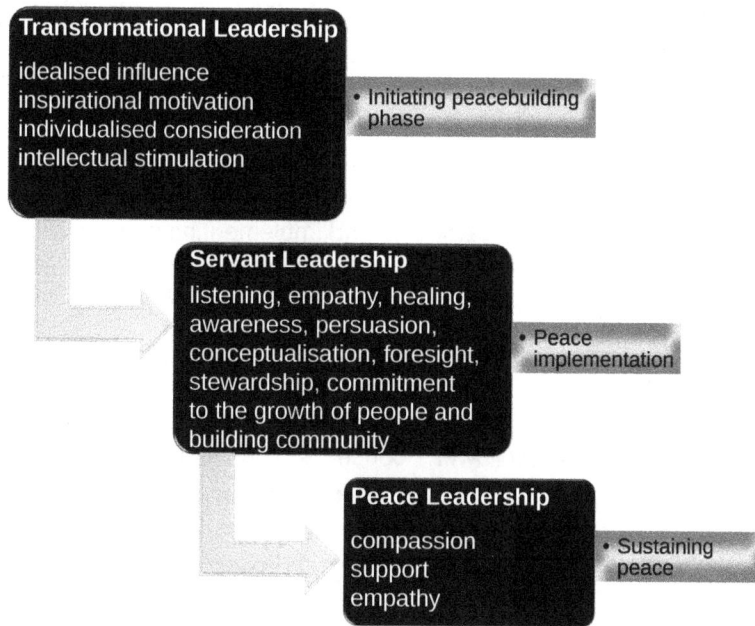

Figure 7.1 A conceptual integrated model of peace leadership

Figure 7.1 shows the interaction between the dimensions of transformational leadership and the components of servant leadership, and how the two may be applied in different phases of peace efforts. The first phase of initiating peace and building peace requires more transformational leadership elements that include involving individuals in active participation in the process of peacebuilding. Thus, transformational leadership through inspirational motivation and intellectual stimulation can encourage the masses or the community to take part in formulating policies and providing strategies for building peace. As the process for peacebuilding strives for new attitudes and practices among leaders, the application of servant leadership becomes more relevant where empathy, commitment to the growth of people and persuasion are applied to implement peace. Both servant and transformational aspects of leadership provide peace leaders with a number of flexible, consultative and collaborative approaches to peacebuilding and implementation that can operate from a contextual understanding of the root causes of conflict to the restoration of peace. As displayed in Figure 7.1, this can include the transformative approach of terminating something undesired (violence) through idealised influence and inspirational motivation and then the building of something desired through the transformation of relationships and construction of new conditions by serving the needs of others (servant leadership).

As indicated in Figure 7.1, the transformational leadership approach could be beneficial to initiating peace in the early stages of the program's development in order to generate widespread stakeholder support and negotiate the change process that may be necessary to launch peace programs[48]. Then servant leadership becomes more relevant during the implementation of peace initiatives where the needs of people are realised. Transformational leadership again becomes relevant where leaders emphasise task accomplishment and personal development. It may be beneficial for enabling close monitoring and follow-up on myriad administrative and management tasks, perhaps ideally suited for overseeing and implementing peace events requiring coordination across multiple stakeholder groups, vendors, facilities, local government agencies and community leaders.

Consistent with that, in the individualised consideration element of transformational leadership, a leader attends to each follower's needs, acts as a mentor or coach to the follower and listens to the follower's concerns. Thus, in both leadership theories, leaders pay huge and special attention to followers' needs for development and achievement. In addition, similar to the qualities of peace leadership discussed in chapter one and depicted on Figure 7.1, Spears[49] defined the characteristics of servant leadership as including listening, empathy, healing (follower wellbeing); awareness (of the environment); persuasion; and conceptualisation (being visionary). He further highlighted foresight, stewardship, commitment to the growth of people and building community of those individuals as characteristics of servant leadership. As indicated in Figure 7.1, peace leaders, with the guidance of servant leadership components, also provide needed compassion, support, empathy and guidance to influence their respective followers in the process of sustaining peace[50]. Therefore, servant and transformational leadership both influence peacebuilding and peace implementation processes.

Additionally, Autesserre[51] emphasised that the transformational leadership theory can never be ignored in peace leadership, because one of the most important needs for peacebuilding is to find ways to understand peace as a change process based on relationship building. In this process, the leaders with idealised influence are honoured, appreciated, trusted, and the followers admire them and listen to them. Such qualities can never be compromised in peace negotiations. Transformational leaders make the followers see an appealing future and offer them opportunities to see meaning in their work; they inspire and motivate followers, stimulating teamwork, pointing out positive attitudes, and emphasising aims and advantages[52]. This suggests that transformational leadership is relevant to the peacebuilding, and facilitates cooperative peaceful efforts required among community leaders so that they influence followers. Recent research indicated that project managers who exercise the transformational leadership behaviour of inspirational motivation enjoy peacebuilding missions[53].

In addition to the discussion, the situational leadership theory indicated that in peace contexts, servant leadership could also be augmented by other leadership styles, such as transformational and transactional leadership[54]. Transformational leaders are adept at marshalling support around a unifying vision, demonstrating charisma, and in astutely navigating the change process. A very good example is Jane Addams who believed in the inclusion of followers into the transformation process and the need to diagnose their wishes, needs, values and abilities in the right way. Similarly, servant leadership is concerned with analysing the needs of followers and making an effort to address such needs. As a servant leader, Jane Addams was of the opinion that achieving peace required that humanity and all nations move in the direction of compassionate tending to citizens[55]. She maintained that as nations tended to the needs of citizens, the possibility of war became more remote and peace would definitely prevail.

Recommendations and directions for future research in peace leadership

Given the benefits of transformational and servant leadership in peace contexts, as a viable leadership theory, a combination of both transformational and servant leadership can perhaps provide the ethical grounding and leadership framework needed to help address most of the challenges that are threatening peace in the twenty-first century. It is thus recommended that peace leaders in practice adopt elements such as idealised influence, inspirational motivation and intellectual stimulation during the peace initiation phases. Combining both transformational and servant leadership elements like empathy, stewardship, listening and practising them just like Jane Addams would, yields peace. The two leadership theories are concerned with commitment to the growth of others, which is a significant notion in peace leadership. However, serving others should take the lead following Jane Addams' sentiments that serving others can resolve problems related to economic globalisation, rising terrorism, war and violence, disease and starvation, as well as closing the gap between the rich and the poor worldwide.

In addition, implementing servant leadership will help to eradicate the traditional leader-first paradigm that values power more than service and applauds Darwinism's individualistic and capitalist approach to life. These approaches are the main contributors to most modern tragedies, which imply that only the strong will survive. As discussed in the integrated model, depending on situations, peace leaders should be flexible enough to adopt the most suitable leadership approach. In the initial stages, transformational leadership will be more applicable to mobilising the people in support of peace initiatives, and during implementation phases, servant leadership becomes more relevant. With the proper application of transformational and servant leadership the possibility of achieving peace is probable. It is therefore recommended that, when nurturing peace leaders, the policy makers should organise and initiate coaching in transformational and servant leadership qualities to equip them with the necessary skills to negotiate peace. This will influence the morale of followers for conflict settlement on peacebuilding.

Additionally, a number of servant leaders such as Mother Teresa and Jane Addams recognised the role of women in war, and had very clear beliefs about women and their contributions in times of war[56]. Jane Addams emphasised that women brought an important perspective to social life and problems, and can be good facilitators of peaceful negotiations. It is therefore recommended that more women be identified to play the roles of peace negotiators and peace leaders across the world. Jane Addams also believed in recognising social amelioration as a way to pursue needed change both at the national and international level. Present-day initiatives should not turn a blind eye to the process of social amelioration to bring together diverse groups to identify shared concerns and to work jointly toward finding appropriate ways to cooperatively address these concerns.

Instead of passively observing and commenting on the need for social change, Jane Addams actively engaged in the change process. Just like Addams, contemporary peace leaders should openly expose and challenge oppressive and unjust systems. Such efforts require individuals to actively engage in public discourse as a means of raising consciousness, leaders need to focus on serving those who are oppressed and treated unjustly through engaging, and this will facilitate the process of advocating for peaceful nations.

Organising coalitions that can develop, present and advocate for needed changes will be of great importance. Leaders need to continue the tradition of Jane Addams as an advocate for peace and justice. Peace leaders should emulate and have among their role models individuals who were actively involved, like the former president of South Africa, Nelson Mandela, and His Holiness, the Dalai Lama, two of the most influential peacemakers the world has ever known. The great legacy of these extraordinary individuals was the end of war, violence and the transformation of life, as humanity reaches for the Golden Goal of Global Peace.

Concluding remarks

In conclusion, the chapter's main objective is to demonstrate how transformational leadership and servant leadership theories can be utilised by peace leaders in the process of building, implementing and sustaining peace. The chapter concludes that an integrated model approach should be utilised for peace leadership. The initial phases of peacebuilding should apply transformational elements such as inspirational motivation while the implementation phase should apply servant leadership elements such as empathy, stewardship, foresight and commitment to growth of community. Even though the efforts discussed in the integrated peace leadership framework are more theoretical and may be difficult to practise, adopting transformational and servant leadership qualities accordingly will provide a clear path to successful peace leadership. However, it should be noted that peace leadership is a lifetime commitment and it requires effort that starts from within and goes beyond to the community.

With the example of Jane Addams who believed in character before leadership, we can all mould ourselves and influence others to do the same for the sake of peace. Jane Addams believed that we only make our way in the world through self-discipline and self-control, which will attract those around us to follow suit. Leaders need to serve before they lead and peace will be achieved.

References

Addams, J. 1922. *Peace And Bread In Time Of War*. New York: The Macmillan Company.

Allen, S.J. 2008. Leadership development: An exploration of sources of learning. *SAM Advanced Management Journal*, 73(1): 10.

Amaladas, S. and Byrne, S. eds., 2017. *Peace Leadership: The Quest for Connectedness*. London: Routledge.

Autesserre, S. 2014. Going micro: Emerging and future peacekeeping research. *International Peacekeeping*, 21(4): 492-500.

Barbuto Jr, J.E. and Wheeler, D.W. 2009. Scale development and construct clarification of servant leadership. *Group & Organization Management*, 31(3): 300-326.

Benner, T., Mergenthaler, S. and Rothmann, P. 2011. *The new world of UN peace operations: Learning to build peace?* Oxford: Oxford University Press on Demand.

Brooks, D. 2017. The Jane Addams Model. *The New York Times*.

Bloom, B.R. 2011. WHO needs change? *Nature*, 473(7346): 143.

Brown, V.B. 2010. *The Education of Jane Addams*, Philadelphia: University of Pennsylvania Press, p.194.

Chu, R.I.M. 2011. *Conflict management styles of pastors and organizational servant leadership: A descriptive study*. The Southern Baptist Theological Seminary.

Ebener, D.R. and O'Connell, D.J. 2010. How might servant leadership work. *Nonprofit Management and Leadership*, 20(3): 315-335.

Elshtain, J.B. and Elshtain, J. 2002. *Jane Addams and the dream of American democracy*. Basic Books.

Farid, S.A. 2014. Toleration or recognition. Towards a new account of religious diversity in contemporary Egypt. *European Scientific Journal*, 8(1): 14-16.

Febres, G.E. 2017. *Relationship between the Transactional Leadership Styles, the Transformational Leadership Style and Subordinates' Job Satisfaction* (Doctoral dissertation, Northcentral University).

Greenleaf, R.K. 1977. Servant leadership in business. *Leading organizations: Perspectives for a new era*, Vol: 87-95.

Johnson, E.C. (ed.) 1960: Jane Addams a centennial reader. New York: The Macmillan Company.

Joslin, K. 2010. Reading Jane Addams in the Twenty-first Century. *Feminist Interpretations of Jane Addams*, Vol: 31-53.

Kelloway, E.K. 2012. Transformational leadership and employee psychological well-being: The mediating role of employee trust in leadership. *Work & Stress*, 26(1): 39-55.

Knight, L.W. 2005. Citizen: Jane Addams and the Struggle for Democracy. Accessed 11 February 2018, http://press.uchicago.edu/ucp/books/book/chicago/C/bo3615179.html (Accessed on 12 March 2018)

Lanctot, J.D. and Irving, J.A. 2010. Character and leadership: Situating servant leadership in a proposed virtues framework. *International Journal of Leadership Studies*, 6(1): 28-50.

Linden, E. 2008. Showcasing leadership exemplars to propel professional practice model implementation. *Journal of Nursing Administration*, 38(3): 138-142.

Northouse, P.G. 2015. *Leadership: Theory and practice*. Sage publications.

Reychler, L. and Stellamans, A. 2008. Researching peace building leadership. *International Peace Research Association*, 23(71): 7-18.

Russell, R.F. 2001. The role of values in servant leadership. *Leadership & Organization Development Journal*, 22(2): 76-84.

Samatar, E.H. 2018. Influence of transformational leadership on peace building in Somalia. *Strategic Journal of Business and Change Management*, 5(1): 799-826.

Sendjaya, S. and Sarros, J.C. 2002. Servant leadership: Its origin, development, and application in organizations. *Journal of Leadership and Organizational Studies*, 9(2): 57-64.

Smith, B.N., Montagno, R.V. and Kuzmenko, T.N. 2009. Transformational and servant leadership: Content and contextual comparisons. *Journal of Leadership and Organizational Studies*, 10(4): 80-91.

Stone, A. 2004. Transformational versus servant leadership: A difference in leader focus. *Leadership and Organization Development Journal*, 25(4): 349-361.

Spears, L.C. 2002. Tracing the past, present, and future of servant-leadership. *Focus on leadership: Servant-leadership for the twenty-first century*, pp. 1-16.

Tawney, E. 2014. The Business Roundtable: Viewpoints on US Economic Policy from America's Leading Business Association. *Chicago Policy Review* Available from https://www.taylorfrancis.com/books/9781134941681. (Accessed 20 February 2018).

Van Dierendonck, D. 2011. Servant leadership: A review and synthesis. *Journal of management*, 37(4): 1228-1261.

Warrilow, S. 2012. Transformational Leadership Theory – The 4 Key Components in Leading Change and Managing Change. Available from. http://EzineArticles.com/expert/Stephen_ Warrilow/361805. (Accessed 12 March 2018).

Welty Peacy, J., Bruening, M. and Burton, L. 2011. Servant leadership in sport for development and peace: A way forward. *Quest*, 69(1): 125-139.

Zhu, W., Riggio, R.E., Avolio, B.J. and Sosik, J.J. 2011. The effect of leadership on follower moral identity: Does transformational/transactional style make a difference. *Journal of Leadership and Organizational Studies*, 18(2): 150-163.

Endnotes

1 Kent, 1994.

2 Joslin, 2010.

3 Brooks, 2017.

4 See endnote 3.

5 See endnote 2.

6 See endnote 3.

7 Allen, 2008.

8 See endnote 3.

9 Ibid.

10 Adams, 1922.

11 See endnote 5.

12 See endnote 3.

13 Bloom, 2011.

14 Samatar, & Kising'u, 2018.

15 Bryman, 1992.

16 Northouse, 2015.

17 Smith, Montagno, & Kuzmenko, 2009.

18 See endnote 16.

19 See endnote 15.

20 Warrilow, 2012.

21 See endnote 16.

22 Farid, 2014.

23 Chu, 2011.

24 Tawney, 2014.

25 See endnote 16.

26 See endnote 24.

27 See endnote 16.

28 Zhu et al., 2011.

29 See endnote 16.

30 Ibid.

31 Amaladas & Sean Byrne, 2017.

32 Greenleaf, 1977.

33 Sendjaya & Sarros 2002.

34 Stone, 2002.

35 Linden, 2008.

36 Russell, 2001.

37 Keith, 2008.

38 Ebener & O'Connell, 2010.

39 Lanctot & Irving, 2010.

40 Barbuto & Wheeler, 2009.

41 Dierendonck, 2011.

42 See endnote 39.

43 Elshtain, 2002.

44 See endnote 9.

45 See endnote 44.

46 Ibid.

47 Benner, Mergenthaler & Rothmann, 2011.

48 Welty Peacy, Bruening & Burton, 2011.

49 Spears, 2002.

50 Kelloway, 2012.

51 Autesserre, 2014.

52 Febres, 2017.

53 See endnote 52.

54 See endnote 49.

55 See endnote 44.

56 See endnote 44.

CHAPTER 8

IMPROVEMENT OF CULTURAL INTELLIGENCE AMONGST PEACE LEADERS

Martha Harunavamwe

"Once you begin the work of cultural intelligence, you can no longer be the same person; you cannot go back to who you were and pick up the pieces as you left them. Your leadership story is different, and how you engage with people of different cultural backgrounds will be different"[1].

Spotlight: Joseph Samuel Nye Jr.

Joseph Samuel Nye Jr. was born on 19 January 1937 in Northern New Jersey. Nye thinks of life as having an inner core, which facilitates the ability to have human love extending to those around you. His life was greatly influenced by his desire to share the love and peace he was experiencing internally. While growing up, Nye had no clear career plans,[2] but was interested in understanding the relationship between politics and economics. He is passionate about peace and managed to interview leaders like Julius Nyerere and Milton Obote in East Africa on issues of peace. He also watched the independence ceremonies for Uganda and Kenya and, as an analyst, he accurately predicted the fall of East Africa's independence. Thus, he wrote his thesis on pan-Africanism and East African federation with a gloomy conclusion.[3]

Joseph Nye is a co-founder of the international relations theory of neoliberalism, which was developed in 1977 in his book *Power and Interdependence*. It was through this book that he displayed his interest in the power of interdependence and unity as a way to eliminate conflict. He stressed the idea of co-existence.[4] He developed the concepts of asymmetrical and complex interdependence and explored transnational relations and world politics. Interestingly enough, he explained the distinction between hard power and soft power, and coined the term "soft power", which became very popular. Thus, Nye was the pioneer of the theory of soft power, which describes an alternative path that leaders can use to effect political outcomes. Soft power works by shaping preferences rather than using military force. Establishing and shaping preferences of others tends to be associated with intangible assets such as an attractive personality, understanding the culture of others, and policies that are seen as legitimate or having moral authority. Thus, by having cultural intelligence a leader possesses what it takes to establish and shape preferences and win the hearts of the other. Nye therefore advocated for peaceful ways of resolving conflict[5].

His idea of smart power, explained as the ability to combine hard and soft power into a successful strategy, became very popular among members of the Clinton and Obama administrations and it was at the heart of their foreign policy vision. What makes him unique and worth highlighting in this chapter is that he emphasised that cultural diplomacy was an important soft power tool that countries may use to obtain the desired outcomes in world politics. He viewed soft power as a staple of daily democratic politics and culture and as a resource that produces attraction. He highlighted that in international politics, the resources that produce soft power arise from the values of a country expressed through culture. He greatly emphasised that soft power depends on understanding the minds of others. The best public and cultural diplomacy is based on understanding other people's beliefs, values and norms. Without sensitivity to the needs of others, peace leadership is threatened, but with pure cognitive analysis and tolerance of the other, peace leadership is guaranteed to succeed.[6]

Nye contributed greatly because in recent years, the utilisation of cultural intelligence and other methods of soft power have been endorsed. Above that, it is widely encouraged as a primary tool of statecraft as opposed to more coercive forms of national power. Development of soft power is being stressed as a primary exercise of power as opposed to the expensive (politically and financially) coercive options such as military action or economic sanctions.

Introduction

At the heart of human behaviour is the mind-set and the mind-set is greatly influenced by a set of things people value, believe in and hold on to as important principles. Such values, norms and beliefs are jealously protected by any society. Based on values or priorities, individuals behave and act in different ways. Therefore clashes and conflicts are inevitable but peace is what we all desire and long for. The idea of individuals sharing different values, beliefs and norms has led some cultures to be undermined, resulting in conflicts, mistrust and difficulties as well as fruitless collaboration across the world[7]. Thus, cultural differences play an enormous role in stirring conflict in diverse communities and cultural intelligence can potentially play a role in resolving such conflict. The more complex and differentiated a society is, the more numerous are potential groupings made up of various subcultures. The overlapping and crosscutting character of multicultural social relationships highlights the effects of cultural difference on communicational competence, mutual understanding, shared metrics and perceptions.

The role of culture, in both causing and resolving conflict, is quite dynamic. Underestimating the complexity of multicultural effects and failure to respect each other's values and beliefs breeds conflict, and the opposite breeds peace[8]. Joseph Nye, an advocate for inter-dependency, stressed the idea of co-existence and how much human beings need each other for survival. If utilised properly, culture can function constructively and meaningfully. Malan[9] clearly noted that, when a breakthrough to mutual cultural understanding and respect has taken place, much more than an ad hoc peace agreement can be reached. At present wars are being fought across nations, within nations, and there exists a never-ending news supply of civil wars motivated by ethnic, racial, cultural, religious and political differences among people[10]. Ethnic divisions and hatred, cultural superiority and tribal animosity all create favourable conditions for violent confrontations in several communities[11]. However, the mere existence of cultural differences is not necessarily the primary cause of conflict between groups. Rather, it is the failure to respect the culture of another group. Thus, cultural clashes and the ability to effectively respect each other and work together is one of the seminal issues of our day.

Though cultural differences are not the autonomous cause of conflict, culture is usually a refracting lens through which the perceptions according to which conflict is pursued, are formed. It provides the context in which conflict actually occurs[12]. Since culture affects major communicational or interlocutory processes that lie at the heart of most conflict-resolution techniques, understanding the impact of cultural difference has become central and crucial, especially for analysts or practitioners of conflict resolution and peace preservers who serve in intercultural contexts.

As society seeks to operate efficiently in the global community, leaders need to have an understanding of the surrounding cultures. Cultural competence is something we can learn and practise; a lot depends on our willingness to stretch[13]. Cultural intelligence and its implications for achieving everlasting peace have increasingly become crucial. It has been identified as an important framework for achieving cross-cultural competencies among peace leaders. Not only do individuals with high cultural intelligence survive the twists and turns of cross-cultural conflict in the world, they thrive on them. It is a key cross-cultural leadership competency for effective leaders[14] and intercultural negotiation effectiveness[15].

With cultural intelligence as the ability to spot cultural differences and potential breakdowns in communication and adapt to them, it is clear that cultural intelligence is possibly the most important skill peace leaders can develop to build strong and stable relationships in the 21st century. It is no doubt the surest way for us to learn to truly communicate with each other and live together in everlasting peace. Consistent with that, Joseph Nye noted that the solution to world problems lies in being sensitive to the needs of others. Without that sensitivity, peace leadership is threatened but with pure cognitive analysis and tolerance of the other, peace leadership is guaranteed to succeed.

This chapter presents how the improvement of cultural intelligence can influence peace leadership. It begins with the conceptualisation of cultural intelligence, followed by a discussion of the cultural intelligence model (motivation, cognitive, metacognitive and behaviour). The discussion will then focus on linking cultural intelligence and peace leadership. The chapter closes with future directions and trends in the area.

Conceptualising cultural intelligence

Cultural intelligence has its roots in Sternberg's[16] theories of intelligence which propose that there are different "loci" of intelligence within an individual. This theory became the basis upon which Early and Ang[17] developed the construct of cultural intelligence and conceptualised that it is made up of metacognitive, cognitive, motivational and behavioural dimensions. Metacognitive, cognitive and motivational cultural intelligence are mental capabilities and behavioural intelligence refers to the overt actions displayed by individuals.

The concept of cultural Intelligence has attracted research attention from a wide range of disciplines and this has resulted in different definitions of the concept. As far back as 2006, Brislin, Worthely and MacNab[18] defined cultural intelligence as a concept that focuses on a set of skills that enables individuals to transfer social skills from one cultural context to another. Consistent with that, Ang and Van Dyne[19] referred to cultural intelligence as an individual's ability to function effectively across different cultures, including national, ethnic and organisational culture. This involves the individual's ability to recognise the shared values, beliefs, attitudes and behaviours of a group of people and the application of this knowledge towards a specific goal[20]. From the definitions provided, it is clear that cultural intelligence provides an understanding of how and why individuals and groups act in a particular way.

Within the peace context, cultural intelligence should be viewed as a multi-dimensional construct, going beyond the basics of cultural sensitivity and cultural awareness because it is broader and seeks to respond to the broad and diverse challenges facing the world. This is in line with[21] those who posit that cultural intelligence is a multidimensional construct referring to the ability that individuals possess to adapt and function effectively in intercultural settings. It consists of metacognitive, cognitive, motivational and behavioural facets. Together; the four capabilities make up one's overall cultural intelligence quotient.

True cultural intelligence becomes a core capability needed when moving from positions of domestic leadership towards leading in global contexts. Therefore, peace leaders are encouraged to decode cross-cultural complexities in order to lead and influence peace negotiations more effectively[22]. It is no doubt clear that the idea of peace leadership is a global issue that requires cross-collaboration between regions to ensure that society works effectively, and does not crumble into dysfunction. When considering a move into new geographies, trying to diffuse peace initiatives from domestic to global, the cultural considerations are infinitely more complex and call for high cultural intelligence. The basics, however, encourage the understanding of one's own culture and acceptance of individual differences, which guarantee inner peace that individuals can spread to the next person.

A model of cultural intelligence

As highlighted earlier in the definition, the cultural intelligence model comprises four factors: metacognitive, cognitive, motivational and behavioural cultural intelligence[23]. These facets represent different types of capabilities that can be aggregated into a single construct to capture overall cultural intelligence[24] and they will be discussed in detail below. Figure 8.1 below represents the four dimensions of cultural intelligence indicating that the motivational dimension is expressed through intrinsic, extrinsic motivation and self-efficacy. The cognitive aspect displays an understanding of cultural systems, norms and values while the metacognitive is concerned with awareness, planning and checking. The behavioural reflects both verbal and non-verbal behaviour as well as speech acts.

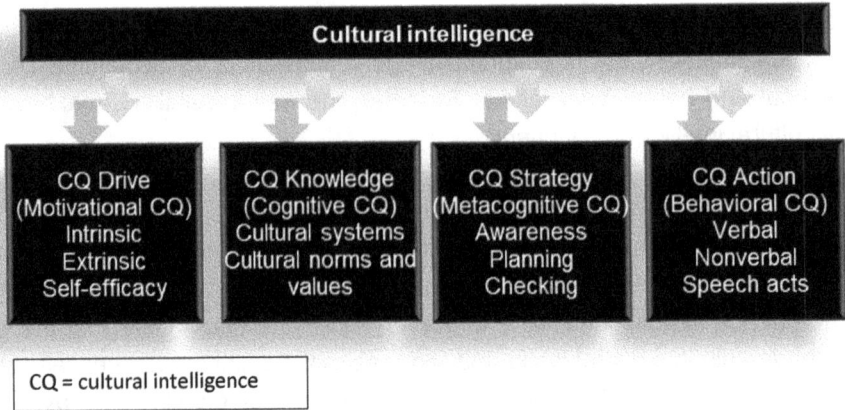

```
┌─────────────────────────────────────────────────────────────────┐
│                      Cultural intelligence                        │
└─────────────────────────────────────────────────────────────────┘
        ↓               ↓                ↓                 ↓
┌───────────────┐ ┌───────────────┐ ┌─────────────────┐ ┌───────────────┐
│   CQ Drive    │ │ CQ Knowledge  │ │   CQ Strategy   │ │   CQ Action   │
│(Motivational  │ │ (Cognitive CQ)│ │(Metacognitive   │ │ (Behavioral   │
│     CQ)       │ │Cultural       │ │      CQ)        │ │     CQ)       │
│  Intrinsic    │ │ systems       │ │   Awareness     │ │    Verbal     │
│  Extrinsic    │ │Cultural norms │ │    Planning     │ │   Nonverbal   │
│ Self-efficacy │ │  and values   │ │    Checking     │ │  Speech acts  │
└───────────────┘ └───────────────┘ └─────────────────┘ └───────────────┘
```

CQ = cultural intelligence

Figure 8.1: Four-step Dimensional Model of Cultural Intelligence (Source: Stevenson, 2015)

Motivational cultural intelligence (CQ)

The motivational facet of cultural intelligence refers to an individual's ability to show interest, confidence and direct efforts in understanding cultural differences in order to operate effectively in a given situation[25]. It refers to the intrinsic interest to acquire knowledge about other cultures and the sense of enjoyment one experiences when learning more about other cultures[26]. It requires the necessary drive, energy and tenacity to be adaptive to the different cultural environments. Individuals with motivational CQ reflect the capability to direct their attention and energy towards learning about and functioning in situations characterised by culturally diverse settings. They are motivated to learn about the similarities and differences that exist in these cultures. It all begins inside the human heart, when a decision is made to learn more about others, and the necessary drive and energy are released through intrinsic motivation. Motivation therefore lays the foundation of the development of cultural intelligence because without the ample drive to take on the challenges that inevitably accompany multicultural situations, there is no probability of success.

The motivational facet can be broken into three parts, which include enhancement, efficacy and consistency[27]. These components in turn direct and influence an individual's adaptation to new cultural environments. Thus, a high score on the motivational CQ dimension is reflective of a possible high level of the other cultural intelligence dimensions. Research indicates that individuals with a high motivational component direct attention and energy toward cross-cultural situations based on intrinsic interest[28] and confidence in their cross-cultural effectiveness[29].

Cognitive intelligence

Another dimension of cultural intelligence is the cognitive CQ which refers to one's knowledge about cultural systems, practices, norms and values in different cultures and how cultures are similar and different at the same time[30]. The idea is not to become an expert on every culture one encounters, but the extent to which the individual understands some core cultural differences and their impact on themelves and others. It reflects knowledge of norms, practices and conventions in different cultures acquired from personal experiences as well as education. This knowledge could also include religious beliefs, legal and economic systems, and sociolinguistic and interpersonal systems of different cultures and subcultures[31]. Individuals with cognitive cultural intelligence will be able to assess and understand cultural similarities and differences and respond accordingly. Thus, a rich mental orientation of cultural differences will influence appropriate behaviours[32].

Metacognitive intelligence

The third cultural intelligence facet is metacognitive, which refers to the higher-order cognitive processes involved in acquiring the cultural knowledge monitoring and controlling individuals' thought processes[33]. It involves how individuals make sense of culturally diverse experiences and occurs when one makes judgments about their own thought processes and those of others. The relevant capabilities include being able to plan, monitor and revise mental models of cultural norms for countries or groups of people. Individuals high in metacognitive intelligence are consciously aware of others' cultural preferences before and during interactions. They question cultural assumptions and adjust their mental models during and after interactions[34]. This aids in the development of the skills and cultural knowledge needed to interact in culturally diverse situations. Individuals with high metacognitive intelligence are more creative in a culturally diverse environment. Metacognitive intelligence also assists peace leaders with creative skills to plan, monitor and revise mental models and to come up with alternative solutions when establishing peace in culturally diverse environments.

Behavioural intelligence

Behavioural intelligence is the extent to which individuals are able to adapt their verbal and nonverbal behavioural practices, such as the use of words or expressions, in intercultural settings[35]. It reflects the individuals' capability to exhibit appropriate verbal and nonverbal actions when interacting with people from different cultures and to be able to do that, an individual should have the necessary verbal and non-verbal skills to communicate and interact with diverse people[36]. Individuals with behavioural CQ exhibit situationally appropriate behaviours based on their broad range of verbal and nonverbal capabilities. Behavioural CQ can help peace leaders to adapt their behaviours to meet the expectations of others and provide them with the know-how to utilise culturally appropriate words, tones, gestures, and facial expressions[37]. From the above, it is clear that behavioural CQ is a very important component that enhances social interactions and focuses on how individuals modify their behaviour to adapt to cultural differences, thus enabling them to behave appropriately in cross-cultural settings.

Cultural intelligence and peace leadership

The cultural intelligence model discussed above indicates different dimensions of cultural intelligence. These dimensions all contribute to peace leadership in a way. The motivational CQ shows interest, confidence and direct efforts on the part of an individual to gain knowledge about other cultural groups. This allows peace leaders to identify the cultural scripts that are hidden and to recognise when to turn them off. Thus, peace leaders need to know how cultures are created, interpreted and shared, as well as how cultural interpretations, meaning and symbols can influence behaviours and attitudes of individuals. With the motivation and cognition CQ peace leaders will be enabled to understand individual and group differences as a foundation towards negotiating common ground.

The other dimension discussed is the meta-cognition component which assists the peace leaders' ability to strategise across cultures using the facts of a given case to assemble, order, organise, interpret and act accordingly. This component can assist peace leaders in building awareness of their surroundings through preparation and planning. They need to suspend their judgments and biases, reflect upon their assumptions, and listen carefully to others. The behavioural component emphasises the leader's ability to perform new behaviours based on new cultural surroundings[38]. Culturally intelligent leaders are like chameleons in social environments, changing their behaviours to mimic their surroundings, and so should peace leaders.

The model also indicates that individuals assess knowledge through a cognitive process, and then behave accordingly, reassessing what transpired based upon the nonverbal cues communicated by the other parties[39]. A culturally intelligent leader must build upon knowledge obtained from another culture and go beyond merely learning facts, analysing their behaviour and reflecting on it in order to build that repertoire of skilful behaviour. The four dimensions are different aspects of the overall capacity to function and lead in different cultural settings[40]. Individuals with high CQ have an integrated view of the world and they appreciate both the similarities and differences among people. Rather than being threatened by differences, they look for what they can learn from them. There is no doubt that having individuals in positions of leadership who understand the knowledge and practices of another group of people will facilitate peace negotiations and other effective diplomatic efforts to sustain peace.

In practical terms, and consistent with the above, historical events in Iraq, Afghanistan, Somalia, Bosnia and Sudan have proven that a lasting and genuine peace can only be achieved if the peace leaders and peacekeepers have a clear understanding of the origins of conflict and the cultural clashes leading to this conflict[41]. Peace leaders should have the motivation QI to know who they are and what they believe, and be equally interested to discover that in others. A thorough analysis of the events in Iraq clearly supports the above proposition. In March 2003, the United States and her North Atlantic Treaty Organisation (NATO) allies officially declared war on Iraq. One of the primary objectives was to bring peace, stability and democracy to Iraq. However, to this day, almost 17 years since the war began, there is still no peace in Iraq. Democracy is still a dream that might never materialise and one cannot even begin to talk about stability. Peace analysts have noted that a lack of understanding of the local population and their culture was the primary cause of this failure of mega proportions.

It has therefore become clear that the success or failure of a peace operation is largely dependent on the relationship between peace keepers and the local population. This relationship can be influenced most importantly by cultural and ethnic motivated behaviour[42]. Thus cultural intelligence must form part of the initial plan prior to any initiatives aimed at restoring peace, with individuals high in cultural intelligence as drivers of peace projects. In line with the above, General Anthony Zinni, former commander of operations in a mission called 'Restore Hope', stressed the importance of cultural intelligence. He said: "…during the process of building peace, it is crucial to know the local people's languages, their way of life, and their needs and aspirations so as to win their minds and hearts and understand how far they are willing to go to achieve peace."[43]

In addition to that, lack of cultural knowledge at a strategic level in countries such as Burundi and Sudan is also a concern. These are countries where religious, race and cultural intolerance are at the core of the conflict that has facilitated the development of policies that fuel an insurgency and derail the peace process[44]. In the African context, many conflicts have come about as a result of failure to understand and tolerate different cultural groups[45]. Therefore, mission failures and an unnecessary loss of lives position cultural intelligence as an important element of strategy and not just another "expendable" casualty in the planning process.

Benefits of cultural intelligence that can be
utilised in peace leadership initiatives

- Cultural intelligence provides the lens through which individual leaders can expand their capacities and raise their levels of collective cultural consciousness to become better cross-cultural leaders. A very good example is that during peace-building missions, to facilitate smooth transition, leaders should first seek cultural awareness by analysing their relationship with their own culture and then try to understand the culture of the affected group in order to generate possible solutions. This may be helpful in understanding how most important systems and institutions work in that particular place.

- When one is culturally intelligent, the differences in cultures promote a diversity of thinking, innovative practices, and ideas that take you out of mindlessness. A very good example is that a leader will listen to the views of other leaders from different cultural perspectives and use a combination of ideas to come up with solutions to problems. Cultural intelligence keeps you alert and attentive to challenges in order to help you reach your highest potential.

- High cultural intelligence has a direct correlation with the ability to adapt to various situations and environments where the assumptions, values, and traditions differ from those with which one is most familiar[46]. This can assist peace leaders to have more success in forming collaborative environments across a diversity of cultures – a capability that contributes significantly to successful cross-cultural negotiations and the acquisition of which is non-negotiable for leaders pursuing peace.

- Cultural intelligence provides the ability to respectfully and effectively connect with individuals and situations from various cultural backgrounds and thus enhances peace leaders' ability to be more effective at whatever they pursue. For example, social attitudes towards filial obedience would imply that power and hierarchy are very important to such a culture and having such knowledge makes peace leaders more alert.

- When faced with the ambiguity of intercultural communication, individuals high in cultural intelligence are more likely to persist and invest greater effort in reaching a win–win situation despite the absence of cues that help to negotiate effectively in a more familiar environment. Cultural intelligence provides a better understanding of how to read the nonverbal cues during a negotiation. Such Individuals are also more aware of how to motivate other groups of people. For example, a culturally intelligent individual can easily identify displeasure within crowds through gestures, and may be aware of how to calm people down. In addition, understanding how certain norms and attitudes influence the origins of certain behaviours may shed light on how to resolve certain problems.

The value of cultural intelligence lies in grasping a true understanding of the human terrain, and what makes it more unique as a useful tool for successful peace leadership is that it improves communication, cooperation and teamwork, enables the development of trust, and facilitates effective leadership in multicultural groups. Peace leaders should embrace the fact that cultures are not necessarily meant to clash and are capable of merging, and while they may clash, they can be understood, and objectives through intelligent engagement may be achieved. Joseph Nye clearly indicated that, in international politics, the resources that produce soft power arise from the values of a country that are expressed through culture, including internal practices and the way the country handles its relations with others. Therefore, culture should never be overlooked in peace negotiations.

Solutions and recommendations

With reference to the model of cultural intelligence discussed above, it is critical to facilitate the development of all four dimensions of cultural intelligence among peace leaders starting with the motivational component. The investment theory of intelligence indicates that motivational cultural intelligence is critical in facilitating the growth of cognitive and metacognitive cultural intelligence; thus it can be used as the foundation when trying to boost cultural intelligence among leaders. If peace leaders possess the motivation CQ, it becomes easier for them to have the zeal and energy to learn more and be informed about the surrounding cultural differences as well as to have confidence in their own culture and respect for the cultures of others. That desire to learn will provide more knowledge on the root of conflict and inform peace leaders on possible resolution strategies. Therefore, it is recommended that cultural intelligence be fostered among peace leaders starting with the motivational component, which then facilitates the development of other dimensions, as the first step towards peacebuilding.

The utilisation of cultural intelligence techniques on a larger scale can bring about systematic change in peacebuilding and implementation processes. Comprehensive discussion on the improvement of cultural intelligence levels among peace leaders may provide practical guidelines to leaders across the world on how to tackle peace challenges posed by cultural barriers. Below is a discussion of how the 3 Ds can be applied to peace leaders.

Developing Cultural Intelligence

From a corporate perspective, cultural intelligence of leaders can be developed through the 3Ds which refer to Discover, Develop and Deploy[47]. The same path can be followed to develop the cultural intelligence of peace leaders. These 3 Ds are related to the dimensions of cultural intelligence. 'Discover' is linked to motivational CQ and 'Develop' is linked to cognitive and metacognitive CQ, and 'Deploy' is aligned to behavioural CQ. The only desired outcome is change in the leaders' mind-sets, skills, knowledge and behaviours leading to measurable performance improvement and collaboration that is more effective.

The first D, which represents 'discover', is the stage where leaders are requested to define cultural intelligence and focus on the key elements of attitudes, awareness, knowledge and skills. Practical activities that peace leaders may engage in during the 'discover' stage include attending cultural intelligence seminars, meeting other expats who have already been exposed to new cultural practices and asking them about "best practice" tips. This stage can also be associated with reading travel guides on local traditions. Learning this might reveal a lot about deeper social issues that might be threatening peace. In short, this stage assists peace leaders to discover the new world around them and beyond and then use that knowledge to generate solutions to the prevailing peace challenges.

In the second phase, which is 'develop', participants learn to recognise their own cultural tendencies and those of others. This correlates well with cognitive and metacognitive CQ in the model discussed above. At this stage, peace leaders need to be aware of their cultures and how they differ from the new culture they will be operating under. This can be facilitated through thought-provoking activities and encouraging discussions that enable peace leaders to acquire cross-cultural skills and develop action plans. This phase can be addressed in a workshop setting where individual leaders, through the use of the ADAPT model, leverage value from differences. The ADAPT model includes Analysing cultural differences, Deciding on a way forward, Applying our approach, Processing what happened and Tuning as we go along. At this phase, peace leaders are expected to acquire intercultural skills. However, acquiring practical intercultural skills is the hardest part of cross-cultural learning. It is not as simple as deciding between a bow and a handshake or between gripping your business contact's hand firmly and touching it cautiously. It means being able to analyse misunderstandings and set them right, or being able to avoid them in the first place. While good seminars may provide the opportunity to practise these skills in role-play situations, for peace leaders, this should be an ongoing process of learning by doing when actually handling challenges threatening peace.

The last D, which is the deploying aspect, is concerned with teaching leaders to control their responses, providing them with strategies for managing potentially conflicting situations in a cross-cultural group and the 'platinum rule' of treating others the way they want to be treated. Peace leaders need to get deeper insight into the respective cultures at hand and ensure that there is clear understanding of the individual and collective values because this is central when resolving conflict in multicultural conditions. The deploying aspect assists peace leaders to adapt their individual behaviour and leadership-related expertise to local conditions. This can be achieved through the understanding of sensitivity and respect, as well as being committed to applying the theoretical expertise to everyday practice. Peace leaders should amass, absorb and use local knowledge to their advantage, getting to know the people they operate with and always asking: What drives these people and what are their needs at the moment?

Peace leaders are recommended to attend the courses constituting the Developing Cultural Intelligence Learning Path, which makes use of the above-discussed 3Ds. This will assist them to use cultural intelligence to enable effective communication and build trusting relationships as well as modifying their own behaviour to make the most out of cultural differences. This can also equip peace leaders to work confidently with cultural differences in virtual and face-to-face environments and achieve desired results by acting out of choice and not out of habit.

Future directions and trends

The above discussion clearly emphasises that, in order to achieve peace, individuals should be zealous to know more about other cultures, motivational CQ, and understand the community environment and be open to adjust to it. The implications that this will have for peace leaders is that learning the local language, history and cultural nuances is crucial to gaining a local population's trust, and eventually achieving peaceful negotiations. This also discourages leaders from making generalisations and oversimplifying the customs of a diverse group of individuals. Therefore, future research should focus on identifying the different methods through which peace leaders can develop cultural intelligence collection and analysis capability. This will provide the necessary information about the human terrain, and provide guidance and serve as a point of departure towards the design and provision of peace leadership programs.

Recent research in peacebuilding indicated that success largely depends on leaders' ability to interact with people from different cultures and also their ability to function effectively in culturally diverse situations[48]. Thus, cultural intelligence has become a non-negotiable skill for leaders involved in peace, suggesting that the more aware individuals are of differences in their cultural environments, the more they will assess these differences and respond accordingly, and eventually achieve peace. Future research should therefore focus on the provision of international study tours and global awareness programs as a way to facilitate the development of cultural intelligence among leaders.

A well-developed cultural intelligence knowledge and set of skills will result in better cross-cultural respect and recognition. Cultural intelligence knowledge can be achieved through participation in awareness workshops that enable the leaders to engage in informed, impartial and non-partisan discussions, which will ultimately create a viable environment for a community-based and long-term peace. Therefore, future research should consider identifying critical topics and issues that can be designed for such workshops. Research also highlights that anyone can grow his or her cultural intelligence. However, it does not happen automatically, but with a little effort, individuals can experience several benefits by increasing their cultural intelligence[49]. Based on this, future research should focus on providing a systematic process on how individuals can develop their own cultural intelligence. Through cultural intelligence peace leaders can learn the traditional methods of resolving conflict and reconciling through restoring relationships and social harmony. The greatest resource for sustaining peace in the long term is always rooted in the local people and their culture, hence cultural intelligence is a strong and essential building block of peace leadership.

Concluding remarks

In conclusion, the main objective of this chapter was to provide knowledge on how improving cultural intelligence can influence peace leaders. The chapter explained the concept of cultural intelligence together with its dimensions indicating how those dimensions can be used to promote peace. The cultural intelligence model was applied to explain the relationship between cultural intelligence and peace leadership, indicating that the motivational CQ component can be used as the foundation to understand other cultures. The model discussion concluded that cross-cultural understanding, tolerance as well as respect are crucial aspects of maintaining peace and peace leaders may focus on improving such aspects. Understanding the mind-sets of both parties involved in a conflict is one step forward towards resolving conflict.

It was recommended that, just like in the business environment, peace leaders' cultural intelligence can be developed through 'discover', 'develop' and 'deploy' (the 3Ds). These 3 Ds, when aligned with the cultural intelligence model, can facilitate the improvement of cultural intelligence, which eventually translates to peaceful negotiations. Training on cultural intelligence helps to counteract divisive elements such as superiority, discrimination and exclusiveness and promotes loyalty to one's own culture while allowing people of other cultures to also be loyal to their cultures. Cultural intelligence is a non-negotiable skill for peace leaders, and one which can assist them to achieve peace through harmonious negotiations.

References

Adebajo, A. 2012. *UN Peacekeeping in Africa: From Suez Crisis to the Sudan Conflicts*. Jacana Media.

Ang, S., Van Dyne, L. and Tan, M.L. 2007. Cultural intelligence. In R.J. Sternberg and S.B. Kaufman (eds.). *The Cambridge Handbook on Intelligence*.

Avruch, K. 2010. Cultural Pluralism 3rd ediition, Social Justice. *Peace and Conflict Studies*, 6(1): 24-41.

Bandura, A. 2002. Selective moral disengagement in the exercise of moral agency. *Journal of moral education*, 31(2): 101-119.

Bogilovic, S. and Skerlavaj, M. 2016. Metacognitive and Motivational Intelligence: Superpowers for Creativity in a Culturally Diverse Environment. *Economic and Business Review*, 18(1): 55-76.

Brislin, R., Worthley, R. and Macnab, B. 2011. Cultural intelligence: Understanding behaviours that serve people's goals. *Group & Organization Management*, 31(1): 40-55.

Carlson, S.M. 2005. Developmentally sensitive measures of executive function in preschool children. *Developmental Neuropsychology*, 28(2): 595-616.

Carmel, E. 1999. *Global software teams: collaborating across borders and time zones*. Prentice Hall PTR.

Chao, M.M., Takeuchi, R. and Farh, J.L. 2017. Enhancing cultural intelligence: The roles of implicit culture beliefs and adjustment. *Personnel Psychology*, 70(1): 257-292.

Coles, B., 2005. *Youth and Social Policy: Youth citizenship and young careers*. Routledge.

Deng, L. and Gibson, P. 2009. Mapping and modeling the capacities that underlie effective cross-cultural leadership: An interpretive study with practical outcomes. *Cross Cultural Management: An International Journal*, 16(4): 347-366.

Deci, E.L. and Ryan, R.M. 1985. The general causality orientations scale: Self-determination in personality. *Journal of research in personality*, 19(2): 109-134.

De Brito, A.B. 1997. *Human rights and democratization in Latin America: Uruguay and Chile*. Oxford University Press.

Duff, A.J., Tahbaz, A. and Chan, C. 2012. The interactive effect of cultural intelligence and openness on task performance. *Research & Practice in Human Resource Management*, 20(1): 43-45.

Donais, T. 2012. *Peacebuilding and local ownership: Post-conflict consensus building*. Routledge. Available from. http://library.fes.de/pdf-files/id/ipa/09522.pdf [Accessed 11 March 2018].

Erez, M., Lisak, A., Harush, R., Glikson, E., Nouri, R. and Shokef, E. 2013. Going global: Developing management students' cultural intelligence and global identity in culturally diverse virtual teams. *Academy of Management Learning and Education*, 12(3): 330-355.

Earley, P.C. and Ang, S. 2003. *Cultural intelligence: Individual interactions across cultures*. Stanford University Press.

Gooden, D.J., Creque, C.A. and Chin-Loy, C. 2017. The Impact of Metacognitive, Cognitive and Motivational Cultural Intelligence on Behavioural Cultural Intelligence. *The International Business & Economics Research Journal*, 16(3): 223.

Nye, J. 2012. Faculty Page. *Harvard Kennedy School (online)*. Available from. *https://www.belfercenter.org/person/joseph-s-nye*. [Accessed 23 March 2018].

Livermore, D.A. 2009. *Cultural intelligence (youth, family, and culture): Improving your CQ to engage our multicultural world*. Baker Academic.

Mashishi, M.M. 2012. *Assessment of referrals to a district hospital maternity unit in South Africa* (Doctoral dissertation).

Malan, C. 2012. Between conflict and compromise in the Philippines. *Indian Journal of Asian Affairs*, (online). Available from https://www.jstor.org/stable/41950521?seq=1#page_scan_tab_contents. 25(1/2): 59-82.

Moon, J.A. 2013. *A handbook of reflective and experiential learning: Theory and practice.* Routledge.

Ng, K.Y. and Earley, P.C. 2006. Culture + intelligence: Old constructs, new frontiers. *Group & Organization Management*, 31(1): 4-19.

Ng, K.Y., Van Dyne, L., and Ang, S. 2012. Cultural Intelligence: A Review, Reflections, and Recommendations for future Research. *Conducting Multinational Research: Applying Organisational Psychology in the Workplace* (29-58). Washington, DC, American Psychological Association.

Smart Power. *The Huffington Post*, November 29, 2009.

Schellhammer, E.P. 2016. A culture of peace and leadership education. *International Journal of Public Leadership*, 12(3): 205-215.

Sternberg, R.J. and Detterman, D.K. (eds). 1986. *What is intelligence?: Contemporary viewpoints on its nature and definition*. Praeger Pub Text.

Spencer, L.M. and Spencer, P.S.M. 2008. *Competence at Work Models for Superior Performance*. John Wiley & Sons.

Stevenson, J. 2015. Four-step model to cultivate cultural intelligence. Available from http://asq.org/quality-progress/2015/06/quality-in-the-first-person/become-the-change.html. [Accessed 11 April 2018].

Triandis, H.C. 2006. Cultural intelligence in organizations. *Group & Organization Management*, 31(1): 20-26.

Tuleja, E.A. 2014. Developing cultural intelligence for global leadership through mindfulness. *Journal of Teaching in International Business*, 25(1): 5-24.

TMA, 2015. Cultural Intelligence. Work productively with people from different cultures. Available from http://www.tmaworld.com/cultural-intelligence. [Accessed 12 April 2018].

Endnotes

1   Ng, Van Dyne & Ang, 2012.
2   School, Harvard Kennedy, 2017.
3   Ibid.
4   Joseph Nye Faculty Page.
5   Ibid.
6   Ibid.
7   Gooden, Creque & Chin-Loy, 2017.
8   Malan, 2012.
9   Ibid.
10   Adebajo, 2011.
11   Carmel, 1999.
12   Avruch, 2010.
13   Schellhammer, 2016.
14   Deng & Gibson, 2009.
15   Moon, 2013.
16   Sternberg & Detterman, 1986.

17   Earley & Ang, 2003.
18   Brislin, Worthely & MacNab, 2011.
19   Ang & Van Dyne, 2008.
20   Spencer, 2008.
21   Ang et al., 2007.
22   Chao, Takeuchi & Farh, 2017.
23   Livermore, 2009.
24   See endnote 23.
25   See endnote 20.
26   See endnote 24.
27   Ng & Earley, 2006.
28   Deci & Ryan, 1985.
29   Bandura, 2002.
30   See endnote 20.
31   Ibid.
32   See endnote 22.
33   Bogilovic & Skerlava, 2016.
34   Triandis, 2006.
35   Duff, Tahbaz & Chan, 2012.
36   See endnote 20.
37   See endnote 22.
38   Carlson, 2005.
39   Tuleja, 2014.
40   See endnote 18.
41   Mashishi, 2012.
42   De Brito, 1997.
43   Coles, 2005.
44   See endnote 43.
45   Donais, 2012.
46   See endnote 8.
47   TMA, 2015.
48   See endnote 8.
49   Erez et al., 2013.

CHAPTER 9

WOMEN AND PEACEBUILDING

Magda Hewitt

"She held fast to the ideal of peace even during the difficult hours when other considerations and interests obscured it from her compatriots and drove them into the conflict. She felt that women have a special role as peacemakers, speaking of "that love, that warm maternal feeling which renders murder and war so hateful to every woman. Jane Addams combines all the best feminine qualities which will help us to develop peace on earth." (Professor P Halvdan Koht on Jane Addams, Nobel Prize winner[1])

Spotlight: Amina J. Mohammed

Amina J. Mohammed is the first-born of five sisters. Soft spoken and a mother of six. Her father is a Nigerian veterinarian-herdsman and her mother a British nurse. After studying in Italy her father demanded that she return to Nigeria and promised her a job at the consulate in Kaduna[2]. There was no job when she returned and she started by doing all sorts of jobs in various industries (retail, insurance, managing restaurants, even working in an old people's home). She obtained a job in an architecture and engineering firm and after eleven years she founded Afri-Projects Consortium in 1991.

Currently, Amina J. Mohammed is the Deputy Secretary-General of the United Nations. She is 57 years of age and is considered one of the world's most well-known African faces and amongst the top 100 world-ranked influencers. Her authority on global issues and her fight for the rights of the underprivileged, women's rights, climate change and governance issues are well known. She was instrumental in shaping the current World Sustainable Development Goals.

Prior to her current role Amina resigned from the Nigerian Federal Executive Council in February 2017 to take up the post of Deputy Secretary-General of the United

Nations. Before that she was the Minister of Environment of Nigeria from November 2015 to December 2016. During 2015 she held several positions such as being a special advisor to UN Secretary-General Ban-Ki-moon, founded and was the CEO of the Center for Development Policy Solutions and was appointed as an adjunct professor at Columbia University for the Master in Development Practice Programme. During 2005 she coordinated Nigeria's debt-relief funds towards Nigeria's Millennium Development Goals and she headed the Task Force on Gender and Education for the UN Millennium project.[3] Many people impacted on her life and she shared the following wisdom:

> *"People will help you if you are brave enough to ask them."*
>
> *"When you have ambition, you will acquire the talent and the skills to deliver on it."*

She considers the greatest challenge of our time to be indifference as it breeds a lack of leadership to address challenges.

Introduction

As Amina is illustrating, women have the potential to lead formally[4]. Throughout history it is women who pledge peace and call for the ending of conflict.[5] When women bond together they tend to focus on ecology, consumer protection, women and children development and rights. The real-life example of Amina J. Mohammed is exemplary of the characteristics peace leaders display and the skills they possess.

As the United Nations Deputy Secretary-General, Amina J. Mohammed has a huge task on her shoulders. Terms that are associated with the United Nations (UN) and which are aligned with peace leaders are: human rights; peacekeeping; creating conditions for peace; prevention of conflict; and the solving of economic, social and cultural international problems. Miller[6] reflects on the phenomenon of peace leadership cited in the work of Jean Lipman-Blumen who asked the question: "What might be obtained by leadership if it is not for peace?"

Amina possesses traits of a peace leader as unpacked by Lieberfeld cited in Miller (ibid) such as empathy, forgiveness, emotional self-control, optimism that things can change for the better and inclinations toward reconciliation. Her ability to build organisational capacity is illustrated by her, amongst others, founding her own company, serving as Nigeria's Minister of Environment assisting the previous United Nations Deputy Secretary-General and now serving as the UN Deputy Secretary-General.

The focus of this chapter is not solely on the traits and characteristics of a peace leader such as Amina, but also covers the existing gender equality gap; women's participation and women's presence in leadership positions; how women may increase their feminine presence; women, peace and dealing with others; women and conflict; and lastly concluding remarks.

Gender equality gap in leadership positions

Besides women leaders in politics such as Angela Merkel of Germany and Amina J. Mohammed of the UN, there are many women in the corporate world who lead. However, worldwide, the gender equality gap is not closing. It is in fact increasing[7] irrespective of the fact that globally women increasingly hold high positions in national leadership and join organisations in executive positions.[8]

Research conducted[9] on a data set that included CEO transitions in Fortune 500 companies over a 20-year period does not support the fact that women leaders are more likely to be appointed to organisations that are struggling, or that are at risk or that seem destined to fail. Findings also do not support the belief that a woman will be replaced by a male if the company she heads is experiencing a decline in growth. Findings did support the notion that diverse boards increase the duration of women leaders' tenure as well as allowing them an opportunity to demonstrate their leadership capabilities.

Amina J. Mohammed expressed her concern that more women than men leave higher education with degrees and diplomas, yet less of them enter the world of work or are seen in leadership positions. As for April 2018, female CEOs in Fortune 500 companies represent only 4.8 percent or 24 out of every 500 CEOs. They are mainly white with the exception of two women, Geisha Williams of PG&E and PepsiCo's Indra Nooyi.[10] No African female CEOs appeared on the Fortune 500 companies' 2018 list. Yet, the question remains: Can women lead?[11]

When Amina delivered the 15th Nelson Mandela annual lecture in Cape Town, South Africa, on 25 November 2017 her chosen topic centred on gender inequality and the inclusion of youth, and it reflected her care and concern for the rights of the less fortunate.[12] She seeks to answer the question: *'What is needed to break down institutional and attitudinal barriers and invest in the core contribution of women and girls to their societies and their countries?'* She emphasised that global leadership is required to enhance transformation and change in this area[13].

Supporting her argument on factual figures such as that women hold less than one third of senior leadership positions and that less than a quarter of all parliamentarians are women, Amina J. Mohammed advocates for leadership to invest in the potential of women, thereby contributing to Sustainable Development Goal five: namely, to achieve gender equality and to empower all women and girls.

Women's participation and presence in leadership positions

Women's participation in various areas in life and business is steadily on the increase, despite resistance from certain societies.[14] In the past women entered the leadership space, but in order to retain and exhibit their womanly attributes such as child-centredness, compassion and motherly characteristics, they typically chose careers such as teaching and nursing. Not surprisingly, this was also a career choice made by Amina J. Mohammed which ultimately set her on her path to become the current UN Deputy Secretary-General.

Regine[15] used the term 'feminine presence'. She refers to women who make their 'feminine presence' known as 'iron butterflies'[16]. Iron butterflies invite participation to seek answers together. This approach sets egos aside and looks at what others do. Women's leadership styles differ from those of their male counterparts and for this reason[17] their mastery continues to go unseen and unrecognised. It is argued that the term 'leadership' does not encapsulate a woman's work role, family role, wife role and mother role to their fullest extent.

Amina J. Mohammed's story is one that reflects 'feminine presence' as she is faced, along with the UN council, with decisions like when to approve peacekeeping missions, import sanctions, or the use of force to maintain peace. Women tend to show their compassion, offer their collaboration, assist others with self-discovery, and look at other alternatives to personal power. Females like Amina, serving on leadership forums, complete the collective consciousness and their self-mastery comes with their ability to recognise opportunities to grow.

Johnson and Mathur-Helm[18] found that women in senior leadership positions are in general very competitive, but become even more so when they compete against other women. They will not only withhold information and not be available, but also try too hard to adopt their male counterparts' leadership traits. Women leaders tend to be less understanding than their male counterparts, thereby working towards lessening the presence of other women when in leadership forums. From this one can deduct that women leaders do themselves an injustice by minimising the presence of other women amongst their ranks. As Regine[19] points out, men have a masculine leadership style and when it lacks a feminine counterpart, it will soon reach toxic levels of self-importance and arrogance.

Unfortunately, Johnson and Mathur-Helm's[20] study confirms that women as managers or leaders or both are not there yet, and that the occurrence of 'Queen Bee' behaviour and attitudes is very much evident in organisations. 'Queen Bee' is a term used to describe women in senior and executive leadership positions who prevent other women from entering and progressing through the leadership pipeline.

Women also tend to adopt a more holistic approach to leadership and nurture more in context and the person at large. They tend to draw more from the collective, open-ended and learn-as-you-go approach to achieve objectives. Regine[21] warns, though, that women in general try too hard to adopt their male counterparts' leadership traits, instead of connecting to their own experience of their natural feminine presence, which will take them further.

Challenges faced to increase feminine presence

The challenge that faces women according to Boals[22] is that some are trying to get 'justice' by educating, shaming, influencing or persuading those who hold power instead of working to assume power themselves. The question is asked: *'What if women do become like men?'* Would women lose the advocates for feminine values? Boals[23] said that one problem with this 'social justice' is the rationale it is based on. It is argued that women and men have equal capabilities and abilities but female suffrage argues that women are unique and that these unique capacities and sensitivities are what is needed in the political (boardroom) sphere. Boals[24] refers to Erik Erikson[25] who stated that women have a special contribution to make in the decision-making sphere such as: i) the realism of householding; ii) the associated responsibilities of upbringing; iii) resourcefulness in peacekeeping; and iv) a devotion to healing. One can argue here that these special, unique capabilities and sensitivities can be extended to boardrooms of large corporations. Nelson, cited in Ledbetter[26], pointed out in 2000 already that it is critical for business to adopt peacebuilding as part of their strategy and to build it into their leadership development.

Eagly and Carli[27] critique the assumptions implied by the classic *'glass ceiling'* (the frustration of having a goal in sight that is unobtainable) metaphor as coined by the two *Wall Street Journal* reporters Hymowitz and Schellhardt[28]. They argue that the *glass ceiling* fails to include the various barriers women experience on their leadership journeys. It assumes that entry points are the same for men and women which, they argue, is not the case. They promulgate the labyrinth as a better metaphor for what confronts a women's journey to a top leadership position.

Eagly and Carli[29] further single out four barriers women experience in reaching leadership positions: i) prejudice, where men are benefited and women are penalised; ii) resistance to women being the leaders; iii) their leadership style; and iv) the challenge to balance their family responsibilities and work. They advise companies who want to see more women at executive board level to reject the psychosocial drivers of prejudice towards female leaders by i) *Change the long hours norm* – the perception that a person's worth lies in the number of hours she spends at office. Companies are urged to move to more objective measures of productivity. Women who display highly productive work habits but who at the same time adhere to their family's demands must receive rewards and encouragement; ii) *Reduce the subjectivity of performance evaluations* – processes should be designed to eliminate decision-makers' prejudice; iii) *The use of open recruitment tools,* such as employment agencies, to fill positions rather than referrals to fill vacancies as research supports the notion that more women will be appointed in managerial roles if they have been recruited via employment agencies; and iv) *Increase the critical mass of women in leadership positions to avoid tokenism.* For the sake of diversity companies tend to spread their women leaders across teams but this only leads to women being under-represented on boards and women's voices getting lost. Evidence supports the fact that male boards will tend to appoint only males who are similar to themselves[30] thus not enabling transformation and change.

It is concluded that women remain under-represented in top leadership positions, irrespective of predictions in 2009[31] that the percentage of women CEOs would reach more than 10 percent by 2016. There is thus an urgency for diverse boards and diverse leadership communities to assist companies in achieving their goals. As women experience an increasing demand to balance work and family, their presence on boards can contribute to organisational effectiveness. Amina J. Mohammed sets an example of a leader who maintains her 'feminine presence' yet balances work and family life as the mother of six children and some grandchildren.

How women may increase their feminine presence

Six ways[32] women can adapt to increase their own feminine presence are: *Embrace the paradox of vulnerability*: this refers to the ability to see challenges as an opportunity for growth and evolution (increase their self-mastery). *Couple mastery with nurturing:* use talents to empower all. *Engage holistic thinking:* Embrace the full person, situation, when engaging with business, thereby influencing the quality of the discussion to include the personal. *See self and the other:* This holistic perspective strengthens the ability to see the bigger picture and to remind others of the overall objective. Regine[33] points out that men tend to focus more narrowly on questions.

Women assume many roles and physiologically, as a rule, men rely more on the left brain and women on the right brain. Studies support the fact that women have an ability to see more options and solutions to challenges than men. The complex world we live in today calls for a feminine presence and a holistic approach to decisions. *Be rooted and wandering*: Women's capacity to adapt to situations is a strength, yet caution is expressed here not to be seen as compromising on integrity. Lastly, *cultivate the collaborative spirit*: Women must learn to work together in the workplace. One of their current challenges is the long isolation from positions of authority in mainstream organisations. When in those positions the strong women (iron butterflies) should nurture a collaborative environment for other women as opposed to the exclusionary approach of the 'queen bee'.

Further to this, women leaders can strengthen their 'presence' by improving on their mindfulness. Paris and Hewitt[34] interviewed ten senior women leaders with the aim of exploring the practice of mindfulness amongst them. Their findings suggest that even if women were not familiar with the concept 'mindfulness', this did not mean that they did not practise mindfulness. It is suggested by them that mindfulness is a tool women leaders can acquire to enhance their skills set as mindfulness can assist them to not only anchor themselves in the present moment but also enables them to rise above their personal and professional challenges. Bhikkhu[35] refers to mindfulness as being aware of the present moment and what is happening around you without being judgmental. Santorelli[36] suggests that leadership, personal mastery and mindfulness are three inseparable concepts and that the one complements the others. Mindfulness includes such practices as meditation, health walks, etc. It is argued here that if women are more present in the moment and are fully aware of their circumstances (by being prepared for an upcoming meeting, for example) they will meet the situation with an equal frame of mind, strengthening them to express and calmly respond to the situation, and thereby enhancing the concept of peacebuilding within their organisation.

Women, peace and dealing with others

Peace is normally a topic associated with politics and policy makers.[37] Peace, as defined in chapter one of this book, specifically refers to the ability of a person to firstly influence oneself, the people around you and the available resources to facilitate peace with others and within the community. The aim is also to challenge conflict in order to promote peace. One of Amina J. Mohammed's major role models is the late Kofi Annan[38], the former United Nations Secretary-General who, in 2000, challenged businesses to link to the Global Compact's ten principles which include issues such as labour, human rights, environment, and anti-corruption to the advancement of society and building peace.

Research supports the fact that women do contribute meaningfully in the conclusion and implementation of peace agreements contributing to sustainable peace. Women are considered change agents who can drive communities to recover after conflict. Yet, their presence during negotiations and around the table in board meetings and peace meetings is only occasional. Amina J. Mohammed called for 'urgent action' during her trip in 2017 to Nigeria to place the focus on women, peace and security. The focus should be to develop women to participate meaningfully in peace relations in all aspects of society.[39]

Lieutenant Colonel Felicia Maganwe of the South African Defence Force (SADF) serves as a special advisor to the United Nations (UN). She highlights three qualities which she believes add to women being better at peacekeeping than their male counterparts. They are: i) women are less aggressive; ii) their communication and persuasion skills seem to reap fruits in hostile situations; and iii) they are better placed to deal with victims exposed to violence. Major Shikha Mahrotra, an Indian officer with the UN, categorically states that the difference between men and women during conflict lies in *"emotional intelligence and empathy-traits"* which do not come naturally to her male counterparts[40].

Emotional Intelligence (EI) forms part of the trait approach to leadership (also see chapter 2 where emotional intelligence is discussed as an important building block for peace leaders). The trait approach focuses on identifying the qualities and behaviour portrayed by great leaders. Amina J. Mohammed had the following to say during an interview:

> *"People see you doing, and you then become an essential commodity, because not many people are getting up and doing. There are more people waiting to be asked to do."*

The most widely accepted definition of Emotional Intelligence (EI) as stated by Mayer, Salovey and Caruso[41] is:

> *"the ability to perceive and express emotion, assimilate emotion and thought, understand and reason with emotion and regulate emotion in oneself and others."*

McCleskey[42] cites a mixed-model of EI developed by Bar-On[43] which includes emotional and social competencies (ESCs) and which can be fully aligned to the peace leadership definition as set out in this book:

> *"the ability to be aware of, to understand, and to express oneself; the ability to be aware of, to understand and relate to others; the ability to deal with strong emotions and control one's impulses; and the ability to adapt to change and to solve problems of a personal or social nature".*

This definition also encapsulates the empathy aspect very well. Amina J. Mohammed said that when people indicate that they will be doing something in two or three weeks that might relieve the suffering and waiting of others, they would not be able to live the lives of those that suffer. The positive relationship between leadership and EI[44] has been supported by various scholars[45] and, as an ability, it is suggested that people who are more sensitive to their emotions than others will be more effective leaders.

Daniel Goleman cited in McGrath[46] points out that those with high EI build lasting meaningful relationships (a highly required skill for peace leaders) and they build healthy careers. He also noted that studies found that EI is a stronger predictor for leadership success than relevant business experience, academic qualifications and Intelligence Quotient (IQ). Leaders[47] with a strong EQ earn on average 134 percent more than their counterparts. EI and cognitive intelligence, especially when both are present, are strong contributing indicators of a person's potential success in life.[48]

Goleman's[49] conceptual model of EQ represents EQ and its associated emotional competencies as: the recognition of emotions in self and in others. The four skills that make up EQ (as also discussed in chapter 2) are: Self-awareness; Self-management; Social Awareness; and Relationship Management. Self-awareness is considered to be the foundational element of EQ on which the other elements are built. *Self-awareness* refers to one's ability to be aware of one's own strengths and weaknesses, your inner emotional life and self-confidence. *Self-management* refers to one's ability to control emotions. The eruption of uncontrolled emotions positively correlates with the derailment of promising leaders. *Social Awareness* refers to one's ability to sense other people's feelings and emotions, and to act in an empathetic manner; understanding the organisational politics; and acting in a service-minded manner towards others. *Relationship Management* refers to the ability to act as a positive influence in a conflict situation by developing interrelationship understanding amongst members during a period of conflict.

All of these characteristics are evident in the life and work of Amina, J. Mohammed.[50] Various YouTube video analysis illustrates how she uses her calm soft voice to address audiences. She is composed, knowledgeable and factual. She portrays self-confidence, yet shows empathy and concern for those suffering from actions that erupt in conflict-stricken areas. She does not hesitate to take responsibility for difficult decisions such as the recent crisis in Nigeria with regard to the export of their endangered rosewood. She calmly faced the media and environmentalist groups, explaining the reasons for signing export permits of Nigeria's endangered 'rosewood' to China amid accusations that she betrayed what she stood for.

Research evidence produced by Goleman[51] could find no supportive evidence that indicates that there is a difference in terms of EQ with regard to gender. However, men and women did show different strengths and weaknesses in the various areas. Goleman attributed it to the instruments that were used and to the fact that males have a tendency to score themselves higher in most areas.

Social intelligence (SQ) is a key skill[52] for successful intercultural communication (also see chapter 2 where **social intelligence** as an important building block for peace leaders is discussed). Social intelligence was first labelled by Edward Thorndike in 1920 and refers to the ability to understand one's own behaviour and the behaviour of other people. However, the term evolved and now also includes one's ability to navigate complex social relationships or measures a person's ability to understand and manage people. Levinson[53] refers to SQ as the ability to navigate the workplace culture. She believes that women and minority groups specifically need to have high SQ to empower them to navigate the workplace and need to take action to realise their SQ. People who make a difference, like Amina J. Mohammed, who was elected as the most influential person on the African continent[54] and whose activities had a transformative effect outside her main calling, demonstrate high SQ. The changes effected by such leaders (like breaking 'glass ceilings' with determination, bravery and sacrifices) affect the perceptions of people across cultures and serve to inspire others.

The belief is that social intelligence is mostly learned, often referred to a *'common sense'* yet if common sense was so 'common' why do most people not possess it? Key elements[55] of social intelligence are: the ability to interact in conversation with a variety of people in the same social setting; the ability to play various social roles – 'knowing how to play the game'[56], possessing effective listening skills and allowing people to express and converse with them without saying too much themselves; really trying to understand the other's behaviour and feelings. The socially intelligent person allows herself to be confident in all walks of life, thereby demonstrating self-confidence and the belief that she is connected. The element most challenging to the SQ person is the art of impression management[57] which refers to the delicate balance of being authentic to oneself. Women aspiring to improve their SQ can learn skills such as becoming more active listeners, acquiring better communication skills and learning from successes and failures in social settings.

Social intelligence considers SQ as a path to peace education and a culture of peace. Albrecht refers to SQ as an ability to get along with people and at the same time to win their cooperation. His recommends five dimensions, known as SPACE, to describe, assess and develop SQ. These are: Situational awareness (read situations and read people); Presence (know how people read you); Authenticity (how others judge you, based on what they see); Clarity (communication of your views); and Empathy (know how others feel, connect with them). A woman like Amina J Mohammed displays high SQ. People connect with her, she knows how to interact from the highest board levels to simple children in a children's home. She shows empathy with the ones she interacts with and is able to communicate her views across all levels of humanity. She understands people and her understanding is reflected in her dealings with people.

Women and conflict

Conflict is considered a state of disharmony between people's ideas, views or interest. In 2000, the UN Security Council adopted Resolution 1325 recognising, for the first time, women's role in conflict prevention and resolution. Conflict is part of each and every person's daily existence. How conflict is dealt with is not an inborn skill, but rather a learned skilled. Poor management of conflict has major effects on companies such as high absenteeism, lower turnover, unsolved grievances, lawsuits, vandalism, decrease in productivity and greater societal challenges arising outside organisations.[58] Conflict competencies enable leaders to improve relationships using constructive communication behaviours and emotional intelligence. Conflict is complex[59] as people's thoughts are skewed by their emotions.

A study conducted on the conflict styles[60] used by men and women at six organisational levels of work (entry-level to executive) revealed that men scored moderately higher on competing than women. Thomas et al. (ibid) specifies five conflict styles: *Competing* (satisfying one's own concerns at the others' expense); opposite of it is *Accommodating* (high in accommodation and low in assertiveness); *Avoiding* (low on cooperativeness and low on assertiveness); *Collaborating* (high cooperativeness and high assertiveness) and *Compromising* (middle-ground settlements). The study revealed that women score higher on compromising, avoiding and accommodating (Thomas et al., ibid). At higher organisational levels (executive and top executive level) scores are higher for both men and women on competing, but men's are still higher than women's. To illustrate this, women, will tend to negotiate lower salaries for themselves but will be more assertive than men when negotiating salaries for their staff. This tends to lead to lower pay and fewer promotion opportunities. Amantullah[61] cited in Thomas et al.[62] found that women did not negotiate higher salaries for themselves out of fear of their male counterpart's reaction. Women find themselves in a no-win situation because if they are seen as competitive they are viewed as lacking social skills and if they are competitive they are seen as lacking leadership competence. Women can take note of conflict-resolution techniques to enhance their capability to deal with areas of conflict and in so doing embrace the *'femine presence'* and avoid adopting male leadership traits.

The difference between men and women[63] is phrased by Miller as *"from the male perspective, control of conflict should lie in the hands of the offended; from the female's perspective, control should reside in the hands of the offender as well"*. A conflict-competence model developed by Runde (ibid) is presented in Figure 9.1. The model displays three stages – cool down phase; slow down and reflect phase; and the engage constructively stage.

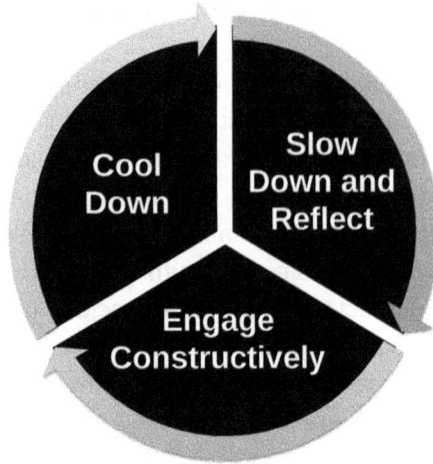

Figure 9.1 Conflict-Competence Model[64]

The cool down phase refers to people taking control of their emotions, reflecting on what happened, acknowledging the feeling (mindfulness is also a term that comes to mind here), and then proceeding to engage constructively with the other party. At this point a series of cognitive, emotional and behavioural skills underpins the constructive communication techniques that will foster understanding, the promotion of good listening skills, well-chosen words, creative solutions and the implementation thereof (Figure 9.2). Amina J. Mohammed was chosen for her skill in dealing with other countries on improving relations and reducing conflict on the African continent. It was important to choose a person like Amina J. Mohammed who will be able to voice issues firmly coming out of Africa. She is considered as a person with strengths, willpower and determination[65]. When someone like Amina J. Mohammed mobilises available resources for the good of the planet it is considered as peace leadership. Peace leaders are those who are mostly faced with difficult political decisions. Important traits for peace leaders in times of conflict are emotional self-control; empathy and cognitive complexity; the ability to effect change and reconciliation as well as the ability to forgive.[66] Phase two refers to 'slow down and reflect'. The practice of mindfulness can assist the woman leader during this phase. Revisiting the moment without being judgmental may assist her to consider and rethink the other person's point of view. With new insight gained, the woman leader can re-engage constructively (phase three) with communication.

Concluding remarks

As conflict is on the rise throughout the globe, businesses can embrace peace-building actions by tapping into the unique peace-building skills that women can provide. More women are needed around boardroom tables as evidence supports the fact that where women are present there is a 35 percent better chance that peace will last[67]. Women, on the other hand, need to understand that being highly competitive (adopting male traits) leads to dysfunctional outcomes. If competing is combined with collaboration it will lead to meeting the needs of both parties, moving from reunification to reconciliation[68]. Women need to embrace their *'feminine presence'*, become *'iron butterflies'* and avoid *'queen bee syndrome'* as this will enable them to contribute to peace-building leadership actions. Mindful practices can aid them further to strengthen their feminine presence within organisations:

> *"…more peace, more work, and production, more vocational education, more exports, more security, and higher standard of living"*[69]

References

Abrams, I. 1997. Heroines of Peace – The Nine Nobel Women. Available from: https://www.nobelprize.org/nobel_prizes/themes/peace/heroines/ [Accessed 16 April 2018].

Anonymous. 2018. Africa: Magazine announces list of 100 most influential Africans of 2017; Available from: http://allafrica.com/stories/201712080111.html [Accessed 25 April, 2018].

Allison, S. 2015. *Are women better peacekeepers? These UN officers think so. The Guardian* International Edition. Available from: https://www.theguardian.com/world/2015/sep/17/women-better-peacekeepers-un-officers-think-so [Accessed 20 March 2018].

Amanatullah, E.T. 2006. *Negotiating assertively: exploring benefits of representing another to women in salary negotiations*, paper presented at the Academy of Management meeting, Atlanta, GA, August 15.

Anonymous. 2017. We need more women leaders to sustain peace and development. Available from: https://www.un.org/development/desa/en/news/sustainable/women-leaders-to-sustain-peace.html [Accessed 1 May 2018].

Bar-On, R., Brown, J., Kirkcaldy, B. D. and Thome, E. 2000. Emotional expression and implications for occupational stress: An application of the Emotional Inventory (EQ-i). *Personality and Individual differences,* 28(6): 1107-1118.

Boals, K. *Some reflections on women and peace.* PDF download. 56-59 Place: Unknown, Publisher, Unknown.

Booyatzis, R.E. 2006. Using tipping points of emotional intelligence and cognitive competencies to predict financial performance of leaders. *Pscothema,* 18(sup): 124-131.

Bhikkhu, B. 2011. What does Mindfulness really mean? A canonical perspective. Contemporary Buddhism: *An Interdisciplinary Journal,* 12(1): 19-39.

Citizen Reporter. 2017. Nelson Mandela Foundation welcomes UN deputy chief Amina J Mohammed. Available from: https://citizen.co.za/news/south-africa/1739727/nelson-mandela-foundation-welcomes-deputy-secretary-general-of-un-amina-j-mohammed/ [Accessed 24 April 2018].

Cook, A. and Glass, C. 2014. Women and top leadership positions: towards an Institutional Analysis, *Gender, Work and Organization.* 219-10, doi:10.1111/gwao.12018: 91-103.

Cote, S. and Miners, C.T.H. 2006. Emotional Intelligence, cognitive intelligence and job performance. *Administrative Science Quarterly,* 51(1): 1-28.

Development agenda must address causes of migrant crisis, says UN adviser. Available from: https://www.theguardian.com/global-development/2015/jul/13/development-agenda-must-address-causes-migrant-crisis-amina-j-mohammed [Accessed 25 April 2018]

Eagly, A. and Carli, L.L. 2007. Women and the Labyrinth of Leadership. *Harvard Business Review*. Available from: https://hbr.org/2007/09/women-and-the-labyrinth-of-leadership [Accessed 24 April 2018]

Elmuti, D., Jia, J., and Davis, H.H. 2009. Challenges women face in leadership positions and organizational effectiveness: An investigation. *Journal of Leadership Education*, 8(2): 167-187.

Erikson, E. "Inner and Outer Space: Reflections on Womanhood," DAEDALUS, Spring, 1964. 582-83.

Fortune Editors. 2017. These are the women leading the CEOs leading the Fortune 500 companies. Available from: http://fortune.com/2017/06/07/fortune-500-women-ceos/ [Accessed, 25 April 2018]

Goleman, D. 2001. Emotional Intelligence: Issues in paradigm building. In Stys, Y. and Brown, L.S. 2004. A review of the emotional intelligence literature and implications for corrections. PDF. [Accessed 25 April 2018].

Hymowitz, C. and Schellhardt, T.D. 1986.The glass-ceiling: Why women can't seem to break the invisible barrier that blocks them from top jobs. *The Wall Street Journal*. 57, D1:D4-D5.

Jalalzai, F. and Krook, L.M. 2010. Beyond Hillary and Benazir: Women's Political Leadership Worldwide. *International Political Science Review*, 31(1): 5-23, Available from: http://www.mlkrook.org/pdf/jalalzai_krook_10.pdf [Accessed 5 May 2018].

Johnson, Z. and Mathur-Helm, B. 2013. Queen Bees: the reluctance of women executives to promote other women. Leaders' LAB. Available from: http://www.usb.ac.za/thoughtprint/ThoughtPrint%20Multimedia/PDF%20media/QueenBee.pdf   [Accessed 1 May 2018]

Lacey, H. 2017. Amina J Mohammed on Nigeria, leadership and the UN. Available from: https://www.ft.com/content/f8caadca-da0f-11e7-a039-c64b1c09b482 [Accessed 16 April 2018]

Ledbetter, B. 2016. Business leadership for peace. *International Journal of Public leadership*, 12(3): 239-251.

Levinson, P. 2014. Smart is not enough. Why social intelligence (SQ) may be the key to career success for women and minorities. Available from: http://www.diversityjournal.com/14203-smart-enough-social-intelligence-sq-may-key-career-success-women-minorities/ [Accessed 25 April 2018]

Lieberfeld, D. 2009. Lincoln, Mandela, and qualities of reconciliation orientated leadership. Peace and conflict: *Journal of Peace Psychology*, 15(1): 27-47.

Mayer, J.D., Salovey, P., and Caruso, D. 2000. *Models of emotional intelligence*. In J.R. Sternberg (ed.), *Handbook of Intelligence*, 396-420. Cambridge, UK: Cambridge University Press.

McCleskey, J. 2012. Emotional intelligence and leadership. A review of the progress, controversy and criticism. *International Journal of Organisational Analysis*, 22(1): 76-96

McGrath, F. 2013. Emotional Intelligence and Conflict Resolution. Available from: http://c.ymcdn.com/sites/www.aclea.org/resource/collection/A8C75F24-5FFF-4686-814A-D153A57D21C3/49_-_Emotional_Intelligence_-_Conflict_Resolution.pdf [Accessed 5 April 2018].

Miller, W.M. 2016. Toward a scholarship of peace leadership. *International Journal of Public Leadership*, 12(3): 216-226, https://doi.org/10.1108/IJPL-04-2016-0013

Miller, J.B. 1991.Women's and Men's scripts for interpersonal conflict. *Psychology of Women Quarterly*, 15: 15-29

NA. 2016. Amina's candidature for AU job generates multiple narratives. Teach Conflict. Available from: https://www.nation.co.ke/news/amina-candidature-for-au-job-generates-multiple-narratives/1056-3458306-11rijoi/index.html [Accessed 17 April, 2018].

NA. 2017. *Joint UN–AU high-level delegation to Nigeria and the DRC to spotlight women, peace and security agenda*. Available from: http://www.unwomen.org/en/news/stories/2017/7/un-high-level-delegation-to-nigeria-and-the-drc-to-spotlight-women-peace-and-security-agenda [Accessed 17 April, 2018]

Ngunjiri, F.W. 2014. *"I Will Be a Hummingbird": Lessons in Radical Transformative Leadership from Professor Wangari; Leadership in Postcolonial Africa*. Palgrave Macmillan.

Northouse, P.G. 2017. *Leadership. Theory and Practice*, 7th Edition. SAGE Publications Inc.

Paris, J. and Hewitt, L.M.M. 2018. *The Mindfulness of Senior Women Leaders in South Africa – An Explorative Qualitative Research Study*, Unpublished paper.

Peters, S. 2017. UN's Amina Mohammed stirs leadership to invest more in women and girls. *Inclusion, Equity and Human Rights News*. Available from: http://www.bizcommunity.com/Article/196/712/170600.html [Accessed 24 April 2018].

Regine, B. n.d. Leadership cultivating female presence. *Interbeing*, 3(1): np

Ricke-Kiely. T. 2016. New developments in peace leadership. *International Journal of Public Leadership*, 12 (3): 197-204.

Permanent link to this document: https://doi.org/10.1108/IJPL-06-2016-0025

Riggio, R.E. 2018. What is social intelligence and why does it matter? *Psychology Today*. Available from: https://www.psychologytoday.com/us/blog/cutting-edge-leadership/201407/what-is-social-intelligence-why-does-it-matter [Accessed 1 May 2018].

Runde, G.E. 2014. Conflict competence in the workplace. *Employment Relations Today*, 40(4): 25-31.

Santorelli, S.F. 2011. 'Enjoy Your Death': Leadership Lessons Forged in The Crucible of Organizational Death and Rebirth Infused With Mindfulness and Mastery. *Contemporary Buddhism*, 12(1): 199-217.

Seddon, M. 2017. Why is she here? The Nigerian herder's daughter who became UN deputy chief. Available from: https://www.theguardian.com/global-development/2017/may/26/why-is-she-here-nigerian-herders-daughter-un-deputy-chief-amina-mohammed [Accessed 16 April 2018]

Spreitzer, G. 2007. Giving peace a chance: organizational leadership, empowerment, and peace. *Journal of Organizational Behavior,* 28: 1077-1095

The Global Gender Gap Report. 2017. Available from: http://www3.weforum.org/docs/WEF_GGGR_2017.pdf [Accessed 24 April 2018]

Thomas, W.K., Thomas, G.F., and Schaubhut, N. 2008. Conflict styles of men and women at six organizational levels. *International Journal of Conflict Management*, 19(2): 148-166.

Van Vianen, A.E.M., and Fischer, A.H. 2002. Illuminating the glass ceiling: The role of organizational culture preferences. *Journal of Occupational and Organizational Psychology*, 75(3): 315-337.

Wawra, D. 2009. Social Intelligence: the key to intercultural communication. *European Journal of English Studies,* 13(2): 163-177.

Endnotes

1   Abrams, 1997.
2   Allison, 2015.
3   Lacey, 2017.
4   Ricke-Kiely, 2016
5   Jalalzai & Krook, 2010.
6   Miller, 2016
7   The Global Gender Gap Report, 2017.
8   See endnote 4.
9   Cook & Glass, 2014.
10   *Fortune* Editors, 2017.
11   Northouse, 2017.
12   *Citizen Reporter*, 2017.
13   Peters, 2017.
14   Ngunjiri, 2014.
15   Ibid.
16   Ibid, p.5.
17   Regine, n.d.
18   Ibid.
19   See endnote 6.
20   Johnson & Mathur-Helm, 2013.
21   Ibid.
22   Boals, n.d.
23   Ibid.
24   Ibid.
25   Erikson, 1964.
26   Ledbetter, 2016
27   Eagly & Carli, 2007.
28   Hymowitz & Schellhardt, 1986 in Eagly & Carli, 2007.
29   See endnote 26.
30   Van Vianen & Fischer, 2002.
31   Elmuti et al., 2009.
32   Ibid.
33   Ibid.
34   Paris & Hewitt, 2018.
35   Bhikkhu, 2011.
36   Santorelli, 2011.
37   Spreitzer, 2007.
38   Seddon, 2017.
39   NA, 2017.
40   See endnote 2.
41   Mayer et al., 2000.
42   McCleskey, 2012 p: 80.
43   Bar-On et al., 2000.
44   Cote & Miners, 2006.
45   Northouse, 2016.
46   McGrath, 2013.
47   Booyatzis, 2006.
48   See endnote 38.
49   Goleman, 2001.
50   *The Guardian*, 2015.
51   Goleman, 1998.
52   Wawra, 2009.
53   Levinson, 2014.
54   All Africa, 2017.
55   Riggio, 2018.
56   Ibid.
57   Ibid.
58   Runde, 2014.
59   See endnote 31.
60   Thomas,et al., 2008.
61   Amanatullah, 2006.
62   See endnote 55.
63   Miller, 1991.
64   See endnote 53.
65   NA, 2016.
66   Lieberfeld, 2009.
67   Anonymous, 2017.
68   Ibid.
69   Ibid, p. 246.

CHAPTER 10

PEACE LEADERSHIP IN THE PUBLIC AND PRIVATE SECTORS

Liezel Lues

"Peace is costly, but is worth the expense." (African proverb)

Spotlight: Chancellor Angela Merkel

Angela Merkel, born in Hamburg 1954, is a German stateswomen and chancellor of Germany since 2005 serving for three terms. She has been described as the *de facto* leader of the European Union (the longest-serving incumbent head of government). Merkel has twice been named the world's second most powerful person following Vladimir Putin by *Forbes* magazine, was named *Time* magazine's Person of the Year[1], and "the most powerful woman in the world" by *Forbes*[2]. Former US Secretary of State, Hillary Clinton, described Merkel in 2017 as "the most important leader in the free world". She is currently the senior G7 leader.

Merkel was appointed Germany's first female chancellor. One of her priorities has been to strengthen transatlantic economic relations. She also played a significant part in managing the financial crisis at the European and international level. On a national level, healthcare reform, future energy development and, more recently, her government's approach to the ongoing migrant crisis have been major issues during her Chancellorship.[3] Her leadership is now under fire amid the refugee crisis engulfing Germany and Europe more generally. In 2015, at least 1.1 million 'refugees', mostly from Syria, but also from Afghanistan, the Balkans, Pakistan and increasingly North Africa, arrived in Germany. Chancellor Angela Merkel announced during her summer press conference on August 31st, 2015, that no refugees from Syria would be stopped from entering Germany with immediate effect, regardless of EU law to the contrary[4]. However, she is known for being pragmatic and having a strong sense of duty[5]. For this reason she confirmed that her Grand Coalition partners would review her European negotiation for many reasons, but also to make progress in Europe.

Introduction

Today, countries in the world are characterised by 21st century challenges of which the depletion of natural resources, violation of human rights, violence, war and corruption are but a few. These challenges in the world have brought about revolutionary leadership concepts, as well as expectations, that have had a considerable impact on the role and disposition of the peace leader. To view a peace leader as a politically neutral force, mainly responsible for executing policies that were put in place by political rulers, is no longer viable. The reason for this is that the task of a peace leader (in the public or private sector), involves more than the mere execution of legislation – he/she plays an active role in policy-making, implementation, monitoring and evaluation.

Improving the quality of life of society, improving political and economic well-being, and rendering affordable services, together comprise the primary aim of every government. In order to achieve this aim, government functions have typically been divided into two groups, namely maintenance and development functions. Maintenance functions include the upholding of law and order and ensuring that living conditions do not degenerate to such an extent that living standards decline. Development functions refer first of all to socio-economic development functions and secondly, to functions aimed at improving the general welfare of society. The latter can be achieved, for example, by the creation of job opportunities and the improvement of education and health standards, as well as by improving the circumstances of the homeless and taking purposeful action to promote economic growth, hopefully within a peaceful environment. Governments typically have to have a strong leader to steer the prosperity of the country assisted by a cabinet (ministers) that gives structure to the operational aspects of the vision of the government of the day. It is evident that governments utilise more than just state departments and ministers to achieve their objectives; several role-players, including the the private sector, which plays a critical role, participate in achieving this aim.

It is important to note that the difference between public and private sectors lies not so much in the nature of administration, as in the environment within which each functions. The public sector strives towards the achievement of higher-order goals and activities and differs from the private sector in that it operates within a highly legal framework, in the absence of competition, and is service-delivery-orientated. In the private sector, however, the core function of business should be to strive for excellence in support of making profit. The overall level of the performance of both sectors and its leaders is highly dependent on a stable and peaceful environment.

It is noted that leaders in both the public and private sectors assume an authoritative and responsible position, which refers, inter alia, to the control that a leader exercises over resources. It entails directing and leading the activities of an institution towards the achievement of identified objectives. This process is guided by compliance with legislation, as well as the availability of capital and other resources.

The purpose of this chapter is to conceptualise the concepts important to this chapter i.e. peace, leadership and activists. The demarcating of the boundaries of peace leaders and activists as well as the generations of peace leaders in the public and private sectors will be discussed. The paper will conclude with an agenda for building a peace culture and developing peace leaders and activists in the 21st century.

Conceptualising the concepts of peace, leadership and activists

It is imperative to demarcate the concepts of peace, leadership and activists within the public and private sectors respectively for the purpose of this chapter, although peace leadership has been extensively delineated in chapters 1–3. As independent concepts, they indicate a strong emotive stance, to accomplish what it is set out to achieve. According to the Oxford English Dictionary[6] the concept 'peace' means: "[in singular] a treaty agreeing peace between warring states: support for a negotiated peace"; "a state or period in which there is no war or a war has ended"; "the state of being free from civil disorder: police action to restore peace". For the purpose of this chapter, the concept peace is best described as: "the state of being free from dissension ... peace with the union".

Without ever over-simplifying the meaning of leadership, it can be explained as "the action of leading a group of people or an organisation. An activity whereby a group of persons in a specific situation, at a specific time and under certain circumstances, are influenced by another person to voluntarily follow the ideologies of that person." The most important deduction that can be made from this definition of leadership is that a group of persons must be influenced in such a way that they will individually and collectively undertake certain activities without being forced to do so. The question thus arises of whether the concepts of a leader and an activist can be seen as having the same connotative meaning. Whereas "denote refers to the literal, primary meaning of something; connote refers to other characteristics suggested or implied by that thing".[7]

Defining the concept of activist, the connotative meaning refers to people who have proactively advocated diplomatic, philosophical, and non-military resolutions of major territorial or ideological disputes through non-violent attempts. Activists usually work collectively with others to put focus on an issue and gain attention from the world. They initiate and facilitate a wide range of public dialogues aimed at peacefully ending conflict of ideas. As a noun, an activist is "a person who campaigns to bring about political or social change" by "organising solidarity events"[8]. Thus, one might say that the concept of 'activist' denotes similar characteristics to those of 'a peace leader' and vice versa. However, an activist's main focus connotes qualities such as 'protection' and 'affection', whereas that of leaders connotes qualities such as 'vision' and 'enhancement'. Adding the concept 'peace' to the words 'leader' and 'activist' respectively gives rise to a whole new meaning to that evoked by merely referring to a leader and an activist. Thus it is expected that a peace leader and peace activist nearly always aspire to act within a non-violent environment and further, also strive towards a positive outcome. This differs from the roles of a leader or activist in other spheres who endeavour to achieve an aim no matter what it takes, even when a hostile environment needs to be created.

The conclusions that could be drawn from well-known historically identified peace leaders and activists such as Woodrow Wilson (1919), Mother Teresa (1979), and Kofi Annan (2001), to mention but a few, is that they (i) acted as leaders to many ordinary citizens; (ii) acted as activist to passionate followers; and (iii) most of the time aimed to foster a peaceful transition from what they might define as an unwanted, negative or a detrimental environment to a favourable, more positive and sustainable place. However, it should be noted that not all peace leaders and activists denote the same meaning to ordinary citizens. You might have a group of citizenry who view the intention of a peace leader or activist as acting favourably towards a marginalised group but to the detriment of others, for example, Martin Luther King (non-violent civil rights leader) and at present Angela Merkel (advocating peace in a time of turmoil). Thus, to conclude in laymen's terms: the concepts 'peace', 'leader' and 'activist' are best defined in the eyes of the beholder, the follower and the antagonist.

Demarcating the boundaries of peace leaders and activists

Peace leaders and activists all over the world, although functioning independently in many ways, religiously believing in their unique ideology, fortunately or unfortunately are confined and influenced by certain environments. Whether in the public or private sectors, peace leaders and activists need to recognise that the following environments, amongst others, will determine to a large extent, the borders of their efforts (Figure 10.1):

Constitutional environment — Uphold constitutional values — Respect constitutional principles

Political environment — Accountable — Adhere to the demands of customers

Statutory environment — Portray ethical decisions in line with laws — Obey rules

Economic environment — Do more with less — Create job opportunities

Social environment — Become more sensitive — Learn to respect

Public sector — Private sector

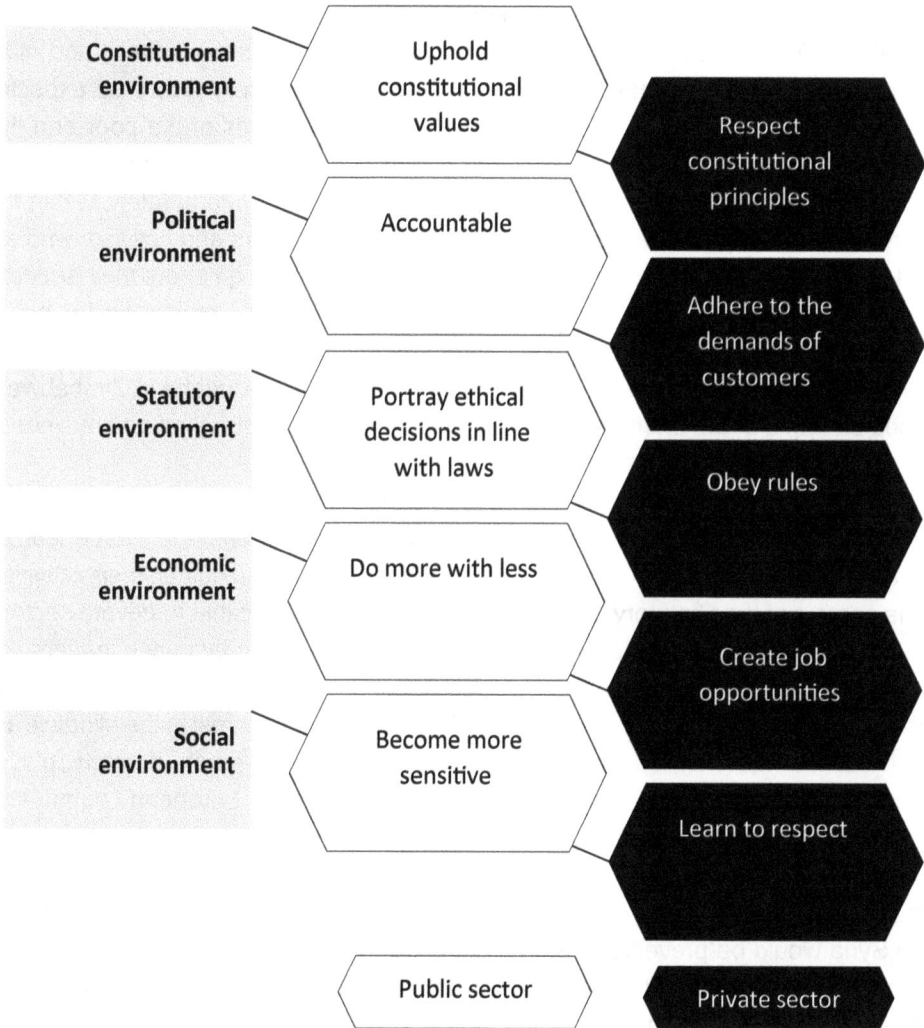

Figure 10:1 The environments influencing the efforts of peace leaders and activists in the public and private sectors

Figure 10.1 attempts to capture the most influential environments in which peace leaders and activists function. The Constitutional environment demands that the exercise of any power must have its origin in lawful authority. Therefore, peace leaders and activists may not exceed their powers and are only allowed to do what the law authorises them to do. For example, functioning within a Constitutional environment such as South Africa will call upon public-sector peace leaders to uphold constitutional values and principles as captured in chapter 10 of the South African Constitution[9]. Private-sector peace leaders within this environment, for example, need to adhere to human rights principles, especially concerning the wellbeing of their workforce, as stipulated in chapter two of the Constitution.

Within the Political environment, accountability is expected from and enforced by the citizens from legislators, ministers, members of the executive council and other political executive office bearers (column 2, Figure 10.1). Also, it would be expected that peace leaders and activists take cognisance of the needs of the poor and that they would try to adhere to the demands of the community, the latter often called the 'customer' in the private sector (column 3, Figure 10.1). Unfortunately, within this environment, it often appears as if public-sector peace leaders and activists who are loyal to the ruling party, have more freedom to function and to go about their agendas than, for example, those who form the opposition. Typically, private-sector peace leaders and activists who support the ruling regime often benefit financially from this affiliation. The recent takeover from the long-serving Robert Mugabe in Zimbabwe is a good example of the often complex relationship between politicians and business.

The Statutory environment, which is dictated by legislation and the courts of a country is also regarded as an integral part of a constitutional environment. Peace leaders and activists need to be familiar with legislation that affects and guides their activities. In the context of the Statutory environment (and equally applicable to private sectors) this environment aims to enforce ethical decisions to be taken by peace leaders and activists in line with laws, with the ultimate purpose of benefiting those who reside within the borders of the country (column 2, Figure 10.1). The unrest in the Middle East, which caused many Syrian migrants to travel to Europe in search of safety, placed an enormous responsibility on the statutory position of many European countries. In order to deal with the huge influx of migrants, the European Union (EU) introduced the European Agenda on Migration in 2015, a statutory intervention to serve as a form of control[10]. However, it was the 2015 announcement by Angela Merkel that no refugees from Syria would be prevented from entering Germany, which suspend pertinent EU law on the conduct of asylum policy in EU member states. This unprecedented influx still poses challenging economic, fiscal, political, socio-cultural and legal difficulties[11].

In the Economic environment (Figure 10.1), in which economic prosperity and employment opportunities need to be established, the public sector is sometimes forced to render services and goods to communities which lay people may regard as an effort to oppose the free market system. Government institutions are these days responsible for rendering ever-increasing services with fewer resources and they also have to ensure that those resources are utilised efficiently and effectively within the context of the economic environment. The private sector plays a vital role within this environment, especially in securing a healthy GDP and supporting the public sector in their objectives aimed at economic prosperity, such as job creation. The Economic environment, especially in a country such as the United States of America (USA), not only sets the trend in this regard, but also determines the prosperity of each citizen. Many USA established private-sector companies such as Apple, Microsoft, Starbucks and Facebook have not only raised the bar for future innovations, but have contributed directly to the prosperity of the economic environment of their country.

The social environment (Figure 10.1) is mainly influenced by culture, gender and religion. It is the task of government to create an environment where citizens live in peace, harmony and good order. The social environment is based on values and needs, understanding the uniqueness of individuals and supporting the enhancement of individuality. The private sector is frequently at the forefront within the social environment, often capitalising on people who naturally form relationships. Churches today are an example where peace leaders and activists will focus their attention on a specific cohort or generation (a naturally formed relationship). Countries within the Middle East have over the years shown that religious and social ideologies determine the boundaries of the social environment for leaders and activists respectively.

Within the mentioned environments it should be noted that several individuals have contributed towards improving the lives of ordinary people. These environments were and still are a valid reality in setting the boundaries within which a peace leader and activist may and can function. What is interesting to observe is that, at a specific time in history and to a greater or lesser extent, these environments swayed a specific cohort of individuals (a generation) to adopt a noteworthy cause at the time. The following sections will focus on the role of peace leaders and activists from a specific generation and how they contributed to raise awareness of a particular issue.

Generations of peace leaders in the public and private sectors

Contemporary society accepts the notion of a generation as a form of demarcation or association. The concept of a generation is also used to locate particular birth cohorts in specific historical and cultural circumstances. However, there are also psychological and sociological dimensions in the sense of belonging and identity that can define a generation[12]. While all generations have similarities, it is too simplistic to say they are the same[13]. The generally used terms to describe the generations currently living in the UK are: GI (born 1900–1920s), Silent or Veteran (born 1929–1945), Boomers or Baby Boomers (born 1946–1960s), Generation X (born 1968–1989), the Millennials or Generation Y (born mid-1980s–2000s) and Generation Z or Gen Z (also known as iGeneration or iGen and Post-Millennials) which is the demographic cohort after the Millennials (Generation Y) demarcated as the generation born during the mid-1990s to the mid-2000s[14]. Figure 10.2 captures several generations of peace leaders and activists and portrays how they were driven by their association and/or relationship with an ideology within a specific time. The latter is depicted within six clearly demarcated environments.

Politicians often dominate the scene when one thinks of examples of peace leaders. In nearly all countries there are well-known peace leaders and activists aiming to either create: (i) peace, (ii) a stable milieu or (iii) a post-war environment. They all function within a constitutional environment (Figure 10.2, column 1). In the United States of America historical political figures such as Thomas Jefferson, Woodrow Wilson, Abraham Lincoln, Jimmy Carter and Martin Luther King come to mind (Figure 10.2, column 3). In England, Winston Churchill, through remaining opposed to Hitler, enabled the eventual defeat of Nazi totalitarianism; in Russia, Mikhail Gorbachev led the transition of Soviet Communism to democracy and paved the way for peace in Eastern Europe; in South Africa Nelson Mandela ended apartheid and created a peaceful transition to democracy (Figure 10.2)[15]. The mentioned figures were all born before 1931 – a cohort of leaders before the Baby Boomers. The 1990s saw Baby Boomer politicians in most democratic countries around the world[16].

A close association with politicians and policy-makers creates an ideal situation for journalists to render inputs as part of an awareness function. Journalists, often acting as activists, focus on increasing awareness of a worthy cause and of issues at hand. Indirectly, journalists all over the world work to activate a movement towards an improved society, a contribution which does not always receive the acknowledgement it deserves. Journalists are forced to operate within both constitutional and political environments and simultaneously often need to challenge the boundaries set by the statutory environment. Dorothy Day (1897–1980), an American journalist, is an example of a social activist and co-founder of the Catholic Worker Movement who enabled citizens to participate meaningfully and called on them to take action (Figure 10.2). The tremendous impact that journalists and the media have, not only on citizens within a country, but even outside the borders of a country, is of utmost importance. The journalist Howard Morland (1942-), for example, was influenced by the World Wars and therefore used the media to campaign for nuclear weapons abolition.

Constitutional environment	Historical figures	Thomas Jefferson (1743-1826) Woodrow Wilson (1856-1924) Winston Churchill (1874-1965) Martin Luther King (1929-1968)
Political environment	Political leaders	Nelson Mandela (1918-2013) Mikhail Gorbachev (1931-) Kofi Annan (1938-2018)
Statutory environment	Activists	Feminists Artists Journalists	Susan Anthony (1820-1906) Malala Yousafzai (1997-) John Lennon (1940-1980) Cat Stevens (1948-) Dorothy Day (1897-1980) Howard Morland (1942-)
Economic environment	Innovators	Sir Richard Branson (1950-) Bill Gates (1955-) Steve Jobs (1955-2011) Elon Musk (1971-) Mark Zuckerberg (1984-)
Social environment	Spiritual leaders	Mahatma Gandhi (1869-1948) Pope John Paul (1920-2005) 14th Dalai Lama (1935-) Desmund Tutu (1931-)

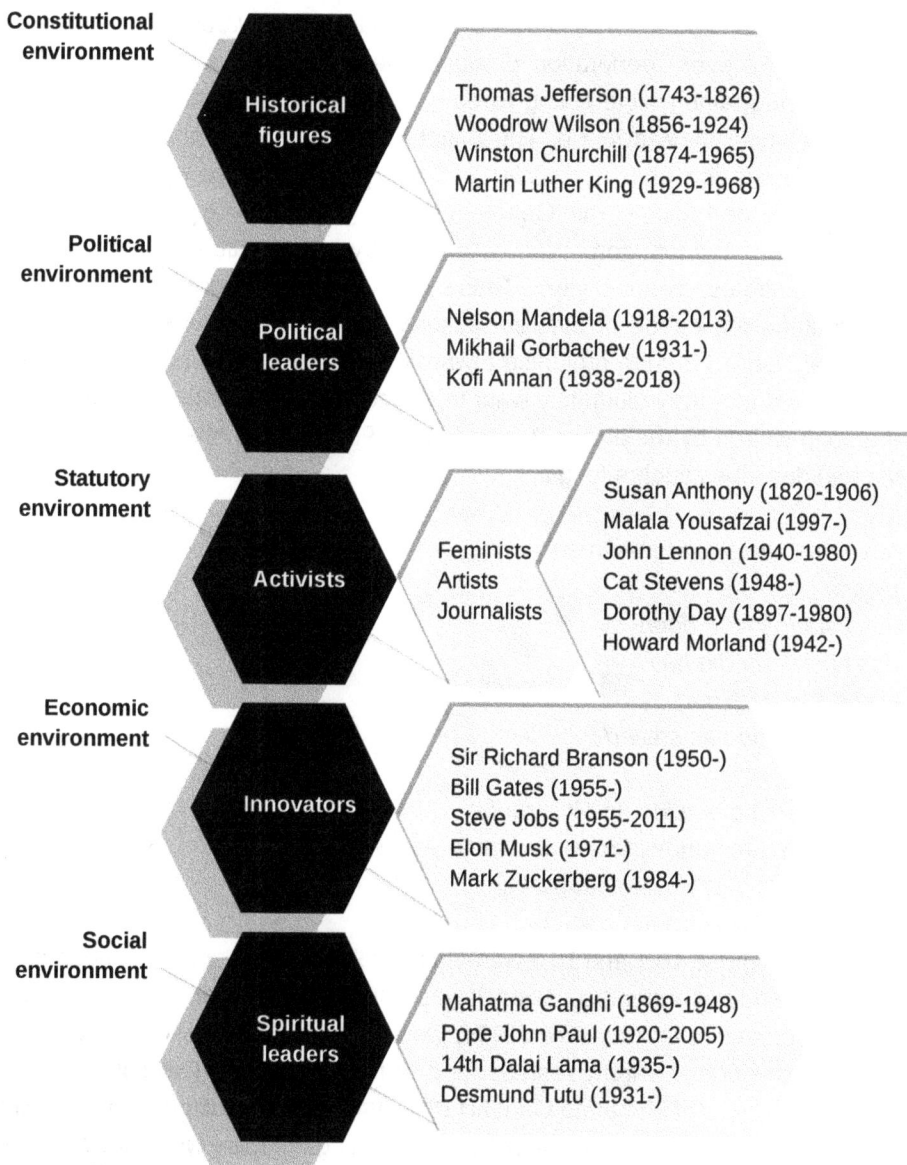

Figure 10:2 A synopsis of public and private sector peace leaders and activists

It is also noteworthy that a cohort of entertainers also act as peace activists. Actors Paul Newman (1925–2008), Jane Fonda (1937-) and Charlize Theron (1975-) support several charities. Songwriters and singers include John Lennon (1940–1980) who was a well-known artist but also anti-war protester and Cat Stevens (1948-) who converted to Islam and became an activist for humanitarian causes. Sir Paul McCartney and Bono also exemplify the longstanding trend of popular entertainers who advance political and social causes. These are merely a few examples of entertainers who took a deliberate decision to dedicate their time and effort towards worthy causes and it is noted that every generation produces peace leaders and activists. The focus of these entertainers, interesting to note, is predominantly influenced by the environment in which they grew up. The Silent Generation was mostly influenced by the Great Depression and World War 2; Baby Boomers by post-war freedoms such as drugs, sex and rock 'n' roll; Generation X by global realities, techno-literacy and women entering the workforce; the Millennials by globalisation, communication technology and wireless connectivity[17]. These peace activists, more often than not, clearly understand the needs of different cultures, vulnerable groups and causes, and deliberately aim to reduce prejudice towards gender, religion and marginalised groups. It appears that they ultimately want to create social tolerance. The following lyrics of a song written by the singer Bob Dylan in 1964 with the title *The times they are a-changin* describes such a focus:

"come senators, congressmen
please heed the call
don't stand in the doorway
don't block up the hall
for he that gets hurt
will be he who has stalled

there's a battle outside and it is ragin'
it'll soon shake your windows and rattle your walls
for the times they are a-changin"[18].

The intentions of Figures 10.1 and 10.2 were mainly to demarcate some boundaries in order to grasp the matter under discussion. It was indicated that the social environment influences those causes that Maslow (1954) would define as higher-order needs in his theory of motivation hierarchy (esteem and self-actualisation). Religious leaders and activists of the likes of Mahatma Gandhi (1869–948), John Paul II (Polish Catholic Pope), Desmond Tutu (1931-), and the 14th Dalai Lama (1935-), are well-known peace activists (Figure 2)[19]. As much as religion is practised all over the world, so is the issue of women's rights recognised in all countries. Generation X, Leymah Gbowee (1972-) is an organiser of a women's peace movement in Liberia and was awarded the Nobel Peace Prize in 2011, and Millenial Malebogo Molefhe (1980-) is a Botswanan activist against gender-based violence.

As the times are indeed changing, new buzz words, dynamic innovations and technology tend to set the tone for what is now defined as peace, leadership and activism. People in the 21st century are driven by money, by inventions, by being the first to propose an innovative idea (clearly defined by the economic environment; see Figure 10.2). Within this fast-changing environment, several unique dangers emerge.

War and peace is still a reality but war now appears even deadlier and crueller, more cunningly waged than in the past. Living in the so-called fast lane necessitates peace leaders and activists with 21st century skills. These are people who will be able to identify a danger to humankind and come up with solutions to prevent a war, or to cure a disease, or to solve problems before they become apparent. Functioning in this economics-driven environment are well-known entrepreneurs such as Baby Boomers Sir Richard Branson (1950-), known for not letting any obstacle get in his way and living his mantra: "Screw it, let's do it!", Bill Gates (1955-) and Steve Jobs (1955–2011). Elon Musk (Generation X, 1971-) and Mark Zuckerberg (Millennial, 1984-) have also became known for their innovation, dreaming big, focusing on the social good and engaging stakeholders[20]. Could these entrepreneurs now be called the peace leaders and activists of the 21st century?

Although several remarkable deductions may be made from the above-mentioned (including Figure 10.2), for the purpose of this paper, the following appear significant:

- What is noted so far is that although public-sector peace leaders tend to set the pace with regard to the direction a country will take in the future, peace leaders and activists in the private sector do not neglect opportunities to give prominence to well-deserving causes (for example gender, sexual orientation and the environment). There are seemingly equal numbers of examples of peace leaders and activists in both sectors.
- It appears that there is a significant number of peace leaders and activists amongst the generation born before the Baby Boomers (1945). These include the Nobel Prize laureate Albert Einstein (1879–1955); Emily Hobhouse, British welfare campaigner (1860–1926); Henry Dunant, founder of the Red Cross (1828–1910); Harry Belafonte (1927-); Nelson Mandela, South African statesman (1918-2013); and David McTaggart, co-founder of Greenpeace International (1932–2001).
- A large birth cohort linked to specific historical circumstances are those influenced by the First and Second World Wars. Consequently, these peace leaders and activists campaigned against war and sought to to abolish nuclear weapons, and they focused the world's attention on the irrationality of violent conflicts, decisions and actions. Baby Boomers played an influential role during this period[21]. Kate Hudson (born 1958) became known as a political activist and was General Secretary of the Campaign for Nuclear Disarmament. Other known peace leaders are anti-Vietnam war activist Suzanne Arms (1945-); nuclear weapons abolitionist Howard Morland (1942-) and Palestinian activist Sari Nusseibeh (1949-).
- The Xers born in the 1960s through to the mid-1970s grew up in the 1980s. They entered the work force in the 1990s and will continue to work until 2030[22]. They have about 51 million members. This generation is characterised by women who enter the workforce seeking economic equality with men, contrary to the traditional way in which they were raised. Peace leaders and activists from this generation include Vittorio Arrigoni (1975–2011), an Italian reporter and anti-war activist;

Rachel Corrie (1979–2003) an American activist for Palestinian human rights; and Liberian Leymah Gbowee(1972-), the 2011 Nobel Peace Prize recipient.

- The 'Millennial Generation' (also called the 'Y or Next Generation' or the 'iGeneration'), is generally distinguished by an increased use of and familiarity with communications, media, and digital technologies[23]. In most parts of the world, their upbringing was marked by an increase in a neoliberal approach to politics and economics, cultural diversity, and more personal freedom and choices. Although this generation will produce its own future peace leaders and activists, the bravery of Malala Yousafzai (1997-) is prominent[24].

Although it might have been anticipated that peace leaders and activists in the 21st century would concern themselves with new causes such as managing foreign aid and managing "development silos"[25], there are some causes that remain on the peace leaders' and activists' agenda, such as poverty, hunger, diseases, promoting gender equality, education, and environmental sustainability.

Ordinary people do great things for the future

So far it is realised that the world has become a transparent system, embedded in thriving environments. The main drivers are technologies and social networks which are creating new ways of living faster whilst simultaneously destroying old ideologies. These not only set the pace but also outline the actions to be taken by peace leaders and activists within. How will Twitter, Facebook, WhatsApp, Pinterest, LinkedIn and the Apple iPhone influence peace leaders and activists in the future? However, no one can foresee what is in store for the world in five, ten, thirty, and a hundred years into the future.

Although we might anticipate what the future might be like, several peace leaders and activists have not waited for the right moment to start. There are already several highly successful projects that are making great strides in creating peace. Building leaders4peace (BL4P) is an initiative looking for innovative ways to spur one another on toward working for peace. They define a leader as someone who demonstrates what is possible and believes that everyone can be a peacemaker. However, they proclaim that it is very important that before mobilising others, you first model peace in your own life. BL4P hosts, amongst others, peace camps where they train participants in practising five peace values: celebrating diversity, collaboration, conflict resolution, catalytic leadership through reconciliation and forgiveness, and changing the world[26].

A second project worth mentioning is The Elders, who are independent global leaders brought together by Nelson Mandela. They offer their collective influence and experience to support peacebuilding, help address major causes of human suffering and promote the shared interests of humanity. Many of the Elders' (Martti Ahtisaari, Kofi Annan, Ban Ki-moon, Ela Bhatt, Graça Machel, to name but a few), work is dedicated to supporting the efforts of other campaigners and advocates, giving them a platform to make their voices heard. Nelson Mandela mandated these leaders to speak truth to power, raise the voices of the voiceless and offer hope where there is despair[27].

Rotary International, a humanitarian service organisation, is dedicated to world peace. This organisation works to make peace a reality by training the next generation of peace leaders. The Rotary Club of Tsawwassen, for example, is now recruiting for the Rotary Peace Fellowship, a program that gives up to 100 fellows the opportunity to obtain professional development certificates or master's degrees in peace and conflict resolution.[28] Another international organisation is called Never Again International and aims to ensure that children are never again manipulated by adults to become agents of war but instead become soldiers for peace. The focus is on educating how to prevent hate speech and undermine prejudice by weakening the grounds for ignorance, by promoting learning to live together and by cultivating respect for all people[29].

The agenda for building a peace culture and developing peace leaders and activists in the public and private sectors

The deadline for achieving the Millennium Development Goals (MDGs) adopted in September 2000, during the Millennium Assembly of the UN, came and elapsed at the end of December 2015. The MDGs were pursued with relative success, but world leaders acknowledged that poverty eradication is still the greatest challenge facing the world[30]. As the world embarks on the second leg of the 2030 Agenda for Sustainable Development Goals (SDGs), all role players, and even more so peace leaders and activists, will come to realise the impact that respective environments and generations will have on the achievement of these goals.

The 2030 Agenda for Sustainable Development, which contains 17 goals and 169 targets, is applicable to all countries irrespective of their development status. It has replaced, and is building on, the achievements of the MDGs to guide development efforts by all countries of the world for the next 15 years, beginning in January 2016. Thus, the framework goes far beyond the MDGs. Alongside continuing development priorities such as poverty eradication, health, education and food security and nutrition, it sets out a wide range of economic, social and environmental objectives. The work ahead for every country is now to implement the 2030 Agenda for Sustainable Development and achieve the SDGs agreed on and adopted by world leaders meeting at the United Nations Summit for the adoption of the post-2015 development agenda in September 2015[31].

Political and economic crises all over the world show that maintaining stability is no easy task. This might only be possible if countries can find consensus on their behaviour towards each other and the use of force. How can a country maintain stability or start a war? A country cannot do anything but its leaders and inhabitants definitely can. The coming decade may well see an ideological renaissance. The agenda for building a peace culture and developing peace leaders and activists requires actions by both the public and private sector. More recently the role of Higher Education Institutions in setting the platform for peace initiatives has been questioned. For the public sector, the development of rules of the game is a matter of common interest and urgency. Transparency of borders, availability of technologies, the universal expansion of democracy as a form of social organisation, and the total domination of communications means that everyone can contribute to peace initiatives.

Peace and leadership in the 21st century is not something that only governments need to pursue. The role of the private sector will also be critical. Private-sector companies have to become security conscious and responsible with their application of technology and information. Resource scarcity and climate change will place tremendous responsibility on organisations' social and environmental conscience.

Concluding remarks

It is sometimes wrongly alleged that leadership is an inherent gift that finds expression in personal characteristics such as intelligence, creativity and emotional strength. Followers of this approach are of the opinion that the above-mentioned and other personal characteristics, even to the exclusion of all other characteristics, could have a decisive influence on the ability of a person to lead. This predicament is highly applicable to peace leaders and activists. It is impossible, for obvious reasons, to categorise all the requirements of successful peace leaders and activists in the 21st century.

Fortunately, no fixed rules and regulations exist which a person must comply with in order to be labelled as a peace leader and activist. It was also noted that peace leaders and activists are not confined to a certain age or generation. However, an important prerequisite seems to be that a person must be able to realise his/her own shortcomings and make efforts to manage them. When peace leaders and activists reveal this characteristic, it can be expected that they will also be able to exercise a positive influence on the mutual relations they may have with others.

Finally, it appears as if all in the public and private sectors have the same primary interests, and this ideology may well be captured in the lyrics of the song titled *What He Means* by South African band Just Jinjer (Songwriter Ard Matthews, 2006). It is suggested that "With a little bit of ease and a little bit of calm, Acceptance is the key to all we know". Then three questions are posed: "What about a stir of compassion and lenience?; What about some understanding?; What about some sympathy"? The songwriter concludes that "what he means" is needed is "Peace, love, more tolerance, faith, hope, trust".

References

Crawley, H., and Skleparis, D. 2018. Refugees, migrants, neither, both: categorical fetishism and the politics of bounding in Europe's 'migration crisis'. *Journal of Ethnic and Migration Studies*, 44(1): 48-64.

Annan, K. 2017. Leadership and Governance for the Challenges of the 21st Century. Speech given by Kofi Annan. [online]. Junior Chamber International (JCI). Available from: www.kofiannanfoundation.org/annan-work/junior-chamber-international/ [Accessed 6 April 2018].

All Nobel Peace Prizes 2014. Nobelprize.org. [online]. Nobel Media. Available from: http://www.nobelprize.org/nobel_prizes/peace/laureates/ [Accessed 6 April 2018].

Building Leaders4Peace, 2018. Everyone can be a peacemaker. [online]. Available from: bl4p.com [Accessed 20 March 2018].

Delta Optimist, 2018. Rotary Club of Tsawwassen recruits future peace leaders. [online]. Delta Optimist. Available from: www.delta-optimist.com [Accessed 23 March 2018].

Development Dimensions International, 2018. Global Leadership Forecast 2018. [online]. Development Dimensions International. Available from: www.ddiworld.com/glf2018 [Accessed 20 April 2018].

Dylan, B. *The Times They Are A-Changin*. Available from: https://bobdylan.com/songs/times-they-are-changin/ [Accessed 16 April 2018].

Maslow, A. 1954. *Motivation and personality*. New York: Harper Collins.

Matthews, A. 2006. *What He Means* by Just Jinjer www.metrolyrics.com/what-he-means-lyrics-just-jinger.html.

Never Again International, 2018. Educating the Next Generation of Peace Leaders. [online]. Never Again International. Available from: http://www.neveragaininternationalcanada.org [Accessed 20 March 2018].

Oxford University Press. 2018 Oxford Dictionaries. [online]. Oxford. Available from: https://www.oxforddictionaries.com [Accessed 20 March 2018].

PR Newswire, 2017. American Future Leaders Connect in London and Walk for Peace with World Leaders. [online]. PR Newswire. Available from: https://www.prnewswire.com/news-releases/american-future-leaders-connect-in-london-and-walk-for-peace-with-world-leaders-654681163.html [Accessed 5 March 2018].

Stone, J. 29 August 2017. 'Angela Merkel says she wouldn't change the way she handled the refugee crisis'. *Independents News*. Available from: https://www.independent.co.uk/news/world/europe/angela-merkel-syrian-refugees-crisis-million-repeat-do-the-same-again-a7918811.html [Accessed 5 March 2018].

Strock, J. 2018. 21st Century Leaders list. [online]. Serve to Lead Group. Available from: https://servetolead.org [Accessed 6 March 2018].

Time WorldPress.com, 2018. Next Generation Leaders. [online]. Time WorldPress. Available from: time.com/collection/next-generation-leaders [Accessed 21 March 2018].

United Nations, 2018. Sustainable Developmental Goals. [online]. United Nations. Available from: https://www.un.org/sustainabledevelopment/sustainable-development-goals/ [Accessed 30 April 2018].

Worldatlas, 2018. Leaders Who Promoted World Peace and Non-Violence. [online]. Worldatlas. Available from: https://www.worldatlas.com/.../most-revered-leaders-who-promoted-world-peace [Accessed 15 April 2018].

Young, G. 2016. Women, Naturally Better Leaders for the 21st Century. The second White Paper in a new series on Transpersonal Leadership. [online]. Routledge. Available from: https://www.routledge.com/posts/10263 [Accessed 15 April 2018].

Endnotes

1. *Time* magazine's Person of the Year, 2015.
2. *Forbes*, 2016.
3. See endnote 1.
4. Crawley & Skleparis, 2018.
5. Young, 2016.
6. Oxford English Dictionary, 2018.
7. Ibid.
8. Ibid.
9. South African Constitution, 1996.
10. See endnote 1.
11. See endnote 5.
12. Development Dimensions International, 2018.
13. Codrington, 2008.
14. Ibid.
15. Strock, 2018.
16. See endnote 13.
17. Ibid.
18. Dylan, 1964.
19. See endnote 15.
20. Ibid.
21. See endnote 12.
22. Ibid.
23. Ibid.
24. See endnote 15.
25. See endnote 12.
26. Building Leaders4peace, 2018.
27. PR Newswire, 2017.
28. *Delta Optimist*, 2010.
29. Never Again International, 2018.
30. United Nations, 2018.
31. Ibid.

CHAPTER 11

HEALTHCARE FOR THE VULNERABLE AND ITS MEANING AND CONTRIBUTION TOWARDS PEACE LEADERSHIP

Laetus O.K. Lategan and Gert J. van Zyl

"I alone cannot change the world, but I can cast a stone across the waters to create many ripples." (Mother Teresa)

Spotlight: Oath of Hippocrates and the revised Declaration of Geneva

Medical history has represented doctors, nurses and therapists as professionals known for healing and caring for communities. The list of such people is endless. There are also a number of ethical oaths associated with the healing and caring for people. In this chapter the focus is on the well-known *Oath of Hippocrates* and the revised *Declaration of Geneva* as "spotlight figures". These oaths do not apply to any specific person but rather embody the attitudes and values that the community of doctors, nurses and therapists represent when healing and caring for people. In this sense these oaths, like many other oaths, are a metaphorical representation of who doctors, nurses and therapists should ideally be.

Although the Hippocratic Oath may no longer be in official use, the overall welfare of the patient remains the core of this oath. The welfare of the patient is supported through the application of knowledge and practice (identified as "art"): no harm to the patient either through intervention or advice, respect for life and respect for the patient[1]. The Declaration of Geneva adds value by focusing on the autonomy of the patient, the obligation of respect between teachers, colleagues and students, the obligation of doctors' self-care and quality of service[2].

The welfare of the patient will be used as the basis for the contribution to peace leadership. This chapter will build on the Hippocratic Oath and the Declaration of Geneva's emphasis on the welfare of patients. The contribution of this chapter to the theme of the book is to outline what guidelines can be identified from patient care that can inform a peace leadership framework. This is in line with communal intelligence (see Chapters 2 and 3 where communal intelligence was discussed), where it was set out that everyone in the community should be included in peace and peace-related efforts (including patients) and to be fair and just to everyone (including vulnerable groups of people like those in healthcare). This may ultimately lead to feelings of cohesiveness in the community and shared understanding so that everyone in the community may then understand the challenges of those who are vulnerable and that those people need to be supported. The intentional focus is on geriatric patients as part of a vulnerable group of people in healthcare and communities.

Introduction

Demographic studies and reports from the World Health Organisation are in agreement that the global village is facing a growing aging population. This development will bring new healthcare, socio-economic, food security, liveable accommodation and social challenges to the fore.

This development raises the questions as to the future social fabric of society: What kind of healthcare will be required, how can elderly people remain active in community and how can their cure and care contribute to their welfare and essentially the building of a just community?

On top of these questions is another question: how to cure and care for aging people due to their particular *vulnerability*. Their vulnerability is characterised by physical, mental, economic and social challenges, to name but a few. The situation becomes more complex when aging people are not always able to participate in decision-making (because of dementia), have access to medical facilities (for example, due to the absence of basic healthcare, mobility, language or location), take on a new family role (becoming a "parent" to a grandchild) and provide for a family (due to a social grant). This becomes even more problematic when dealing with geriatric patients who are, because of their dependence on healthcare, not in a position to participate effectively in society.

The Constitution of the WHO (adopted and signed in 1946 as amended) puts nine principles forward. It defines health as "a state of complete physical, mental and social well-being and not merely the absence of the disease or infirmity."[3] The Constitution identifies the enjoyment of health as a fundamental human right and it acknowledges health's contribution to the attainment of peace and security. With regard to the public health agenda the Constitution states: "Informed opinion and active co-operation on the part of the public are of the utmost importance in the improvement of the health of people."[4] The role of government is confirmed through the provision of adequate health and social services. From these principles is it evident that health includes physical, mental and social wellness. Medical and social determinants are important for securing health, a healthy society and the general wellbeing of people. Of particular interest in this chapter is the role of social determinants in the healthcare of geriatric patients. The importance is motivated by factors such as access to water and sanitation, waste management, accommodation and social wellbeing to enhance physical, mental and social health. There is no doubt that these social determinants should be developed and promoted. However, this activism is a major challenge due to the economic status of aging people.

This sparks the question of how to keep on mainstreaming aging people into a just community especially where the odds are not even.

The issue is therefore how to promote a healthy community given that not all, in this case geriatric patients, are in a position to participate in creating and maintaining such a community. This dilemma relates to consumerism which opens new challenges, amongst others, a *replacement culture*. If something is not good enough, then it is replaced without asking whether it still has any value. It is for this reason that the end-of-life debate, especially for geriatric patients, is linked to the purposefulness of geriatric patients for themselves or society at large.[5]

The problem is intensified amongst geriatric patients as they are part of a *vulnerable community*. UNAIDS define vulnerable communities as having some or all of the following characteristics: *limited economic development; inadequate protection of human rights and discrimination on the basis of the health status; inadequate community/cultural experience with the understanding of scientific research; limited availability of healthcare and treatment options; limited ability of individuals in the community to provide informed consent.*[6]

Vulnerability therefore includes human experiences such as ethical decision-making, physical suffering, psychological disorders, economic challenges and cultural orientation. These issues are imbedded in the ethical issues associated with geriatric healthcare.[7] Consequently this chapter will provide guidelines on how to deal with vulnerable communities in building a peaceful community. Following from this view is the question on what *ethical* guidelines are needed to promote humanity and dignity amongst geriatric patients.

In this chapter the nature of ethical well-being will first be discussed. Then the problems associated with health and healthcare will be set out whereafter the link between healthcare and peace leadership will be discussed. The chapter will end with solutions as well as recommendations on rethinking the integration between healthcare and peace leadership.

Background: ethical well-being

Medical ethics and bioethics are much debated due to a rapidly growing aging population, technological developments, cultural orientation and religious conviction. The values of Beauchamp and Childress' "Georgetown mantra" (respect for individuals and their autonomy, non-maleficence, beneficence and justice) are leading the discussion.[8] Although the emphasis is on humanity and dignity, there is a need to integrate ethics in all aspects of the healthcare value chain, namely *cure, care, control* (management) and *community* (family, friends and society).[9]

This observation leads to the conclusion that ethical well-being should be a *multi-phased* and *integrated* approach.

A multi-phased and integrated approach has as scope that a singular approach cannot be followed to address and solve a matter. The objective of this approach is to meet the challenge in such a way that it will contribute towards the common good of society.

When this observation is viewed from a public health perspective, one can say that public health puts a responsibility on government (as provider of health) and communities (as recipients of health services) to secure *jointly* the wellbeing of a community. Although the assumption is that the wellbeing of a community is a joint effort, this effort cannot be freed from *personal responsibility.* What is emphasised here is the individual who has a personal responsibility to contribute to a healthy society. Consider smoking, obesity, fitness, sugar consumption, sexual health, etc. The emphasis is on the "I" meeting the "other" in promoting health.

The emerging question is: How can geriatric patients, given their vulnerability with regard to health, access to and benefit from healthcare facilities, social engagement, self-care and self-worth, still live a meaningful and purposeful life if they are not in a position to contribute towards developing and upholding of such a community?

This is then the focus of this chapter: What kind of peace leadership for vulnerable groups, in particular geriatric patients, is needed? In this chapter the doctor, nurse and therapist will take on the role of a peace leader within a vulnerable community.

Health and healthcare: scoping the problem

Benatar comments that in South Africa the health of individuals and populations is a complex social construct:

> "… improvements in overall population health have been compromised by colonialism, apartheid, growing economic disparities, incompetence, corruption, and failure or delay in widely applying the benefits of many medical advances."[10]

He comments that in South Africa there are many reasons for health inequalities. Challenges include access, service delivery and effective usage of resources, new technologies and medicines. The drive to introduce National Health Insurance (NHI) to promote more equitable access to quality healthcare will be challenged by at least four things: (a) run-down and dysfunctional infrastructure must be replaced; (b) management practices must be improved; (c) resources must be used more effectively; and (d) many skilled and motivated healthcare workers must be trained and retrained. To start with, this will demand quality teaching and a changing working environment:

> "A priority must be to strengthen existing facilities and strive for high quality teaching, conditions of service and an ethos of care in clinical services that would encourage dedication by healthcare professionals to excellence, rather than merely to having job security and a salary."[11]

Evidently, it is the frustration of weak services, waste of resources, lack of knowledge of how to be scientific and competitive, a clash of cultures and values, bad management and poor politics that influences people's health. These matters are essentially linked to understanding the sociology of illness.[12]

The organisational challenges, often coupled with an absent work ethic, are further influenced by the many social determinants influencing health. This is based on the philosophy that health gains are better obtained when people's basic needs are met first. Principles of primary healthcare include equity in health service delivery, access to affordable and appropriate services, empowerment of people and sustainability of service provision. Primary healthcare allows for assessment of quality, appropriateness and impact of service delivery, identification of gaps and research development. What cannot be ignored is the impact of neoliberal economic policies and the broader impact of economic forces on primary healthcare delivery:

> "Primary health care requires structural re-organisation, a multidisciplinary team approach with clear lines of accountability, clear referral patterns in a two-way direction, improved access to health insurance to improve health coverage, and developing effective public-private partnerships. The universal core packages of health care should be evidence-based, cost effective and appropriate to local needs."[13]

These comments confirm the challenges that geriatric patients as a vulnerable group are experiencing. This triggers the question of how healthcare should be managed for these patients to optimise the improvement of health and to contribute to an inclusive and just society (peaceful society).

Peace leadership and healthcare

As already indicated, doctors, nurses and therapists can be considered as peace leaders due to the fact that they promote and support the vulnerable in a community context. By doing that, a more stable and flourishing community (and world) can emerge (peace). It was indicated in Chapters 2 and 3 that important communal values (as part of communal intelligence) entail inclusiveness, justness, cohesiveness and shared understanding.

To include, promote and support the vulnerable and, more specifically, geriatric patients in our community, should be seen as an effort to include an important section of our community in peace actions. Letting patients feel their needs are being heard and attended to support the idea of inclusiveness.

Treating these patients fairly is an act of justice that will support the idea of correctness and fairness within a community context. This links up with the role of health professionals and peace leadership.

By including geriatric patients in peace actions (helping and supporting them), as well as always acting in a just and fair way towards them, may lead to feelings of cohesiveness in the community. (In Chapter 3 cohesiveness was defined as: the quality of forming a united whole). Always including geriatric patients and the vulnerable in the community in peace actions and acting fairly towards them may lead to united feelings of "always help the vulnerable in our community".

Cohesiveness may lead to shared understanding. (In Chapter 3 shared understanding was defined as "everyone understands and accept a common problem"). Cohesiveness therefore can lead everyone in the community towards understanding the challenges of being a vulnerable member of the community and accepting the challenge of helping/supporting them.

Peace, as defined by the scope of this book, starts with self-insight and awareness which then cultivates a humanity that will influence community positively. Peace is therefore growing from an individual perspective to a communal perspective. Such a perspective does not imply that a communal perspective does not influence the individual's approach. Peace is therefore created through an ecological approach – meaning the diversity of participants contributes to growing and maintaining peace.

In view of this approach peace is defined as the harmonious relationship between people and structures/institutions in society. Harmonious relationships should lead to righteousness as the basis for peace. Consider economic disparities. As economic differences resulted in an unequal society, economic rights can never be ignored in peace making. In the context of healthcare, the application of economic righteousness is found in equal treatment for all regardless of economic, cultural or societal status. The gaps in healthcare delivery should be closed for those who do not have economic or social status. Peace is therefore essentially about creating and sustaining social justice.[14] This is an ongoing effort. This perspective is further informed by Gabrielle who investigates the contributions J.F. Kennedy and Martin Luther King Jnr. made towards social justice. He says that their acts are well captured by an agricultural metaphor of *planting* and *harvesting*. The actions associated with this metaphor are never-ending. Planting and harvesting are not once-off activities; they are ongoing and never-ending:

> "Much can be gleaned from the land at harvest time. It certainly has its own challenges and immensely hard work. And many a times the harvest is itself another call, a call to embrace and then be nourished so as to continue the rough process of farming into future seasons. You see, the season of ploughing and harvesting never ends."[15]

This metaphor has a significant meaning for peace: peace is *action* (plant and harvest), it is an *engaged* activity (plant to harvest), it creates *expectation* (harvesting), it is *ongoing* (no harvesting without planting) and it is *organised* (plant and harvest). This metaphor can further be aligned with the theme of the book: *multiple contributions are required to maintain, grow and prosper peace.* Peace is therefore not a once-off activity but a continuum of activities.

These perspectives merge into the central framework that healthcare is an important role player in peace.

The next paragraph offers a "statute" as proposed therapy.

Solutions: proposed therapy

The proposed "therapy" is the design of a "statute" for vulnerable groups grounded in healthcare ethics which peace leaders can follow. Healthcare ethics can be defined as the principles informing the moral practices and behaviour of healthcare practitioners towards patients in the performance of healthcare.[16] It is further emphasised that healthcare ethics include Glouberman and Mintzberg's four worlds associated with healthcare (cure, care, control and community – see paragraph 2 of this chapter).

Based on this, the following guidelines can be presented as the basis for such a "statute":

- Due to technological developments and possibilities, cultural orientation and religious conviction, a *single* answer for/solution to a problem is no longer feasible. The proverbial distinction between "right" and "wrong" may not be as straightforward as one may think. "Right" and "wrong" have become very much *context*-specific and influenced by *individual* orientation. This demands the unpacking of the moral dilemma. This comment is well illustrated by MacKinnon and Comer's study (2017)[17] on the role of culture, values and faith in life-ending decisions as these are informed by personal beliefs and orientation. What is more, it is not only the patient who has a specific view of culture, values and faith but the doctor, healthcare practitioners and family too. These values can also change over time. The solution is for the doctor and healthcare practitioner to understand their own culture, values and beliefs and then to understand that of the patient. The pointer here is that there cannot be the claim that one's view is the only view that is correct. Also, regarding decision-making, it is not simply about having a "right" or a "wrong" answer but to contextualise the answer given the particular circumstances. This makes any situation extremely vulnerable. The dictum "do no harm" should prevail under all circumstances[18].
- Ethics can never be removed from the personal meaning or interpretation a person attributes to ethics. Lips[19] comments on this view by saying that one's own ethical view forms the basis of ethical behaviour towards others. His view is grounded in the understanding that a person is part of a bigger group dynamic. Hence ethical behaviour towards other people/the group cannot be divorced from its effect towards oneself. The value of this observation is that healthcare practitioners have a responsibility not only to other people, but also to themselves regardless of what the personal orientation is. The art is not to impose one's own views on patients but to meet them in a context of dual respect and care.
- Identifying the moral dilemma depends on a comprehensive understanding of underlying ethical challenges. Solving one problem can easily grow into a series of ethical dilemmas if one is not careful. An example is life-ending support simply not being provided because it is too expensive to treat geriatric patients, the necessary facilities may not be available or the economic inactiveness of geriatric patients. This requires the repetitive review of a situation. The implication is that healthcare ethics should become a way of living within the medical industry instead of a tick-box approach that will simply confirm compliance. It is therefore appropriate to recall the well-known question of whether one should do what one can do. Technological power and ability should always be subjected to their potential ethical implications.

- Motive, outcome and consequences are three integrated links in the ethical value chain. These links depend on discussion, decision-making and review. This approach implies a team approach rather than an individual approach. Ethics, in general, is still trapped by the public perception that it (ethics) is an individual act, a hollow call against unjust actions, and not able to bring an end to individual and public dilemmas. The lead question should always be: Why was a decision taken, what was the basis for this decision, were the potential consequences calculated before the decision was taken and how did this decision contribute towards the behaviour of either the patients and/or the doctor and healthcare practitioner? What should be listed here is the common approach, which is to jointly own the problem, jointly contribute towards solving the problem and jointly own the solution.

- The ethical value chain must be managed for its quality of outcome but also its quality of relationship. The ethical value chain is characterised by input, process, outcome, outputs and impact. Most important in healthcare is the relationship that should be oriented towards the interaction between those who cure and care and those who are cured and/or cared for. This should be regarded as the impact of all actions within the value chain. To this well-known chain can be added "uptake" and "policy" – what difference is one making and what was put in place to steer a particular activity? A leading question is linked to the sustainability of outcome. Ethics is open, transparent and transformative: it wants to move from where one "is" to where one "ought" to be.

- Ethical decision-making can never be removed from the human "experience". Ethics has its origin in motive (why am I doing this?), habitat (what is the context for the decisions taken?) and the common good (what do I hope to achieve through this decision?). One can refer to motive, habitat and common good as the triple bottom of ethical decision-making. The point stretched with this comment is that decision-making is no sterile action as it has to consider the effect it may have on the individual and his/her situation. Ethical decision-making should be understood against the metaphor of the white cloak which refers to purity of intention, protection and safeguarding. Uvijn[20] comments by saying that it is not so much about which ethical indicators to apply but more about how to address a problem.

- Ethics reflects personal behaviour as an expression of one's personality and personal orientation. Ethics is also behaviour towards the other, organisations and institutions, culture, nature (environment) and structure. "Do not harm" and "do unto others ..." are the cornerstones of all ethical behaviour. The way in which one behaves towards other people is reflected in the statement that the individual's ethical orientation is expressed through the mercy the individual has for other people. The way in which one behaves is an indicator of one's own ethical orientation. Poor behaviour is an indication of one's own ethical armour and an expression of a questionable ethical orientation. Baur, Van Nistelrooij and Vanlaere[21] argue that the various emotions caregivers experience should be allowed to be expressed in the workplace as this conveys the needs and therefore the vulnerability of the caregiver but also forms a basis from which to develop ethical behaviour.

- Managing healthcare cannot be removed from business ethics. Fundamental questions with regard to behaviour, decision-making and profit margins should be asked. For example, does the quality of treatment depend on the money available for the treatment or is it based on both monetary and humanitarian orientations? (An "added" plus or an "integrated" orientation?) Patients and clients want to experience ethics as the safety net for healthcare management. The downside is also important to understand. Sometimes professional disobedience is the only way out of a moral dilemma. This means that when all reasonable attempts have failed to bring a dilemma to the attention of healthcare managers, then the individual may not have any other choice than to be professionally disobedient through, for example, a strike, to highlight the existing challenge.[22]
- The public would like to have confidence in the wellbeing of the patient. One should never forget the anxiety of dealing with an unknown future (outcome of diagnosis and treatment) through unfamiliar devices, apparatus and treatment. This is particularly evident in the fear for technology if a patient has never been exposed to technology before. Healthcare is not only about treatment. It is essentially about healing. Healing is also not limited to physical healing but includes mental, psychological and ecological healing. Egnew[23] highlights the healthcare practitioners' relationship with the patient. Here the focus is on balancing personal responses to patients through their professional engagement. The emphasis should primarily be on what is good for the patient. Here personal choice and opinions should be put aside in the interest of the patient and the care of the patient.
- Ethics demands uptake and innovation. Ethical uptake refers to what the healthcare industry, community and politicians can do to improve on the quality of healthcare as service, as relation and as agent for just health. Given the inequality in a society, one cannot ignore that different systems (private and basic healthcare), access (language, distance, money, comprehension) and improvement (diet, living conditions, mental health) all have an influence on the well-being of a person. Ethics must become entrepreneurial too. Here is it not only about improving the behaviour, but about behaving differently.

This statute will form the basis of the proposed peace leadership framework. The perspectives gained from the discussion on geriatric patients will inform this framework.

Recommendation: rethinking healthcare and peace leadership

It is evident that a new debate is emerging around patient care. The focus is not only on the patient but also the healthcare practitioner, the healthcare service providers, the healthcare managers and the community either as family and friends, or private or public institutions. In short, the emphasis is no longer on the patient only. This is not suggesting a shift away from the patient but rather a strengthening of the relationship with supportive networks.

The purpose is to contribute to a *quality relationship* with the patient.[24] Murphy[25] writes about the leading principle for healthcare: "first, do no harm". She states that this must be the guiding principle for healthcare workers. This can never be separated from the rights of the individual (individualism) and also the rights of the community.

Fundamental values in healthcare are the responsibility of care for others, the burden of knowing privileged information and the feeling of unworthiness, and the necessity to know oneself as a prerequisite to forming a therapeutic relationship with a patient. These matters have been submerged in concerns about emerging technologies, regulatory compliance, metrics and return on investment.

As a result of this shift the focus is now on an integrated understanding of the patient, medicine and healthcare.

This calls for a different look at ethical behaviour in healthcare and how it can contribute towards peace leadership. Three important baseline perspectives can be presented: healthcare ethics as *professional* behaviour, healthcare ethics as *relationship* and healthcare ethics as *compassion*.

For Luban[26] *professional ethics* has two distinct meanings. Firstly, it is an occupational ethics, for example, medicine, and secondly, it is a doctrine with related concepts common to all subjects and sub-fields. A serious concern is the loss of professionalism and the rise of commercialism. Verbruggen[27] refers to professional ethics as the ethical basis of what one does which is different from a personal moral code. Although there can be a central motive to care, for example, personal ethics will inform how it should be done. This cannot be reduced to a private responsibility only. He argues that law, professional codes and ethics cannot be separated and that these parts form the basis for good care. Ethics is therefore regarded as of the highest value. Ethics will supersede the law when it comes to good and just behaviour. The pointer here is that although healthcare is essentially about cure and care, the way it is practised and implemented can never be outside the realm of professional ethics.

A thought-provoking perspective on healthcare as relationship is suggested by Baur, Van Nistelrooij and Vanlaere.[28] Their research is on *care ethical perspectives* for caregivers. They consider care ethics to be "an interdisciplinary field of studies concerning care as a central human practice, with moral and political relevance."[29] They define care as a *relationship*. Care ethics is *relational* and *interdependent*. Care is contextual and bound to particular situations. They argue for an active attention to the caregiver. Caregivers' emotional experiences should be part of caring practices. Care organisations should also create a moral space within which to function. It is important to pay attention to the experiences and emotional wellbeing of healthcare professionals. Doing so will enhance their own well-being and that of their patients. It is here that ethics education can assist to expose healthcare practitioners to as many situations and emotions as possible.

Egnew[30] adds another dimension to healthcare: for him there is a recognisable shift from *expert-doer* to *servant-accompanier*. This requires physicians to attend to how they *behave* towards patients as well as what they *do* for them. This requires a new approach to healthcare. For example: promote access to and continuity of care, provide for home visits, spend time with patients and provide parity in funding for mental health issues.

These perspectives coincide with those of Teboada[31] who argues for a more compassionate medical ethics. Her views coincide with those of Singer who promotes an ethics where the experiences and activities of healthcare practitioners are also acknowledged. Teboada comments:

> "The physician–patient relationship is neither a-historical, a-cultural nor an abstract rational notion; persons are always persons-in-relation, are always members of communities, are immersed in a tradition and belong to a particular culture."[32]

Teboada outlines two key elements of compassion: Firstly, to enter another person's situation in order to understand the person's experience of suffering and secondly, to relieve suffering or at least to support a person. This requires a self-commitment to the other and a continual readiness to perform fundamental acts. For her, compassion is firstly directed to a person and then the suffering.[33]

Although mindful of the emphasis on the quality of care through professional ethics, care ethics and compassionate ethics, no ethical engagement goes without the challenge of power relationships, knowing personal and professional boundaries and knowing how to engage with communities.[34] This is further challenged by the complexity of decision-making where there is not a common platform.[35] Vervotte[36] captures the new relationship between healthcare practitioner and patient well by saying that the patient is now at the helm of healthcare. The shift is first from *providing* care to care on *demand* to *negotiated* care. The caregiver is no longer the one who knows it all but has to co-determine with the patient what the needs are.

The rethinking of healthcare, especially for geriatric patients as a vulnerable group, suggests a framework for peace leadership which will be discussed below.

Direction: foundations for peace leadership

This chapter identified several pointers that can be used as basis for a peace leadership framework for vulnerable groups, especially geriatric patients. The following building blocks can be presented:

- Healthcare has as its aim promoting health and sustaining the wellbeing of patients. In curing and caring for patients it is not exclusively about the prolonging of life but about creating a *relationship* with the patient that will secure wellbeing long after the treatment of a disease.

  Building block 1: establish a quality relationship with the patient.

- Curing and caring for geriatric patients as part of a vulnerable group of people, demands a *respectful relationship* especially in those cases where there is limited or no communication, the patient is in palliative care, or the patient is handicapped or has lost all self-worth (for example, has been reduced to wearing a nappy).

  Building block 2: respect for the patient and his/her situation is part of the relationship.

- Healthcare is not about the patient only, but about all engaged with healthcare to secure health and sustainable living. Respect is therefore extended to all who cure, care, control and to the community.

  Building block 3: A respectful relationship is part of the four worlds of healthcare.

- Geriatric patients are vulnerable due to their circumstances, needs and growing presence in society but declining participation in societal activities.

  Building block 4: Vulnerability due to situation and circumstances requires special leadership to secure wellbeing of the vulnerable.

- Healthcare plays an important role in uplifting the welfare and wellbeing of society. Healthcare is therefore also a contributor to peace in society. If peace is about righteousness, harmony and closing the gap in society, then healthcare is a leading role player to secure peace in society.

Building block 5: Healthcare is a lead player in the promotion of peace.

- Ethical coaching is required to educate society on the new ethical role of healthcare, the multiple role players in healthcare and the shift of emphasis to a doctor who takes the decision on his/her own to play an integrated role where patient, care provider, management and community have to play a role too.

Building block 6: Ethical coaching can establish an integrated approach to healthcare.

- Healthcare ethics has as objective value-driven care for patients. This is now extended to more role players and institutions. This extended view of healthcare ethics has also brought about an extended responsibility. This responsibility is not limited to healthcare providers only, but extends to all who are involved in healthcare either of oneself, the other or the institution/organisation.

Building block 7: The new approach to healthcare requires a shared responsibility.

- An integrated approach to healthcare should change the lived experience of geriatric patients, especially in their vulnerable state. Healthcare has the responsibility to restore justice, dignity and to create meaningful closeness.

Building block 8: Healthcare should secure dignity and foster closeness.

- Geriatric care is not about the doctor, care provider or care receiver only, but also about the institution or organisation. Geriatric care should positively contribute towards changing structures and relationships to secure wellbeing and care.

Building block 9: Care should change people and structures.

- Leadership is the ability to get buy-in, to create expectation and to see the benefits of an endeavour. Healthcare leadership should bring visible change about for the benefit of people and structures.

Building block 10: Leadership should enable people to "see" and "experience" change.

Concluding remarks

The Hippocratic Oath and the Declaration of Geneva were identified as "spotlight figures" in this chapter. The oath and declaration's emphasis on the cure and care for the patient were extended to the care of healthcare practitioners and the recognition that social structures and management should be included in care too.

The chapter builds on the respect for patients by promoting the role that healthcare, in its extended form, can play in patient care. The arguments continued to build an integrated approach to healthcare that can contribute to just medicine. The ten building blocks described as part of the framework of peace leadership can be used to attain this status.

Although not at the centre of this oath and declaration, no peace can prevail if care for the elderly as a vulnerable group but also growing entity is not taken on as a priority in healthcare and society!

References

ASTHO™. 2018. *The economic case for health equity.* 1-11. Available from http://www.astho. org/Programs/Health-Equity/Economic-Case-Issue-Brief/. [Accessed 1 May 2018].

Baur, V., Van Nistelrooij, I. and Vanlaere, L. 2017. The sensible health care professional: a care ethical perspective on the role of caregivers in emotionally turbulent practices. *Medical Health Care and Philosophy.* 1-8. Available from https://www.ncbi.nlm.nih.gov/pubmed/28432482. [Accessed 1 May 2018].

Beauchamp T.L. and Childress, J.F. 2013. *Principles of biomedical ethics.* Oxford: Oxford University Press.

Benatar, S.R. 1998. Global disparities in health and human rights: a critical commentary. *American Journal of Public Health,* 88(2): 295-300.

Benatar, S.R., Daar, A.S. and Singer, P.A. 2003. Global Health ethics: the rationale for mutual caring. *International Affairs*, 79(1): 107-138.

Benatar, S.R. 2013. Editorial: The challenge of health disparities in South Africa. *South African Medical Journal,* 103(3): 154-155.

Burggraeve, R. 2016. *An ethics of mercy: on the way to meaningful living and loving.* Leuven: Peters.

Creplet, J. 2013. *De derde revolutie in de geneeskunde.* Brussel: Pharma.be vzw.

Dookie, S. and Singh, S. 2012. Primary health services at district levels in South Africa. A critique of the primary healthcare approach. *BioMed Central Family Practice.* 1-8. Available from https://bmcfampract.biomedcentral.com/articles/10.1186/1471-2296-13-67. [Accessed 1 May, 2018].

Egnew, T.R. 2009. Suffering, meaning and healing. Challenges of contemporary medicine. *Annual Family Medicine,* 2009 (7): 170-175.

Gabrielle, E.F. 2018. From plough to harvest. *Journal of Human and Health Experience,* 4(1): 19-21.

Glouberman, S. and Mintzberg, H. 2001. Managing the care of health and the cure of disease. Part 1: Differentiation. *Health Care Management Review.* Winter: 56-69.

Hippocratic Oath. Available from https://en.wikipedia.org/wiki/Hippocratic_Oath [Accessed 1 May, 2018].

Holtzer, L. 2015. *De 7 privleges van de zorg.* Leuven: Acco.

Lategan, L.O.K. and Van Zyl, G.J. 2017a. An introduction to healthcare ethics. In Lategan, L.O.K. and Van Zyl, G.J. (eds.). *Healthcare ethics for healthcare practitioners.* Bloemfontein: SUN MeDIA. 5-10.

Lategan, L.O.K. and Van Zyl, G.J. 2017b. Healthcare ethics code. In Lategan, L.O.K. and Van Zyl, G.J. (editors). *Healthcare ethics for healthcare practitioners.* Bloemfontein: SUN MeDIA. 130-131.

Lips, D. Ethiek kan niet worden losgekoppeld van die zin die men aan het eigen leven geeft. *Ethische Perspectieven,* 16(2): 174-188.

Luban, D. 2005. Professional ethics. In Frey, R.G. and Wellman, C.H. (eds.). *A companion to applied ethics.* Oxford: Blackwell Publishing. 583-596.

McKinnon, J. and Comer, A. 2017. The influence of culture, values and faith on end-life decisions. In Lategan, L.O.K. and Van Zyl, G.J. (eds.). *Healthcare ethics for healthcare practitioners.* Bloemfontein: SUN MeDIA. 53- 63.

Murphy, K. 2014. The ethics of infection. *New York Times,* 8 November. p. SR5.

Nys, H. 2013. Medicalisering van levenseinde neemt toe. In Nuyens, Y. and De Ridder, H. (reds.). *Dokter ik heb ook iets te zeggen.* Tielt. Lannoo Campus. 174-186.

Phalime, M. 2014. *Postmortem: The doctor who walked away. A true story.* Cape Town: Tafelberg.

Republic of South Africa. Department of Health. 2004. Ethics in health research: principles, structures and processes. Available from http://learning.ufs.ac.za/FST309_ON/Resources/2%20RESOURCES/2.Study%20Material/1.Ethics/DoH%20Ethics%20in%20health%20research%20-%20Principles,%20structures%20and%20processes%20(2004).pdf [Assessed 17 July 2018].

Scofield, G.R. 2008. What is medical ethics consultation? *The Journal of Law, Medicine and Ethics,* 36(1): 95-118.

Taboada, P. 2004. *How do we conceive a "more compassionate" medical ethics?* International Association for Hospice and Palliative Care Resources. Available from http://www.hospicecare.com/ethics/monthlypiece/ethics2004. [Accessed 1 May, 2018].

Uvijn, K. 2013. Ethiek als actieve praktijk. In Van Kerckhove, C., De Kock, C. and Vens, E. (eds.). *Ethiek en zorg in de hulpverlening. Over taboes gesproken.* Gent: Academia Press. 169-168.

Vanlaere, L. and Burggraeve, R. 2014. *Gekkenwerk: Kleine ondeugden voor zorgdragers.* Tielt: Uitgeverij Lannoo Campus.

Vanlaere, L. and Burggraeve, R. 2017. The quality of healthcare: a care ethics approach. In Lategan, L.O.K. and Van Zyl, G.J. (eds.). *Healthcare ethics for healthcare practitioners.* Bloemfontein: SUN MeDIA. 43-52.

Van Zyl, G.J. and Van Zyl, P. 2017. The difference between right and wrong. In Lategan, L.O.K. and Van Zyl, G.J. (eds.). *Healthcare ethics for healthcare practitioners.* Bloemfontein: SUN MeDIA. 27-41.

Verbruggen, A. 2013. Over de verhouding tussen beroepsethiek, deontologische codes, wetten en een 'goede' beroepsuitoefening. In Van Kerckhove, C., De Kock, C. and Vens, E. (eds.). *Ethiek en zorg in de hulpverlening. Over taboes gesproken.* Gent: Academia Press. 159-176.

Vervotte, I. 2013. We zijn nou anders ziek dan 40 jaar geleden. In Nuyens, Y. and De Ridder, H. (reds.). *Dokter ik heb ook iets te zeggen.* Tielt. Lannoo Campus. 16-29.

World Health Organization. 1946. Constitution of the World Health Organization: Principles. Available from http:/www.who.int/about/mission. [Accessed 13 July 2017].

World Medical Association Declaration of Geneva. 2017. Available from https://jamanetwork.com/journals/jama/fullarticle/2658261 [Accessed 1 May, 2018].

Endnotes

1   Hippocratic Oath
2   World Medical Association Declaration of Geneva, 2017
3   World Health Organisation, 1946
4   Ibid.
5   Nys, 2013
6   Republic of South Africa, Department of Health, 2004: 48
7   Lategan & Van Zyl, 2017a: 9
8   Beauchamp & Childress, 2013
9   Glouberman & Mintzberg, 2001
10   Benatar, 2013: 2
11   Ibid.
12   Phalime, 2014
13   Dookie & Singh, 2012: 4
14   ASTHO™, 2018; Benatar, 1998; and Benatar, Daar & Singer, 2003
15   Gabrielle, 2018: 20.
16   Lategan & Van Zyl, 2017a: 6
17   MacKinnon & Comer, 2017
18   Van Zyl & Van Zyl, 2017
19   Lips, 2006
20   Uvijn, 2013: 175
21   Baur, Van Nistelrooij & Vanlaere, 2017: 1-9
22   See Burggraeve, 2016: 114ff
23   Egnew, 2009: 173
24   Holtzer, 2015; Criplet, 2013; Vanlaere & Burggraeve, 2014; Vanlaere & Burggraeve, 2017 and Lategan & Van Zyl, 2017b
25   Murphy, 2014: SR5
26   Luban, 2005: 583, 585
27   Verbruggen, 2013: 161, 162, 167-168
28   Baur, Van Nistelrooij & Vanlaere, 2017: 1-9
29   Baur, Van Nistelrooij & Vanlaere, 2017: 3
30   Egnew, 2009: 173, 174
31   Teboada, 2011
32   Ibid.
33   Ibid.
34   See Scofield, 2008
35   MacKinnon & Comer, 2017
36   Vervotte, 2013:23

CHAPTER 12

PEACE LEADERSHIP: WORKING FROM HELPLESSNESS TO SERVING THE COMMUNITY

Carol Dalglish and Ebben van Zyl

"While leadership is necessary at every stage, beginning with the first spark that awakens people's hopes, its vital role is to create and expand the opportunities that empower people to pursue happiness for themselves."[1]

Spotlight: Jonas Fortuna Quembo

Jonas is not an internationally known name. Nor are any of the other case studies/ profiles included in this chapter. Each is an example of peace leadership to be found amongst some of the poorest people in Africa. Jonas was born in 1980. He was brought up in poverty by illiterate parents who survived by subsistence farming. He was a second child of a second wife and had one brother and three sisters. One sister has recently died.

One of the greatest challenges Jonas has faced was getting an education as there were no resources and no family imperative. However, he did manage not only to put himself through school, but he also learnt Portuguese and English and has recently graduated from university. Getting married was considered the way of showing adulthood, and in 2002 he married Guida and has one son, Jireldo.

His father was a local unpaid pastor. As he grew up he wanted to follow in the footsteps of his father but did not want the lifestyle his father lived. He really wanted to run away. He went to university to study to be a teacher, then thought he would become an academic, but his background caught up with him. He eventually became a pastor and established a church in 2006. His church has grown from a small congregation to over 200 and he has an active Facebook page that takes his message to a very wide range of people – often the more privileged, who have access to the technology.

He is an interpreter and trainer for Despertai Mozambique, a community organisation that will be the main thrust of this chapter:

> "I believe in the mission of Desperate for I know what it is to live without hope, food and resources for daily living. Seeing old men sending their grandchildren to school; people who were having one meal are having two meals. This makes me happy."

He is committed to the vision of empowering people and giving them knowledge, hope and opportunity. These are also the foundations of peace.

Introduction

The greatest challenge for the world's leaders is the most intractable problem facing humanity in the 21st century: the basic wants of the world's poor[2]. This is particularly relevant in Africa, which has loosened the ties of colonial exploitation but not yet found a way to value and assist the poor. The central strategic failures of past approaches have often arisen from the assumption that money and technology were essential to overcoming poverty.

The human capital existing among the poor is often ignored. An effective peace leadership strategy would provide a host of listeners who would hear the voices of the poor rather than imposing other people's solutions. The poor cannot intellectually lift themselves by their own bootstraps because they have no bootstraps[3]. Leadership needs to listen closely to the wants of the poor and recognise them as actionable needs, and that the poor are both worthy of help and capable of benefiting greatly from appropriate strategies. Then resources, both material and intellectual, can be applied to answer them directly.

In chapter one various descriptions or definitions of leadership and peace leadership are outlined. This chapter focuses on how self-awareness, self-development and self-mastery can lead to 'lead others' and 'lead community'. Lipman-Blumen[4], as cited in chapter one, defines leadership as follows[5]:

> "Peace, as conceptualised here, must be broadly defined to mean far more than the absence of war. Peace must stand on a foundation of justice, equality, sustainability, and all the other societal and human needs required for the world's citizenry to live productively, harmoniously and happily. We must realise Ubuntu in action."[6]

In this chapter background information about the needs and challenges of the poor in Africa and in Mozambique will be discussed. Awaken Mozambique, as a non-profit organisation to assist the urban poor in Mozambique, will then be discussed as an example of a company enhancing peace by helping and supporting the poor. Different real-life case studies of people being helped by Awaken Mozambique will then be discussed to indicate what effect support and empowerment had on their lives. This support also transformed those people described into peace leaders due to their support of others. Lastly, some recommendations and concluding remarks will be given.

African background

If statements are to be made about the poor it is important to understand the nature of the challenges that face leaders trying to overcome the disadvantages of history and the nature of the poverty that is to be found in Africa, whatever its original cause may have been. This will then be narrowed down to Mozambique where the project, Despertai Mozambique, is operating.

Selected facts about poverty in Africa paint a less than rosy view, particularly given the wealth that lies in Africa and the rest of the world[7]:

- More than 50% of Africans suffer from water-related diseases such as cholera and infant diarrhoea.
- Every 30 seconds an African child dies of malaria – more than 1 million child deaths a year.
- Of the 300 million children around the world who go to bed hungry every night, only 8 percent are victims of famine or other emergency situations.
- More than 40 percent of Africans do not have the ability to obtain sufficient food on a day-to-day basis.
- For the African farmer conventional fertilisers cost two to six times more than world market price.
- A woman in Sub-Saharan Africa has a 1 in 16 chance of dying in childbirth or during pregnancy. This compares with a 1 in 3,700 risk for women in North America.
- More than 40 percent of women in Africa do not have access to basic education.

Poverty probably presents the greatest of the strategic leadership challenges if peace is to be achieved. One third of the world (2 billion people) remains trapped in extreme poverty, unrelieved by the global economic growth which has benefited so many. Not only does this cause hardship for the poor, it creates great risks for the rest of us. Burns[8] argued that:

> "No leader can truly lead if they cannot respond to the wants of followers, if they fail to elevate and empower them. No leader can truly lead if lacking in the ability to produce intended change through creative innovation. A leader not only speaks to the immediate wants of followers but elevates people by vesting

in them a sense of possibility – a belief that changes can be made and that they can make them."[9]

The crucial factor in the dynamic comes into play at the outset, the building of efficacy. There is much to suggest that this is not a priority for leaders in Africa (and elsewhere). Prestige for leaders tends to come from the international stage, not giving a voice to the voiceless.

Wangari[10] identified the past as a significant psychological problem that may take decades to overcome. A dangerous and unfortunate psychological process that perhaps affirmed to Africans their inability to be agents of their own destiny. Eventually it may destroy the sense of confidence they should and must have to make progress. Building this confidence and enabling the poor to take greater control of their future is a critical role for leaders and governments[11].

Massinguw[12] claims that if government and leaders made it their mission to provide a latrine for every household and teach basic hygiene, particularly in schools and churches, countless lives would be saved. They can do this. In addition, this would provide all Africans with a degree of dignity that millions do not have at the moment.

Mozambique

Mozambique lies along the Indian Ocean border of Southern Africa and is one of the poorest countries in the world. It is poor even by African standards. This poverty is largely attributable to a history of both human and natural destruction, from slavery and wars to drought and floods. As an economy Beira is struggling; its physical infrastructure is broken and the people are poorly educated. They have limited access to services and few opportunities to advance.

Most ordinary Mozambiquans equated democracy with an improvement in material conditions. Instead, the economic gains thus far seem to benefit a relatively small middle class concentrated around capital cities. The rest of the country has had to adjust to increases in the cost of living and little change in the rudimentary public and social infrastructure. The widening gap between rich and poor may pose a threat to political stability and peace. By the late 1990s the economy had begun sustained growth but social inequality has grown as well[13].

In Mozambique 61 per cent of the population live on less than $1.25 a day[14]. The GNI per capita, in 2012 was $1 020 per annum. The poorest 40% earn 14% of household income and the richest 20% earn 51%. There are 95 dependents per 100 work-age adults[15]. In addition to the problems that arise from this, only 11% have access to electricity, the supply of which is often unreliable. This presents significant challenges for leaders who wish to represent the community as a whole, rather than appealing to old, tribal loyalties. Training and development of self-confidence and self-efficacy become important to effective leadership and followership. The new communications technologies cannot be relied on to share the message – the old ways work[16].

The challenges facing the people and the government of Mozambique, the leaders at all levels, include overcoming low educational standards, high levels of unemployment, weak infrastructure, bureaucratised government, corruption and very high mortality levels from curable diseases such as malaria, tuberculosis, cholera, leprosy and HIV/AIDS. Most of all, perhaps leaders have to demonstrate that things can be different; they need to develop the self-efficacy of their followers[17].

The civil war led to considerable migration from rural areas to the cities. The waves of drought and floods did the same. Urban environments, unprepared for the challenge, had to welcome the ever-rising number of displaced people who were seeking shelter, protection, work and sustenance. Beira was designed for a population of 30,000 but had a population of just under 500,000 according to a 2007 census[18]. Most of these internal migrants are illiterate subsistence farmers who have little opportunity to earn a living in the city.

However, the potential of the poor should not be underestimated. What is needed is an individualised focus on what individuals can achieve given targeted assistance.

Solutions

Awaken Mozambique/Despertai Mozambique

Despertai Mozambique is a small not-for-profit organisation that works with the urban poor in Beira to encourage entrepreneurial activity through the provision of financial services, training and support, and undertakes research to improve understanding of the challenges facing families in this context.

The clients of Despertai Mozambique are the urban poor who desire to set up or grow micro businesses to support their families. The staff in Beira are all local people who live in the poor peri-urban suburbs they serve. Whilst the project is funded from Australia, no Australian wages are paid. Formal employment opportunities in Beira are rare, require good levels of education, and are insecure. Eighty percent of the total economic activity that takes place is in the informal sector. These are the people who must lead or be led if peace is to become the necessary background to effective economic development[19].

The Awaken Mozambique project has clear objectives. They have remained in place while the means of achieving them changes with circumstances. They are:

1. To provide financial and training support to micro-enterprises in Mozambique in a sustainable manner.
2. To build capacity by developing expertise in management, micro-finance and enterprise development. Access to education and training has been very limited in Mozambique, restricting the capacity to develop effective organisations and industries.
3. To develop international linkages between entrepreneurs in Mozambique and the developed world.
4. To collect data and build research into the process of enterprise start-up and growth in a developing economy.

The inclusion of local expertise and support allows individuals to make productive use of the private and local knowledge to which they have access, thereby giving value to their perspective and creating ownership. Recognising and valuing local expertise is critical for access to local networks and to local participation. Leaders need to be connected to those they wish to lead. Chamlee-Wright[20] recognises that tapping into the knowledge embedded within local social institutions lowers transaction costs, saves time, and helps to anticipate and avoid pitfalls. Many African leaders are drawn from the elite and have attempted to widen rather than narrow the gap between them and those they seek to help. Experience in Beira shows that local expertise is initially insufficient as locals do not have access to a sufficiently wide base of knowledge and expertise. Building capacity becomes critically important. Self-awareness and capacity building are equally important among those who hope to lead.

Despertai Mozambique used participative methods involving the local small business people to shift the focus from a deficit approach that focuses on survival and assumption of limited human resources, to one that acknowledges people's resources and agency in the pursuit of business success and the wellbeing of their families and the community. The feedback received offered the opportunity to generate new information about the way in which people see the world and enabled models for delivery of services to be developed in ways that meet the specific needs of the local community[21].

In 2004 Dr Carol Dalglish went to Mozambique to conduct seminars and do research with some of Beira's poorest entrepreneurs. She was very impressed by their courage and willingness to learn and planned to do a long-term study. When she returned in 2006 it was to find that the support for these entrepreneurs had been withdrawn. The local people asked for her help. There was so much commitment and wasted potential that she couldn't say no and that is how Awaken Mozambique was born.

The local staff are drawn from the poor community and have had to learn how to run an organisation and support very poor entrepreneurs. They provide training, interest-free finance and support to some of the poorest people, many of them women with families to support, widowed through war, disease or the mines. The job of Awaken Mozambique in Australia is to provide the expertise, money and training to help the poor of Beira towards self-determination. (It has become a project of the Global Development Group.) Relatively small sums of money can make a big difference in the lives of families, providing a living income that helps prevent malnutrition which is endemic among the children, restricting their potential and that of their country. The ability to support their families and receive training (conducted orally because of low literacy levels) raises people's self-efficacy and self-esteem. They acquire agency and are expected to take responsibility for themselves and their families, and help their community wherever they can. This is the beginning of leadership, a leadership that may prevent the return of civil war which threatens to reoccur.

Next, four real-life examples of people being supported by Awaken Mozambique to make a success of their businesses/lives, will be discussed.

Amina's story

Amina was a 52-year-old widow supporting three children when she received her first loan. She had never been to school, so she cannot read or write. She was very ashamed that she was not doing better and leading a good Christian life. She was one of the first borrowers, and the loan was made without any confidence that she could be successful. Amina, however, had confidence in herself and in her abilities, and believed that she would pay the loan back. The project funded her first business, a small stall selling necessities just outside her home. She said she applied for help because her family were always hungry.

In her own words Amina explained the impact of this assistance:

"Through the loan today my children do not go to sleep with hunger and my children go to school just like other children."

She repaid the loan and never had any repayment problems. Her success was somewhat of a surprise and encouraged others in the local community to try for themselves as few thought that an older woman with no education could succeed. She has become a community leader. Since her first loan she has built up a chicken farm. She provides a local place for people to buy inexpensive protein. She would like to expand her business and build a house in her yard for rental. She is now sixty and two of her children have left home. She has one married son living with her with his wife and baby. She has been waiting for a second loan for several years and was very excited when informed that she was to get a second loan.

The staff comment:

"She is a hard working and self-confident woman who does not live in expectancy of a handout but she goes out and gets things done. She has been asking for a loan for years but has not waited to try to improve things."

Victoria's story

Victoria had an accident as a child which put her in a wheelchair. The limited medical services available in Mozambique were unable to find a cause for her inability to walk. She lived with an elderly grandmother. Victoria came to the attention of Despertai Mozambique when a member of the local advisory committee asked visiting Australians to meet with her. She was in her wheelchair in a parched yard in the poverty-stricken landscape of the peri-urban slums. She was extremely thin and appeared to be losing a whole range of bodily functions. The local Director thought that she was probably starving. She had no way to help herself and her family were very poor. She ate when they gave her something.

Despite her situation, she had a vision and self-determination to become a lawyer but no-one could see how a disabled young woman could study to become a lawyer. Very few people in Beira are able to go to university and most disabled people in Mozambique are entirely dependent on their families, with few opportunities for work or study. And she was a woman. Her background as a member of a 'cursed' family, a young woman and disabled were all against her – but she held onto her dream. She battled against negative thoughts and emotions and persisted with what she was doing.

Awaken Mozambique found a donor for her who has provided the money for housing, food and a carer for three years, so far. She has now completed her second year of law, and is looking well, though still in a wheelchair. She is a role model and may become the first disabled female lawyer in Mozambique. She is most definitely setting an example for others. She is a very determined young woman and is a role model for many about what is possible with a little help and a lot of determination.

Jose's story

Jose is a banana wholesaler and started his business after receiving a small loan. He built a shed to store his bananas. He purchased the bananas from out-of-town farms.

He hired two people to load the bananas onto the truck and drive them to town. People in the neighbourhood helped unload the bananas and took them to market. These people he paid in cash and/or bananas. His small operation provided an income for a wide range of local people as well as making a good food source available. By providing an income to other people in the community he created opportunities for them to also think of starting their own businesses (and he encouraged them to do so).

Seeing the success of his small operations, he wanted to grow his business and start buying in bulk. However, he needed more money to buy larger quantities of bananas and transport them. He also realised that he needed more knowledge: – a better understanding of how much stock to buy at once – since bananas might rot if he could not sell them quickly enough. He was approached to supply a local supermarket with 500 kilos of bananas a week. Jose discovered that he could not raise the necessary initial capital to enable him to take up the offer. The investment capital he was seeking was around 6 000 rand. This would have enriched his whole community.

Felisberto's story

Felisberto Tole was born on 6 March 1960 in Marromeu of illiterate parents who were subsistence farmers. In terms of education, he only managed grade 1. He is the divorced father of three daughters and one son. He moved to Beira 43 years ago as a young man. He became a pastor and is greatly respected throughout the community. He goes everywhere on foot which means he knows his community very well indeed. He has been a pastor for the past 28 years.

He has been working with Despertai Mozambique for the past 8 years. His honesty and courage have a lot to do with the esteem in which the organisation is held in Beira. He has an attitude of trying to involve everyone in the solutions to problems and to be just to the needs of other people. When he was offered the position of Director of the local office of Despertai Mozambique he was very reluctant, citing his lack of formal education. Despite this he is an excellent administrator and mediator and has gone to considerable lengths to learn English. His self-confidence and self-esteem have grown as he has become aware of how much his leadership is appreciated. In his own words:

"It has been a great experience working with Despertai, helping the less privileged people get up on their own feet with the loans. Despite the challenges, seeing them improve their life patterns and supporting them to do so, is my greatest joy. That's why me and colleagues together with Dr Carol, are pushing for a better life for the forgotten people in Mozambique."

Integration

Awaken Mozambique/Desperate Mozambique can indeed be seen as a peace leader organisation, due to the fact that they provide financial services, training and support to the poor in Mozambique. By doing that they empower local people to become successful in what they are doing. Being successful enables them to empower friends, family and other people in the community to do the same.

The example of Amina is a living example of a peace leader demonstrating self-awareness and self-mastery skills. After she obtained a loan from Awaken Mozambique she used this to build up a chicken farm as well as building a house which she is renting out. She had confidence in her own strengths when she applied for a loan from Awaken Mozambique and worked very hard to make a success of her business. She therefore demonstrated personal awareness and personal mastery skills (see chapters 2 and 3 where personal awareness and personal mastery were discussed), by being aware of her own qualities and by creating what she wants in life. She also worked very hard in achieving her goals.

The example of Victoria also demonstrated self-awareness and self-mastery due to the fact that she had a very clear vision of what she would like to become in life (self-awareness). She then demonstrated a lot of self-determination and persistence, defeating negative thoughts and emotions (self-mastery) in order to become a lawyer.

Jose realised that he does not exist in isolation, but in context and in relationship with others. In chapter 3 it was explained that peace cannot be achieved alone, but with and through other people (see chapter 3 where 'lead with others' was discussed).

Felisberto tried to be sensitive to the needs of others in the community as well as to include everyone in the solution of problems. Inclusiveness and justness are important values of communal intelligence and lead community (see chapters 2 and 3 where 'communal intelligence' and 'lead community' are discussed), and he therefore can be seen as a real-life peace leader demonstrating lead community skills.

The abovementioned examples of people living and working in Mozambique can therefore be seen as real-life examples of peace leaders because they demonstrated lead self, lead with others and lead community skills.

Recommendations

Du Plessis and Kaspersen[22] are of the opinion that our youth should be seen as a stabilising factor in the fight against being poor, and therefore be given a quality education, stable employment and a political voice. According to Du Plessis and Kaspersen[23], it is critical to promote an educational system with a strong focus on entrepreneurship and technology in order to optimise opportunities and reframe narratives. Entrepreneurship qualities can help the youth to plan and grow their own businesses and technology can help them in accessing quality education and to connect with important stakeholders[24].

More farmers should be empowered to achieve success in life and in their work[25]. African farmers – mostly women – are paying the price for the lack of investment by their own governments and the international community in agriculture and the rural economy. Women farmers, in particular, suffer from lack of access to credit and tend to use low-yield seed varieties[26].

Training and supporting local people (for instance the youth and women farmers) to become successful, will help in creating more peace leaders.

Concluding remarks

Long-term sustainability requires a move to a model that broadens the base of both economic and intellectual resources through building capacity[27]. Economic prosperity requires peace and stability. For peace to be achieved leaders at all levels in society have to feel secure and competent. They need to understand the context within which they lead and their own strengths and weaknesses. Designing for peace means responding to the community's priorities, investigating individual problems and solutions, and encouraging agency and active involvement in goal setting with ongoing consultation and co-development of solutions[28].

Without peace there can be no prosperity in Africa or elsewhere. Peace requires all citizens to have the basic requirements of life and hope for a better future over which they have some control. Without this they can be manipulated into using aggression because they have no other skills to offer in an attempt to improve their lives and the lives of their children. This is understood in African culture and so peace leaders need to look within as well as without to find solutions to the multiple challenges that face them. As can be seen in the real-life examples (discussed in this chapter), with a little help, no challenges are insurmountable.

References

Burns, J.M. 2003. *Leaders who changed the world*. New Delhi: Penguin.

Chamlee-Wright, E. 2005. Fostering sustainable complexity in the micro-finance industry. Which way forward? *Economic Affairs*, 25(2): 5-12.

Dalglish, C. and Tonelli, M. 2017. *Entrepreneurship at the bottom of the pyramid*. New York and London: Routledge.

Dalglish, C. 2007. From the informal to the formal sector; micro enterprises in a developing economy – research in progress. In *Proceedings of the fourth international AGSE entrepreneurship research exchange*, 6-9 February 2007, Brisbane Graduate School of Business.

Dalglish, C. and Miller. P. 2016. *Leadership modernising our perspective*, second edition. Australia: Tilde Prahan.

Dana, L.P. 1996. Small business in Mozambique after the war. *Journal of Small Business Management*, 34(4): 67.

Du Plessis, A. and Kasperen, A. (2016). Seven trends shaping the future of peace and security in Africa. Institute for Security Studies, Johannesburg.

Elkington, J. and Hartigan, P. 2008. *The power of unreasonable people: how social entrepreneurs create markets that change the world*. Boston, Ma: Harvard Business Press.

Hammersley, M. and Atkinson, P. 1995. *Ethnography: principles in practice*. New York: Routledge.

Lipman-Blumen, J. 2014. *Peace and prosperity: make it happen (a connective leadership strategy for global, enduring and sustainable peace and prosperity)*. Paper presented at the International Leadership Association 12th annual meeting: London.

Massinguw, X. 2013. *Theology of work and poverty alleviation in Mozambique*. Carlisle: UK Langham Monographs.

Matthews, J.H. 2009. What are the lessons for entrepreneurship from creativity and design? In Solomon, G. *Proceedings of the Academy of Management Meeting; Green Management Matters*. Chicargo, Il: Academy of Management.

Millennium Project Sachs J.D. 2008. *Commonwealth*. New York: Penguin Books.

UNICEF, 2017. Peace education in UNICEF, Working paper series, (Education Section), June 2017.

Wangari, M. 2010. *The Challenge for Africa*. London: Arrow Books.

Endnotes

1   Burns, 2003.
2   Wangari, 2010.
3   See endnote 1.
4   Lipman-Blumen, 2014.
5   Ibid.
6   Ibid.
7   Millenium Project Sachs, 2008.
8   See endnote 1.
9   Dalglish & Miller, 2016.
10   See endnote 2.
11   Dana, 1996; Dalglish, 2008; Massinguw, 2013.
12   Massinguw, 2013.
13   Ibid.
14   UNICEF, 2017.
15   Ibid.
16   See endnote 12.
17   Wangari, 2010.
18   Dalglish & Tonelli, 2017.
19   Ibid.
20   Chamlee-Wright, 2005.
21   Hammersley & Atkinson, 1995.
22   Du Plessis & Kaspersen, 2016.
23   Ibid.
24   Ibid.
25   See endnote 17.
26   Ibid.
27   Elkington & Hartigan, 2008.
28   Matthews, 2009.

SECTION 3

TOOLS AND INITIATIVES TO BECOME A HIGHLY EFFECTIVE PEACE LEADER

INFORMATION AND COMMUNICATION TECHNOLOGY: CONTRIBUTING TO PEACEBUILDING?

Andrew Campbell, Ebben van Zyl and Ciara Marie Gallagher

"Technology is a useful servant but a dangerous master."
(Christian Lange, 1921 Nobel Peace Prize Speech)

Spotlight: Elise Hampel

Elise Hampel (née Lemme) was born in Bismark/Stendal, Germany on 27 October 1903, and became part of the German resistance against the Nazi regime during WWII. Following elementary school, Elise worked as a domestic servant. In 1935, she married WWI veteran and factory worker, Otto Hampel. She was a member of the National Socialist Frauenschaft (Women's League) between 1936 and 1940. However, in 1940, when Elise's brother was killed in action during the German assault on France, it prompted her and her husband to launch an opposition initiative against the war and the Third Reich. Together, from their home in Berlin, they pioneered a novel method of civil disobedience and began a clandestine campaign of resistance against the Nazis, writing anonymous anti-propaganda messages on postcards which they placed in mailboxes, on staircases and in streets throughout Berlin. Elise and Otto were arrested on 20 October 1942. Between September 1940 and 1942, when they were ultimately betrayed, they distributed over 200 handwritten postcards and leaflets, encouraging people not to cooperate with the Nazis, to refuse to serve in the army or donate to National Socialist public collections such as Winter Relief, to end the war effort, and to overthrow Hitler. On 22 January 1943 Elise was sentenced to death, alongside her husband, for "demoralizing the troops" and "preparation for high treason". She was executed in Berlin-Plötzensee on 8 April 1943[1].

Introduction

At a time when postcards have evolved to Tweets, Facebook and WhatsApp messages, Elise and Otto Hampel's example remains relevant as one of the power of words and communication in the face of untruths as well as cruel actions of oppressive rulers. The true extent of Elise and Otto Hampel's silent revolt may never be known, but we can see from the force with which their communication was suppressed that words hold a power that strikes fear into even the most brutal of regimes. However, at a time when technological communication has evolved from telegraph to cyberspace, Hampel's example remains relevant in today's complex global environment. The technological advancements of weaponry and war have resulted in some of history's darkest chapters as well as spawned social discourse. To illustrate, the technological communication by a single user organised the anti-government uprising and armed rebellions of the Arab Spring 2011 to demand political reforms and social justice across the Middle East[2]. In the same vein, technological assets used within the Israel-Palestine conflict provide local peacebuilders with the capability to not only challenge conflict narratives but also facilitate communication pathways between group discourse[3].

Thus, the use of technological platforms like social media, logistical assets and cyberspace assets are being used more frequently by local peacebuilders to build communication networks that facilitate pathways towards peace and stability. Basically, technology is a peacebuilder's strategic enabler that brings the conflicting parties together to counteract disparaging violent narratives and enhance local peacebuilding capacity towards conflict resolution and reconciliation[4].

This chapter is divided into five sections. First, the discussion examines the limited literature on information and communication technological innovations that peace leaders employ to lead others within the community towards peacebuilding. Second, important aspects related to information and communication technology are defined. Thirdly, literature on the role and effect of information and communication technology on peace and peacebuilding are discussed. Information and communication technology as a tool for peacebuilding is then outlined. Fifth, challenges and future trends are then discussed. Finally, the chapter will end with concluding remarks.

Literature

The emergence of peace leadership as a field of study is relatively new[5]. As a result, there is limited research on the role and effects of information and communication technological innovations on peace development. Thus, how to identify technological advancement and effectively employ such technologies as part of a peacebuilding strategy needs to be investigated. That said, arguments can be made to the effect that the employment of information and communication technology is a strategic enabler for peace organisational decision-makers to bring civil society actors, affected populations and marginalised groups together, and discuss pathways for conflict resolution and peacebuilding activities[6]. In the same vein, there is data showing that information and communication technological assets can be used to mobilise politico-ethnic discontent and promulgate social discourse[7]. To illustrate, "many examples were cited in which communities were mobilised quickly for both constructive and violent purposes on the basis of the new so-called Web 2.0 collaborative technologies"[8]. As already indicated, the use of social media by one person was used as a tool to initiate a social movement of social justice that sparked the Arab Spring. Likewise, data shows the use of various internet platforms as tools by violent extremist organisations (VEOs) to recruit, propagandise, and plan structural violence towards outer groups in accomplishing a certain political objective[9]. The Islamic State (ISIS) utilises social media channels to both spread its message and to recruit fighters.

Nevertheless, information and communication technological assets are used either to spawn social discourse or to constructively transform (violent) conflicts towards sustainable and developing peace-supporting structures. Basically, our understanding surrounding the technological relationship of initiating social discourse is well developed with very little appreciation of its use within conflict transformation and peacebuilding.

Definitions

The purpose of defining some concepts related to information and communication technology is to make these concepts as understandable as possible to non-technologists.

Information and communication technology can be defined as an umbrella term that includes communication and information devices or the application of these. Radio, television, cellular phones, computers and network (and the associated hardware and software), video conferencing, satellite communication, etc. can be included here[10].

Information technology is the utilisation of technology for the transmission of a message from a sender to a receiver. Communication technology is the utilisation of technology in a bi-directional sequence of transmission of messages. The counterparts are both senders and receivers[11].

Social media refers to websites and applications that generate participation and interaction between people. Facebook, YouTube, Google, Linkedin, Twitter and WhatsApp can be regarded as social media. Social networks are websites and applications that build personal and business networking opportunities (for instance, Facebook and Linkedin)[12].

Web 2.0 is new communication technology (for instance, Orkut and Wikis)[13].

Information and communication technology as a tool for peacebuilding

Information and communication technology (ICT) serves an important role as a force multiplier and as a peacekeeping operation tool to provide a monitoring, situational awareness and intelligence capability to communicate and cooperate directly with each other[14]. The integration of ICT's assets provides the capacity for local actors to digitally organise the sharing of information towards local conflict transformation in developing sustainable peace development activities. Basically, ICT can be used by peacebuilders to empower local actors in changing the conflict narrative to both de-escalate and prevent violence[15].

Information and communications technologies (ICTs) are technological tools that peace leaders can use, not as a solution in and of themselves, but to build peace development strategies connecting conflictual parties and local actors in efforts towards conflict resolution and peacebuilding activities[16]. Thus, many ICT platforms are being used for conflict resolution, governance and peace development. Although not all the information and communication technologies will be discussed here, satellite technology (as part of information technology) will firstly be discussed. Social media and networking (as important communication technologies), will then be discussed.

Satellite information is a type of information technology that is used in human rights protection. Examples of its use include documenting flows of refugees, the torching of villages, the destruction of infrastructure as well as identifying previously unknown mass graves or confirming their existence[17].

Case study: example where satellite information was applied to track human rights violations in Sudan

"The Satellite Sentinel project (SSP) has been regularly monitoring the trajectory of the conflict between the Republic of Sudan and South Sudan from a height of 300 kilometres. The aim was to table evidence of alleged atrocities and human rights violations (for instance, proof of refugees fleeing). The aim of this initiative was to prevent a return to full-scale civil war by informing the world about what is happening. To achieve this, SSP collaborates with the civil society organization

"Enough Project", which focuses on genocide and crimes against humanity. SSP also collaborates with DigitalGlobe, a company producing commercial satellite information systems. Along with satellite imagery and data analysis, unfolding developments within Sudan could be identified. In 2011, SSP drew attention to some dig sites that indicated the presence of mass graves close to the town of Kadugli in the South Sudanese state of Kordofan. Though they were generally treated with caution, these satellite-assisted finds provoked marked political reactions"[18].

Social media and **social networking** are communication technologies that peacebuilder organisations and leaders employ to forge open communication lines to resolve political, economic, social and ideological disputes[19]. Social media and networking are increasingly being used as a medium to spotlight the challenges in building peace and to help bridge the divide between adversaries. With today's youth being one of the most engaged and active users of social media, it is important to encourage their participation towards preventing and ending cycles of conflict. Where social media captures the imagination of citizens, it can be a genuine means to empower communities and take ownership of conflict prevention[20].

It is certainly true that social media alone cannot resolve some of today's most entrenched conflicts; the hard work of classical diplomacy is still very much essential here. However, social media, by virtue of reaching out to all people, is a great facilitator of conflict resolution and diplomacy. For that reason, within communities, conflict transformation can only occur when people of all walks of life start to act on their sentiments for peace. With more people tweeting, noticing and acting upon each other's calls for peace, the power of harnessing social media as a positive "social change multiplier" is realised. Hence, the strategies and toolbox of peace leaders must evolve to combat these new challenges. In essence, if these technological tools are to facilitate communication pathways to share information and ideas, they must incorporate the values of peace itself. As Chinn puts it: "peace is intent, process and outcome"[21].

Case study: example where social media and networks were used to advocate peace in Somalia

"Maryan Mohamed Hussein, 22, is a social media peace ambassador, spreading the good news about Somalia's recovery through Facebook, Google and WhatsApp as well as other platforms popular with young Somalis. Maryan says she wants to be remembered for her contribution to the change taking place in Somalia: 'Mostly, I take photos and videos from important places in Mogadishu like Liido beach, Jazeera beach and the peace garden, among other notable places, and use the images in the media to demonstrate real change, relative peace and stabilization efforts in the country,' she remarks. 'What I share on social media triggers positive conversations about the country. My aim is to influence the youth who are eyeing Europe and want to migrate using the risky high seas and dangerous deserts. I encourage them by telling them that their country is recovering and will soon have abundant opportunities for them,' she adds. 'I urge them to exercise a little more patience, as the peace is returning and things are looking up.' Born in Wanlaweyn district, lower Shabelle region, in South West State of Somalia during the war, Maryan knows too well the consequences of instability and uses every opportunity to preach peace. 'Somalia, being a country that is recovering from insecurity, we need to unite and consolidate our efforts towards peacebuilding. We need to remind ourselves that peacebuilding starts with an individual. So, I urge my fellow citizens to each take the crucial steps in promoting peace,' she states, matter-of-factly. Her efforts at peacebuilding have paid off. As a result of her activism, many youths are empowered and continue to benefit from her leadership. Maryan also takes pride in pioneering the construction of the first FM radio station in her home district of Wanlaweyn. The radio station, which serves Wanlaweyn and surrounding areas, was built in 2016 with support from Mr Hassan Lucky, a director with Radio Dalsan. She urges the youth in Somalia to use social media to make positive change, promote peace and progress. 'I appeal to the Federal Government of Somalia, the international partners and the Somali business community to invest in youth empowerment by providing them with critical life skills and employment. By doing so, the youth will be able to provide for themselves, their families and stay away from criminal activities,' she concludes.[22]"

The advancement of user-generated technological tools (like YouTube, Wiki and Twitter blogs) **as part of social media and social networking**, are media assets that begin with more independent, individualistic production of text messages and blogs[23]. Community media operate on a local level through traditional platforms such as television, radio and print. That said, many examples can be cited in which communities were mobilised quickly for both constructive and violent purposes on the basis of the new so-called Web 2.0 collaborative technologies. In one of the most politically volatile regions in Kenya, Chief Kariuki used the micro-blogging site Twitter to radically transform the historical deliberative space known as *baraza* into a space for peacebuilding and community policing[24]. The intent showed how a local actor (the chief) can use social media with varying degrees of success to fight crime, respond to emergencies, and heal.

Lastly, through well-designed and well-implemented ITC peace-building activities, affected communities can utilise more traditional communication methods and combine these with more modern communication and social media technology in order to implement change and create peace. The following case study is an example of that.

Case study: example where traditional methods of communication were combined with modern technology in Sudan's Blue Nile State

"Conflicts were occurring between farmers and nomadic pastoralists (sheep/cattle farmers) from Sudan and the Sahel region. The cause of conflict was because of the using of land for pasture along the same migratory routes. It emerged that a lack of information and the poor quality of communication was the main cause for the conflict. Information was accessed only through community leaders. By encouraging farmers to access data not only through community leaders but also through other communication technology like cellular phones, WhatsApp messages and local radios contributed to improve the otherwise unreliable and fragmented supply of information. While it was primarily young men who knew how to use a mobile phone and WhatsApp messages, only the elders had the authority in the communities to pass on information. As a way of overcoming this power discrepancy, they were paired in teams. By improving the quality of communication, peacebuilding took place"[25].

Challenges

Peace leaders should be aware of challenges when information and communication technologies are used in peace and peacebuilding[26]:

The first challenge is for peace leaders to integrate information and communication technologies (ICTs) more often into the peace and peacebuilding apparatus. Peace leaders should therefore obtain knowledge about different information and communication technologies and how these can be applied to the benefit of the situation. Formulating a peace strategy that integrates ICT tools can influence the engagement of stabilisation and reconstruction activities in a post-conflict environment. The impact of these ICT tools is that they can provide a strategic capability for peace leaders to navigate the unity of effort that prevents violence, peaceably manages conflict, and opens communication pathways for multi-track diplomacy.

The second challenge for peace leaders is how to use information and communication technology tools (ICT) that connect local actors with civil society networks as peace leaders not only develop a shared approach toward negotiating a way to resolve conflicts but also facilitate coordinated strategies toward stabilisation and reconstruction processes.

The third challenge is how peace leaders leverage the use of ICTs in underdeveloped countries that lack a digital network to support social media applications. Information and communication are critical in planning, staging and responding to humanitarian crises in conflict-afflicted areas. The biggest challenge for peace leaders is to coordinate and deploy limited resources within geographically dispersed areas to provide the basic human service-delivery needs when human security lapses back into violence. Basically, information and communication technology has a diverse implication that can either support or obstruct peacebuilding measures.

The last challenge is how to prevent states, organisations and individuals from stoking conflict through technology. A digital network, for instance, can be created in a conflict-affected region to exchange information about the conflict quickly and adequately. At the same time, however, rumours and negative information can be spread across the region, giving rise to further conflict and violence.

Future trends

The following three trends may be a reality with regard to employing information and communication technology within peace development.

The first trend is that the employment of new technology within peace development will improve communication between all important stakeholders and improve the quality of decisions. This improved communication will allow peace leaders to communicate with more people in more ways, collect better information and to sustain relationships on digital platforms. A new type of citizenship may emerge that is more concerned with fostering relations and taking actions with other citizens than building relations with organisations and participating in institutional processes.

Second, the trend to employ ICT technological assets will enable all important stakeholders to formulate communication strategies that identify and facilitate the exchange of ideas towards countering the promotion of violent extremist ideologies including design, formulation and implementation processes. The importance moving forward is that ICTs used by peace leaders provide a means to build coalitions with local actors and civil society to create conflict-prevention strategies to deter spoiler groups from re-initiating conflict. Whilst many of our most important peacebuilding organisations remain highly centralised, new technologies may encourage us to decentralise and to distribute knowledge.

The final trend is that peace leaders may focus more on assessing the strategic progress of operationalising ICT tools in communicating conflict-prevention strategies and human service-delivery systems among key stakeholders. In moving forward, this is important as peace leaders seek a unity of purpose across the full spectrum of peace development. Basically, the impact of technology on peace should not be overstated or exaggerated.

Concluding remarks

This chapter has explored the possible contributions and challenges of information and communication technologies (ICTs) in peace and peacebuilding. Technology is a strategic enabler as peace leaders, local actors and civil society make connections in leading others towards intercommunal peace and stability. Technology can indeed play numerous roles in peacebuilding – being an information provider, watchdog, mobiliser and promoter. Certain challenges, however (as discussed in this chapter), should always be taken into consideration.

References

Gedenkstätte Deutscher Widerstand, 2016. Available at: https://www.gdw-berlin.de/en/recess/biographies/index_of_persons/biographie/view-bio/elise-hampel/?no_cache=1 [Accessed on please supply date]

Himelfarb, S. & Chabalowski, M. 2008. Media, Conflict Prevention and Peacebuilding: Mapping the Edges. United States Institute of Peace. Available at: https://www.techtimes.com/articles/88794/20150926/zuckerberg-tells-un-universal-internet-access-will-promote-human-rights.htm

Ledbetter, B. 2012. Dialectics of leadership for peace: Toward a moral model of resistance. *Journal of Leadership, Accountability and Ethics*, 9(5): 11-24.

Legatis, R. 2015. Media-related peacebuilding in processes of conflict transformation. *Berghof Handbook for Conflict Transformation*. Colombia.

Lieberfield, D. 2016. Leadership change and negotiation initiatives in intractable civic conflicts. *International Journal of Peace Studies*, 21(1): 4-49.

Narula, S. 2016. Role of Youth in Peace Building via New Media: A Study on Use of New Media by Youth for Peace Building Tasks. *Journal of Mass Communication*, 6: 311-315.

Omanga, D.M., (2015). 'Chieftaincy' in the Social Media Space: Community Policing in a Twitter Convened Baraza. *Stability: International Journal of Security and Development*, 4(1): 32-39.

Parks, L. (2015). Satellite communication and peacebuilding in East Africa. Statebuilding and peacebuilding in Africa. Available at: http://repository.upenn.edu/africaictresearch/7

Puig Larrauri, H. & Kahl, A., 2013. Technology for Peacebuilding. *Stability: International Journal of Security and Development*, 2(3):12-19

Varis, T. 1982. Peace and Communication. *Journal of Peace Research*, 3: 1-5.

Zuppo, C. M. 2012. Defining ICT in a boundaryless world: The development of a working hierarchy. *International Journal of Managing Information Technology*, 4,(3):13-18.

Endnotes

1   Gedenkstatte Deutscher Widerstand, 2016.
2   Narula, 2016.
3   Ibid.
4   Legatis, 2015.
5   See endnote 2.
6   See endnote 4.
7   Puig Larrauri & Kahl, 2013.
8   See endnote 2.
9   Himelfarb & Chabalowski, 2008; Puig Larrauri & Kahl, 2013.
10   See endnote 7.
11   See endnote 2.
12   Ibid.
13   Zuppo, 2012.
14   Parks, 2015.
15   Varis, 2018.
16   See endnote 14.
17   Parks, 2015; Legatis, 2015.
18   See endnote 4.
19   See endnote 14.
20   See endnote 15.
21   See endnote 15.
22   See endnote 4.
23   See endnote 2.
24   Omanga, 2015.
25   See endnote 4.
26   Lieberfield, 2015.

CHAPTER 14

SPORT AS A TOOL IN PEACEBUILDING

Jannie Putter and Ebben van Zyl

"Sport has the power to change the world. It has the power to inspire. It has the power to unite people in a way that little else does. It speaks to youth in a language they understand. Sport can create hope where once there was only despair." (Nelson Mandela)

Spotlight: Lucas Valeriu Radebe

Lucas Valeriu Radebe, born 12 April 1969, is a former Leeds United and South African football player. He was born in the Diepkloof section of Soweto, near Johannesburg, as one of 11 children. His family was very poor and he had no opportunities to play soccer. When he was 15 years old he was sent to the Bantustan of Bophuthatswana by his parents in order to keep him away from the violence that was affecting Soweto during the apartheid era. Radebe was spotted and signed by the Kaizer Chiefs Football Club as a midfielder. In 1991 he was shot while walking down the street, although luckily he was not critically wounded. The motive for the shooting never became clear, but Radebe believed that someone had been hired to shoot him in order to prevent him from moving to another club. His career playing for South Africa started in 1992 when he made his international debut against Cameroon. Soon after, in 1994, Radebe moved to Leeds United. He had been sold by Kaizer Chiefs for £250 000. Radebe became a star player for Leeds and was nicknamed 'The Chief' by its fans due partly to his previous club and partly his absolute rule in defence. In recognition of his leadership and ability, Radebe was appointed captain of the team for the 1998–1999 season.

As captain of Leeds, Radebe was very successful. In the 1998–1999 season Leeds finished fourth in the FA Premier League, qualifying for the UEFA Cup, and during the 1999–2000 season they finished third in the Premier League, and qualified for the

Champions League, reaching the semi-finals. However, in 2000 Radebe sustained knee and ankle injuries, which kept him out of the game for almost two years.

During his years with Leeds United Radebe continued to play on and off for South Africa, and in 1996 he was a member of the South African team that won the African Nations Cup. Radebe was also the captain of the South African national football team, nicknamed ***Bafana Bafana (means "Go Boys" in Zulu)*** in both the 1998 and 2002 FIFA World Cups. He earned 70 caps for South Africa and scored two goals during his international career with his last match being against England on 22 May 2003, and was voted 54th in the Top 100 Great South Africans in 2004. At the end of the 2005 season Radebe retired from professional football in a star-studded testimonial match at Elland Road involving players from all around the world, and Leeds United players past and present. The match was attended by a crowd of more than 37 000 fans.

Lucas also held a retirement match at Kings Park Soccer Stadium in Durban, South Africa, between a South African Invitation XI and the Lucas Radebe All Stars. The match finished 3–2 to the South African Invitation XI. The proceeds from both of these matches were combined with other money raised and donated to charity as part of Radebe's big donation to charity in his final year as a player. After his retirement he was offered a role on the Leeds United coaching staff. He is still a crowd favourite at Elland Road, and fans continue to chant his name there, showing how much he endeared himself to them during his playing career. Similarly, in 2008 a local Leeds brewery asked for suggestions for the name of a new beer and the most popular suggestion was 'Radebeer', again illustrating the Leeds fans' fond admiration of Radebe[1].

Introduction

Peace leadership actions (lead self and lead with others and community), are evident in the real-life example of Lucas Radebe. Lucas had a vision and so set himself objectives on how to become an international soccer player accordingly. He practised very hard and demonstrated both courage and persistence (lead self), despite starting to play at a late stage. Having come from a disadvantaged background with inadequate opportunities he not only relied on his skills but also showed strong character (lead self) in order to overcome his barriers and to become a world figure. He not only understood his strengths but his weaknesses too, and was willing to learn from his mistakes and grow.

Radebe also took an interest in the public, and by donating substantially to charity he showed an interest in empowering others (lead with others), which added to his popularity. His support of charities also served to build systems that, in turn, supported his goals to become a successful world sports figure. He indicated that his donations should support the disadvantaged in the different communities in South Africa, and even indicated how the money should be distributed (lead community). Although the abovementioned show leadership skills, he also demonstrated and implemented management skills by actively implementing his vision. He also allowed himself to be empowered (lead self) when he moved to England, where he constantly developed his skills to become one of the best soccer players in the world.

How did Radebe become such a successful and popular soccer player and world-renowned figure? Much of the answer lies in leading himself (the development of his character) and through the opportunities that opened up in his talent being identified and pursued. He also empowered others (lead with others and lead the community). Lucas Radebe is one of thousands of individuals – coming from a variety of backgrounds – who became world-influencers and idols through their ability to excel at sport. Sport stars are truly world leaders and influencers in every aspect of leadership.

In this chapter, general background information on sport and peace will firstly be discussed. Secondly, the character and nature of sport will be discussed. The question will then be asked as to why sport is such a powerful tool in peacebuilding, and answers will be provided. Current undertakings to create peace via sport will then be set out. Lastly, some future trends and recommendations will be outlined and concluding remarks will be given.

Background

Sport is an enormous industry[2]. Competition and sport stars – heroes and legends who influence society in how we act, what we talk about, what we believe, what we hope and what we buy – are constantly becoming more significant and meaningful.

The stuff our children dream about – becoming champions, people of influence and significance in history – is what fills our daily conversations[3]. The potential for wealth and fame in becoming a sport star has given rise to a movement of interest, commitment and dedication towards mastering sporting skills amongst people of all classes and all races.

Sport stars influence nations, society, cultures as well as the world's economy[4]. History books are written about these people and their accomplishments... What is most fascinating is learning about their character (the values and norms that inform their lives) and the decisions they had to make to become those stars.

Many things happen daily – leaders fall and leaders rise. Wars starts and wars end. There are numerous international talent competitions taking place – almost daily. There are people who move and shock the world with their incredible abilities. An event that has a very big influence (and impact) on humanity and society is surely the Olympic Games. A **sporting event** that takes place every four years with the aim of determining the world's best... Every country in the world hopes to have an athlete representing them in this global sporting event. The performances of a single athlete can change a nation's moral and social atmosphere. Sport influences society in major ways[5].

World champions become the heroes of their time. Their stories become the fantasies of our children's children. Their lives and accomplishments become the inspiration of our youth. Their influence on society is majestic. What they do influences the wealthiest people on our planet. The sport stars determine trends. They set standards. People use their lives as examples of influence and inspiration because these champions are people just like you and me – normal people. People who became heroes by making quality decisions and extreme commitments in their personal lives... By doing this (living exemplary lives) and by hearing their stories, our youth are inspired and motivated to do the same.

Sport participation and the "aura" of excellence surrounding it have the ability to create peace[6]. Sport participation is the platform from where sport stars can communicate messages of peace and peacebuilding.

In recent history there is one person who has truly touched the world with his story of survival and building peace. This person was a MONUMENT to building peace in a nation where division and apartheid had divided different cultures into enemies. Generations into the future will know this name: "MADIBA" (Nelson Mandela). He was a true world-influencer and a true peace-builder. Here's what Nelson Mandela said about sport, hope and peacebuilding[7]:

> "Sport has the power to change the world. It has the power to unite people in order to build peace. It has the power to inspire. It has the power to unite people in a way that little else does. It speaks to youth in a language they understand. Sport can create hope where once there was only despair."

The nature and features of sport

Sport can be defined as follows[8]: "It is a structured physical activity, usually competitive, that requires complex skills and a high level of individual commitment and motivation." This definition can be analysed as follows:

- Structured physical activity: "Structured" means it is organised. All sports have governing bodies that set rules and arrange events. It also requires physical preparation to some extent.
- Competitive: All sports have a competitive element, either between individuals or teams.
- Requires complex skills: Skills have to be learned for an individual to become a performer. Basic skills have to be learned first and later developed into more complex skills.
- High level of individual commitment and motivation: Top athletes get to where they are by training for long hours for many years and often have to make sacrifices. This may lead to rewards such as winning, a sense of achievement, etc., which make all the hard work worthwhile[9].

All types of sports, however, have common features, namely:

- competition between individuals or teams
- physical activity
- winners and losers (in some sports you can have a draw)
- rules to ensure fair competition
- a special place to play
- special equipment[10].

What makes sport such a powerful tool in peacebuilding?

According to Kidombo[11] sport has the potential to create the following:

- Building relationships: Sport works primarily by bridging relationships across social, economic and cultural divides within society, and by building a sense of shared identity and fellowship among groups that might otherwise be inclined to treat each other with distrust, hostility or violence. Some peace researchers view relationship-building as the central component of peacebuilding and highlight the importance of interventions that explicitly focus on strategic networking to build relationships.
- Connecting individuals to communities: Community programmes can provide shared experiences between people that "re-humanise" opposing groups in the eyes of their enemies. By sharing sport experiences, sport participants from conflicting groups increasingly grow to feel that they are alike, rather than different. This shared sense of belonging to the same group on the basis of a shared experience helps to erase the dehumanising effects of negative characterisations of opposing groups.

- Using sport as a communication platform: The profile and influence of elite athletes and sporting events can shine a light on the structural causes of social exclusion and help to promote solutions. The global popularity of elite sport makes it an ideal and extremely powerful mass communication platform to enhance the message of peace.
- Creating a space for dialogue: Elite sport has been used to open the door to peaceful dialogue and to build peace. An example is where the term "cricket diplomacy" has been used to describe the improvement of relations between India and Pakistan resulting from an informal invitation from Prime Minister Singh to General Musharraf to watch an international cricket match between the two nations[12].

The popularity of sport and its convening power contribute to sport being a powerful voice for communicating messages of peace. Sport seems to be an effective element in community-based initiatives that aim to create sustainable peace[13]. The skills and values learned through sport are many of the same skills and values taught in peace education to resolve and prevent conflict and create conditions conducive to peace, from the interpersonal to the international. Well-crafted sports activities teach respect, honesty, communication, cooperation, empathy and how and why to adhere to rules. Sport is a powerful way to communicate these values, especially to young people, in a way that is fun and participatory. For refugees, displaced persons, orphans and former child soldiers, sport offers a sense of normality, providing structure in destabilising environments, and serving as a means to positively channel energies[14].

According to Chawansky, McDonald and Van Ingen[15], sport has the potential to teach people peace-related aspects like respect for other people, how to connect to other people, how to understand other people and how to reframe social relations. In addition to that, Chawansky, McDonald and Van Ingen[16] are of the opinion that sport can serve as an ice-breaker to open channels of communication between opposing groups of people.

Limitations of sport as a peacebuilding mechanism

Kidombo[17] acknowledged the fact that sport, like many aspects of society, encompasses some of the worst human traits, including violence, corruption, discrimination, hooliganism, excessive nationalism, cheating and drug abuse. Vail[18] also indicated that sport can, and is, being used by some groups and nations to promote conflict. A well-known example is where Olympic athletes were murdered at the Munich Olympic Games. Sport may be used to promote nationalism, and in its more extreme forms, to promote acts of racism and violence against members of minority groups.

According to Kidombo[19] for sport to be an effective tool for peacebuilding there must be strategic and planned action together with important stakeholders in the peacebuilding process. With careful design and implementation, sport can play an important role in peacebuilding

Current undertakings to create peace via sport

There are a number of spectacular world-wide campaigns taking place to promote peace leadership and peacebuilding via sport-related actions.

Connecting individuals

The Danish Cross Cultures Project Association and the UEFA support 185 "Open Fun Football Schools" for 37 000 children between 8 and 14 years of age as part of a project to nurture peaceful coexistence in countries such as Bosnia and Herzegovina, Macedonia, Serbia and Montenegro. Young people participate in football training camps that aim to engender team spirit and help bridge ethnic and religious divides. Young people can share their experiences and connect with each other by being involved with football[20].

Another example is where friendly football matches were coordinated between refugees and host communities by UNHCR (UN Refugee Agency) in order to connect people in different countries and to encourage people to understand each other better[21].

Space for dialogue, build relationships and create opportunities to communicate

Sport has on several occasions successfully brought together the two Koreas, most recently seen at the 2018 Winter Olympic Games where the North and South Korean teams marched side by side in the opening ceremony. The Pakistani-Israeli tennis pair, Aisam ul-Haq Qureshi and Amir Hadad, served as positive role models for peace within their countries, known as a "two-man peace initiative", with rackets[22].

The NGO Comvida in Honduras uses national football matches as a communication tool to increase awareness of peacebuilding and respect for other people as an important way to increase peace. UNESCO and UNICEF work together with footballers Ronaldo and Zinedine Zidane as Goodwill Ambassadors to advocate and support efforts for peacebuilding and the reduction of poverty[23].

Another well-known sport initiative to enhance peace is **Peace and Sport[24]**. Founded in 2007 by Modern Pentathlon Olympic Medallist and World Champion Joël Bouzou, Peace and Sport is a neutral and independent worldwide organisation that is operational in using sport and its values as an instrument for peace.

Peace and Sport launched an initiative called **#WhiteCard campaign[25]**. This international initiative invites the entire world to show support for the peace-through-sport movement using the 'white card' symbol. At an official meeting, Joel Bouzou, President and Founder of Peace and Sport and Didier Drogba (international football player) and Champion for Peace, joined HSH Prince Albert II of Monaco, Mr Juan Manuel Santos, President of the Republic of Colombia and winner of the Nobel Peace Prize in 2016 and Mrs Maria Angela Holguin, Colombian Minister of Foreign Affairs. Together, they held up a #WhiteCard which – contrary to the red card – symbolises inclusion, equality and peace[26].

Didier Drogba, Champion for Peace and international football player stated[27]:

> "I am very happy here to be in Cartagena to launch a message via the symbol of the #WhiteCard and to remind people that sport is an invaluable tool for peace and development the world over. As a Champion for Peace, I want to use my voice to unite young people around the positive values of sport and I invite everyone who supports the peace-through-sport movement to hold up a #WhiteCard."

Many celebrities from the world of sport such as Roger Federer (tennis player), as well as Champions for Peace like Christian Karembeu (well-known soccer player) and Balla Dieye (well-known taekwondo athlete) have already raised their #WhiteCard. In 2017, #WhiteCard crossed over borders to reach 43 million people worldwide on social networks, including high-level athletes, international and national sports federations, diplomats and government representatives. The #WhiteCard campaign captures the attention of millions of people each year through social networks, especially on the International Day of Sport for Development and Peace, celebrated on 6 April[28].

More and more, role models and sport heroes throughout the world are dedicating their time, their fame, and their athletic experience to serve projects that use sport to tackle social issues. As an example, a group of over 90 high-level sportsmen personally committed themselves to the peace through sport movement[29]. Through structured action and methods of expression, they work to make sport a tool for dialogue and social inclusion. These sportsmen compiled the "Champions for Peace Charter"[30]:

CHAMPIONS FOR PEACE CHARTER

"As an internationally-renowned athlete, I am aware that sport has been a great chance in my life. It has given me opportunities, enabled me to be a better citizen, and motivates me being a role model for millions of people who play and watch sport throughout the world. In this I have a responsibility towards society.

I firmly believe that sports are not limited to podiums and world records. It builds bridges between cultures and fosters universal values of respect, tolerance, fair-play, discipline, self-confidence and going beyond personal limits.

I am committed to giving back to society so that sport and its ideals can change the lives of a maximum number of people, in particular the lives of vulnerable young people in areas of the world that are dangerous and at risk.

I believe that sport can be a tool for their personal development, education and social integration and that sport played in a structured way, with identical rules for all, can nurture inter-community dialogue, social solidarity and sustainable peace.

This is why I support "PEACE AND SPORT" and I agree to become a member of the club of top-level athletes known as "CHAMPIONS FOR PEACE".

As a "CHAMPION FOR PEACE" I would like to help Peace and Sport's actions by mobilizing my network and making my reputation, my time and my experience available to the organization.

I will act to make sport a tool for dialogue and social cohesion, using the structure of action and expression offered by the organization.

Through field action, advocating, fundraising and promoting values I will work to tangibly demonstrate the federating social and educational impact of sport.

As a "CHAMPION FOR PEACE" I am convinced that, together, members of the peace-through-sport movement can help build sustainable peace and make this a better, safer and fairer world".[31]

The abovementioned examples of peace initiatives by different organisations use sport as a tool for dialogue, for communication, to connect individuals and to build relationships that support peacebuilding.

Future trends and recommendations

The future is in the hands of our educational system and any system which has the power to empower and educate our youth[32]. Sport has in its character the values and disciplines of people who understand pressure, decision-making, consequences and dreams. The sport stars of our era have a tremendous influence on the leaders of today and tomorrow. Educating them and aligning them with a common vision and responsibility (*as outlined in the Champions for Peace Charter*) will ensure that there is a powerful force at work in society to work towards world peace through the leadership of our sport[33]. Furthermore, sport stars can be role models who demonstrate attributes that everyone can follow.

Important attributes of sportsmen that peace leaders can learn from include the following[34]:

- Play fair
- Be a team player
- Stay positive
- Respect the rules
- Never give up.

The following recommendations for using sport as a tool to enhance peace can be considered[35]:

- Include sport as a tool in government strategies to address challenges confronting excluded populations and to prevent conflicts arising from these challenges.
- Review the use of sport for nation-building purposes to ensure that the messages conveyed are peaceful and conducive to preventing conflict both within and outside the country.
- Engage key stakeholders and larger target populations in sport for peace initiatives.
- Ensure an effective sport in peace programme focus, by first undertaking a context analysis that inter alia answers questions like: what is this conflict not about? (so that programmes can build on these commonalities), what needs to be stopped? etc.
- Monitor all the variables of the sport in peace programme and be ready to change them in order to reduce possible negative impacts such as increased conflict

- Ensure that coaches and trainers are well trained in sport, conflict management and peacebuilding techniques.
- Take advantage of opportunities to mobilise high-profile elite athletes to serve as spokesmen and role models for peace.

Concluding remarks

If leadership is influence it means that every sportsperson is a leader. Every sportsperson influences others – whether it is only your opponent, your family or your friends, you have influence. Yes, some have more influence than others – yet they are ALL influencers. Just reading the names of some of the thousands of top sports stars throughout history ignites a feeling of importance, pride, excitement and bravery within us all. Just knowing someone of influence makes you feel important in your own special way. Sports people truly have the ability to be peace leaders (influencers).

According to Maxwell[36] leaders (including peace leaders), should be able to influence others in the achievement of a common goal. Peace leaders should influence others in the attainment of peace by implementing important attributes of sportsmen. Important outcomes of sport like, inter alia, building relationships, connecting individuals, good communication skills and creating a space for dialogue can be taken into consideration by peace leaders when trying to achieve peace.

References

Chawansky, M.L., McDonald, M. and Van Ingen, C. 2017. Innovations in sport for development and peace research. *Sport Research*, 8(9): 1-6.

Giulianotti, R. 2010. *Sport and ethnic studies. Ethnic and Racial Studies,* 34(2): 9-12.

Kidombo, H.J. 2012. The role of sport in peace-building. Centre of Peace and Reconciliation Studies, Coventry University, Coventry.

Malebo, A. 2007. Sport participation, psychological wellbeing, and psychosocial development in a group of young black adults. *South African Journal of Psychology,* 37(1): 188-223.

Maxwell, J.C. 2005. Leadership is influence, nothing more and nothing less. Catalyst Conference, Atlanta, Georgia.

National Institute of Adult Continuing Education. 2009. *"There's Light at the End of the Tunnel"*. Bloemfontein, University of the Free State.

Newman, M., Bird, K., Tripney, J., Kalra, N., Kwan, I., Bangpan, M. and Vigurs, C. 2010. Understanding the impact of engagement in culture and sport: A systematic review of the learning impacts for young people. Department for Culture, Media and Sport: London.

Pawlowski, T., Breuer, C. and Leyva, J. 2011. Sport opportunities and local wellbeing: is sport a local amenity? In Rodriguez, P., Kesenne, S. and Humphreys B.R. *The Economics of Sport, Health and Happiness: The promotion of wellbeing through sporting activities.* Cheltenham: Edward Elgar Publishing Limited.

Peacock-Villada, P., DeCelles, J. and Banda, P.S. 2007. Grassroot Soccer resiliency pilot program: building resiliency through sport-based education in Zambia and South Africa. *New Directions for Youth Development*, 116: 141-154.

Rodriguez, P., Kesenne, S. and Humphreys, B.R. 2011. *The Economics of Sport, Health and Happiness: The promotion of wellbeing through sporting activities*. New Horizons in the Economics of Sport. Cheltenham: Edward Elgar Publishing Limited.

Schulenkorf, N. and Edwards, D. 2012. Maximising positive social impacts: strategies for sustaining and leveraging the benefits of intercommunity sports events in divided societies. *Journal of Sport Management*, 26: 379-390.

Spaaij, R. 2012. Beyond the playing field: experiences of sport, social capital, and integration among Somalis in Australia. *Ethnic and Racial Studies*, 35(9): 1519-1538.

Stander, F.W. and Van Zyl, L.E. 2016. See you at the match: motivation for sport consumption and intrinsic psychological rewards of premier football league spectators in South Africa. *South African Journal of Industrial Psychology*, 42(2): 22-30.

Thompson, S., Aked, J., McKenzie, B., Wood, C., Davies, M. & Butler, T. 2011. *The Happy Museum: a tale of how it could turn out all right*. Stowmarket: Museum of East Anglian Life.

UNICEF, 2017. Peace education in UNICEF, Working paper series, (Education Section), June 2017.

Vail, S.E. 2005. *Promoting the Benefits of Sport: A Collection of Peer-Reviewed Journal Articles and Reports*. Federal Provincial-Territorial Sport Committee.

Van Zyl, E.S. 2016. *Leadership in the African Context*. Second Edition. Cape Town: Juta Publishers.

Endnotes

1   Van Zyl, 2016.
2   Stander & Van Zyl, 2016.
3   Thompson, Aked, McKenzie, Wood, Davies & Butler, 2011.
4   Pawlowski, Breuer & Leyva, 2011.
5   Ibid.
6   Vail, 2005.
7   Ibid.
8   Malebo, 2007.
9   Ibid.
10 Malebo, 2007; National Institute of Adult Continuing Education, 2009.
11 Kidombo, 2012.
12 Ibid.
13 UNICEF, 2017.
14 Ibid.
15 Chawansky, McDonald & Van Ingen, 2017.
16 Ibid.
17 See endnote 11.
18 Vail, 2005.
19 See endnote 11.
20 Guilianotti, 2010; Kidombo, 2012.

21 See endnote 11.
22 See endnote 20.
23 See endnote 11.
24 Schulerkorf & Edwards, 2012.
25 Ibid.
26 Rodriguez, Kesenne & Humphreys, 2011.
27 Ibid.
28 Spaaij, 2012; National Institute of Adult Continuing Education, 2009.
29 See endnote 13.
30 Ibid.
31 See endnote 3.
32 Peacock-Villada, DeCelles & Banda, 2007.
33 Newman, Bird, Tripney, Kalra, Kwan, Bangpan & Vigurs, 2010.
34 See endnote 13.
35 See endnote 15.
36 Maxwell, 2005.

SECTION 4

CONCLUDING THOUGHTS

CHAPTER 15

CONCLUDING THOUGHTS

Ebben van Zyl, Andrew Campbell and Liezel Lues

"Peace cannot be kept by force, it can only be achieved by understanding."
(Martin Luther King, Jnr.)

What have we learned?

This book explores the interplay of leadership within the conflict resolution and peacebuilding process. The contributing authors sketched out the main ingredients intersecting leadership practices within various stages of peace development. This research reflects that leadership theories and practices extend well beyond their traditional domain and into the international affairs of peace and peacebuilding. This book presents cutting-edge research of peace leadership as an emerging field. The fifteen chapters examine the definition and concept of peace leadership, its role in conflict transformation, and leadership approaches towards peace and peacebuilding. Sustainable peace is a process. This process involves focusing on important building blocks for attaining peace, namely lead self (through emotional intelligence), lead with others (through social intelligence) and lastly lead communities through the implementation of communal intelligence (see Figures 2.4 and 3.1). Therefore, peace leadership starts with self-transformation towards peace. If leaders are unable to lead themselves through inter-conflict towards self-peace, how can peace leaders lead others towards intercommunal peace? As a result, self-transformation prepares peace leaders to lead others and intercommunal leaders in conflict-afflicted areas towards peace.

This book is divided into three sections. The first section presents a conceptual understanding of peace leadership. The second section examines how self-transformation to peace can be implemented by discussing lead self, lead with others and lead community. The last section addresses existing and emerging tools and initiatives available to increase the operational effectiveness of peace leaders (see Figure 15.1).

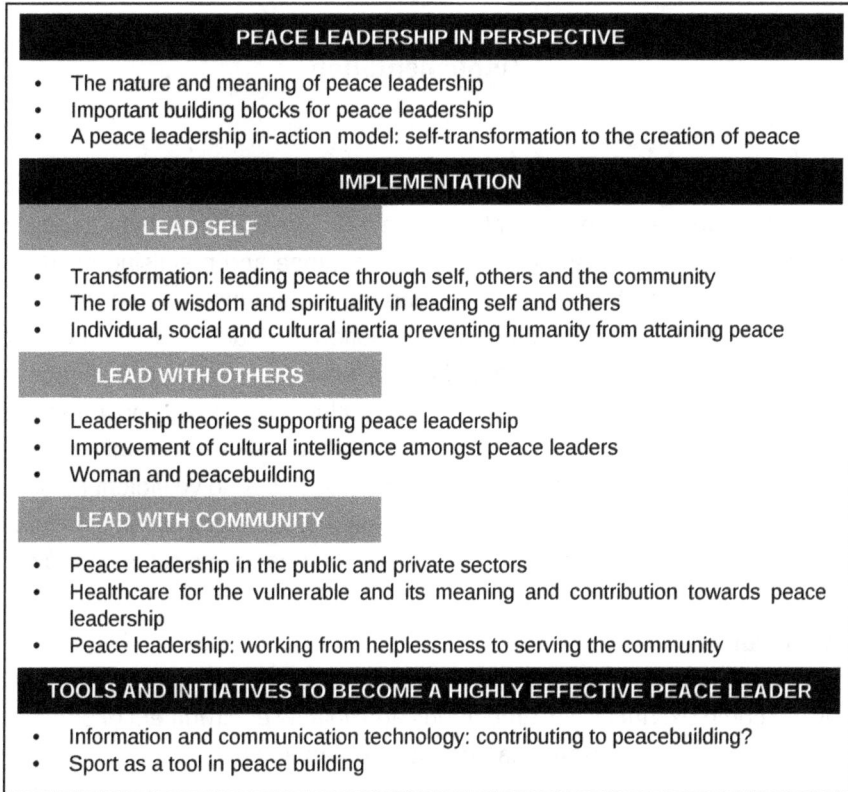

PEACE LEADERSHIP IN PERSPECTIVE

- The nature and meaning of peace leadership
- Important building blocks for peace leadership
- A peace leadership in-action model: self-transformation to the creation of peace

IMPLEMENTATION

LEAD SELF

- Transformation: leading peace through self, others and the community
- The role of wisdom and spirituality in leading self and others
- Individual, social and cultural inertia preventing humanity from attaining peace

LEAD WITH OTHERS

- Leadership theories supporting peace leadership
- Improvement of cultural intelligence amongst peace leaders
- Woman and peacebuilding

LEAD WITH COMMUNITY

- Peace leadership in the public and private sectors
- Healthcare for the vulnerable and its meaning and contribution towards peace leadership
- Peace leadership: working from helplessness to serving the community

TOOLS AND INITIATIVES TO BECOME A HIGHLY EFFECTIVE PEACE LEADER

- Information and communication technology: contributing to peacebuilding?
- Sport as a tool in peace building

Figure 15.1 Lead community

What have we learned with regard to those three sections? This will now be discussed.

Peace leadership in perspective

For purposes of this book peace leadership was initially defined (see chapter 1) as "focusing on the ability to influence the self, people and resources so that a state of peace within the self, with others and the community can be promoted, conflict be challenged and a common notion of and space for a more civilised and flourishing world (peace), can be attained". By focusing on important building blocks (emotional intelligence, social intelligence and communal intelligence), a peace leadership-in-action model was created. This self-transformation model (as basis for this book), focuses on lead self, lead with others and lead community as part of the process of self-transformation to peace. Based on the building blocks and self-transformation model, peace leadership can be conceptualised as: "focusing on transforming self to the attainment of peace (a more civilised and flourishing world) through lead self (emotional intelligence), lead with others (social intelligence) and lead community (communal intelligence).

Implementation

Lead Self

Lead self involves transforming self to lead others within the community through emotional intelligence. Emotional intelligence helps peace leaders to transform their own personal ideological issues through neuroscience and practising mindfulness to not only lead others to forgive but also lead intercommunal leaders towards peace and reconciliation. Furthermore, individual emotional wisdom and cultural spirituality play an important role in recovering from human rights violation. Peace leaders need an awareness of cultural and spiritual influences in leading others towards intercommunal peace and reconciliation. Arguably, ethno-religious influences can be a root cause of conflict or leveraged by peace leaders to resolve violent conflict. Thus, peace leaders who understand the intercommunal cultural and spiritual influence can lead the conflict transformation towards developing peace and reconciliation.

Lead with Others

The next step in self-transformation to peace is for peace leaders to lead others through the complex, uncertain, ambiguous and volatile environment of peacebuilding. This section linked transformational and servant leadership theories to equip leading others as peace leaders. An argument made is that peace leaders who apply transformational leadership as peace leaders not only develop leaders executing peacebuilding activities but also transform the environment from violence to peace. Second, the argument that serving others with humility, relational power and empathy is more important as a peace leader transforms the orientation to lead others through service. Peace leaders are servant leaders. Third, peace leaders need the cultural intelligence to work across different cultures, the cultural savvy to deal with uncertainty and complexity and the cross-cultural skills and knowledge to lead others towards confidence-building measures necessary for sustainable peace. Cultural intelligence helps to prevent negative actions like discrimination, prejudice and exclusiveness. Lastly, there is a gender gap among peace leaders as women play an influential role in promoting peace by leading others within the community to not only collaborate in implementing peace agreements but also to recover from human rights violations. Emotional and social intelligence are, inter alia, being utilised by women leaders seeking to resolve conflict that builds sustainable peacebuilding activities.

Lead Community

In a post-conflict environment, peace leaders must coordinate with the public and private sector in leading the community through targeted institutional governance reform as well as the socio-ethnic environment to sustain peace development. Peace leaders play a critical leadership role in articulating intercommunal interests, initiating accountability, inter alia. That said, the correlation between conflict-ridden states and post-conflict societies rests with the collaborative approaches of the peace leader's ability to facilitate intercommunal conflict resolution strategies towards building stronger local institutions. For example, chapter 11 discussed the integral role peace leaders play in health-service delivery to vulnerable groups within a post-conflict environment. In leading the community towards peace, leaders play an integral role by coordinating with local actors in developing a comprehensive approach that provides health-service delivery programs that meet the basic needs to ensure the social wellbeing of the population within conflict-afflicted areas. The role of leaders working with communities in providing health-service delivery is to coordinate with the public and private sectors towards coordinate structures and resources through capacity-building programs. Lastly, training and supporting the poor in the community to become successful, make organisations and individuals providing the training and support, peace leaders in the real sense of the word.

New Tools and Initiatives

The landscape of technological tools available for peace leaders creates new opportunities for managing conflict and peace development at the local level. The discussion in Chapter 13 showed that information and communication technology is a strategic enabler as peace leaders, local actors and civil society make connections in leading others towards intercommunal peace and stability. The integration of technological advancements provides peace leaders a strategic asset for community engagement that advocates resisting violence, empowering communities in the recovery from conflicts, and communicating the promotion of peace. Furthermore, peace leaders utilise tribal, intercommunal and regional sporting events as a way to enhance peacebuilding. Peace leaders are beginning to understand the value sporting events play in peacebuilding. Important values of sport include participation and inclusiveness. For example, the inclusion of sporting events into peace-building activities brings intercommunal dialogue, intergroup interaction and cohesion and opens channels for relationship-building between separated parties. Basically, the practice of adapting technology and integration of sporting events into the peace leader planning process is a strategic enabler in managing the complex intercommunal peace and security.

Looking ahead

Challenges

Below are some challenges highlighted by contributing researchers in this book:

- The challenge of understanding the individual leadership behaviours and styles inside various contexts as peace leaders establish sustainable peace initiatives at the societal level. The building blocks of collective intelligence, communal intelligence, and cultural intelligence create the space to lead others towards intercommunal peace. This challenge addresses the complexity of developing the peace leadership terrain within an organisation. Thus, researchers developing standardised assessment tools for collective, communal and cultural intelligence grounded in the social learning theory are urgently needed. The reason is that integrating a standardised assessment tool (measuring the ability to lead self, lead others and lead community) into a comprehensive peace leadership development program will strengthen the leader's capability to be an effective peace leader.
- The challenge of developing a theoretical definition and characteristics of peace leadership within conflict prevention, conflict resolution and peacebuilding. Thus, a consensus peace leadership definition will expand the leadership aperture that addresses political, diplomatic, social and ethnic ideological discourse by framing leadership constructs and competency development programs towards peace development.
- The challenge of exploring a theoretical leadership framework for peace leadership to identify the leadership skills and competencies needed is based on the different conflict, political, social and ideological contexts. The authors identified a critical knowledge gap that urgently needs to be examined as peace leaders build self-leadership capabilities (lead self) to lead others towards intercommunal peace and stability. A starting point for future researchers is the need to investigate transformational and servant leadership theories as a viable theoretical framework for peace leadership.
- The challenge researchers addressed throughout this book is the development of peace leaders' emotional, social and communal, as well as cultural intelligence, as a leadership set of skills needed to lead self, lead others and intercommunal leadership. The consensus among researchers is that neuroscience and mindfulness may inter alia be important development tools for individual and collective development as peace leaders build a whole of community (public and private sector) approach to peacebuilding. More research needs to be done on what additional development tools may be relevant for individual and collective development.

Some key conclusions and recommendations

1. Future leadership developments should focus more on the improvement of the quality and availability of humanness (like peace, peace leadership and peacebuilding).
2. Inner skills (like emotional intelligence) should be the starting point for peace leaders to attain peace.
3. Emotional intelligence shapes not only the capabilities of peace leaders' organisational and operational peacemaking, peacekeeping and peacebuilding efforts but also the facilitation of conflict-resolution processes.
4. Peace cannot be attained alone. Therefore, leading with others (social intelligence) and lead community (communal intelligence), should be included.
5. There are universal principles for positive peace that can be derived from the work of spiritual leaders and can be equally applied by followers of other spiritual traditions and secular leaders.
6. An inertia amongst individuals, civil society and states to attain peace can be prevented by adopting a mindset that underlies a culture of peace, a mindset of solidarity and care, as well as to be convinced of the value of human dignity.
7. Inspirational motivation, team-orientation, effective communication and empathy (as part of transformational leadership), honesty, trust, service and empowerment of others (servant leadership), together with cross-cultural understanding, tolerance as well as respect for others, should be practised by peace leaders in the process of building, implementing and sustaining peace between individuals and communities.
8. Women leaders need to focus more on the implementation of their feminine qualities like compassion and empathy as this will enable them to contribute to peacebuilding actions.
9. Caring for vulnerable groups (like the elderly and sick people) are a core value for and core function of peace leadership.
10. Peace leaders are not bound to a certain age or generation. However, an important prerequisite seems to be that a peace leader must be able to realise his/her shortcomings and make efforts to manage that.
11. Peace requires that all people have the same basic requirements of life and hope for a better future over which they have some control. Without that they can be manipulated into using aggression because they have no other skills to offer in an attempt to improve their lives and the lives of their children.
12. The utilisation of information and communication technological advancements provides peace leaders with a strategic asset for community engagement and can be used in the communication/promotion of peace.
13. Important attributes of sportsmen/women peace leaders can learn from include play fair, be a team player, stay positive, respect the rules and never give up.

Concluding remarks

Peace leaders are global leaders who build local and communal partnerships in rebuilding legitimate political, economic, legal and security institutions. This book provides a significant contribution within the emerging peace leadership discipline as the international community, non-governmental organisations, and the public and private sectors struggle to formulate sustainable peace initiatives at the tribal, local and communal societal level. Basically, we hope that peace leaders understand that supporting locally legitimate authorities and peaceably managing conflict depend on leading one's self in order to lead others and leading communities toward sustainable peace.

INDEX

www.ingramcontent.com/pod-product-compliance
Lightning Source LLC
Chambersburg PA
CBHW080246030426
42334CB00023BA/2725